The Annunciation

THE ANNUNCIATION

A New Evangelization and Apologetic
for Mainline Protestants and Progressive Catholics
in Postmodern North America

Larry Hart

WIPF & STOCK · Eugene, Oregon

THE ANNUNCIATION
A New Evangelization and Apologetic for Mainline Protestants and Progressive Catholics in Postmodern North America

Copyright © 2017 Larry Hart. All rights reserved. Except for brief quotations in critical publications or reviews, no part of this book may be reproduced in any manner without prior written permission from the publisher. Write: Permissions, Wipf and Stock Publishers, 199 W. 8th Ave., Suite 3, Eugene, OR 97401.

Wipf & Stock
An Imprint of Wipf and Stock Publishers
199 W. 8th Ave., Suite 3
Eugene, OR 97401

www.wipfandstock.com

PAPERBACK ISBN: 978-1-5326-0547-5
HARDCOVER ISBN: 978-1-5326-0549-9
EBOOK ISBN: 978-1-5326-0548-2

Manufactured in the U.S.A.   03/07/17

New American Standard Bible, copyright © 1960, 1962, 1963, 1968, 1971, 1972, 1973, 1975, 1977, 1995 by The Lockman Foundation. Used by permission.

The Holy Bible: Contemporary English Version, copyright © 1995 American Bible Society. All rights reserved.

The Message, copyright © 1993, 1994, 1995, 1996, 2000, 2001, 2002. Used by permission of NavPress Publishing Group.

Revised English Bible with the Apocrypha, copyright © 1989 Oxford University Press and Cambridge University Press.

To Brenda

Contents

About the Cover | ix
Acknowledgments | xi
Introduction | xiii

PART I: A NEW EVANGELIZATION

CHAPTER ONE
The Practitioner | 3

CHAPTER TWO
The Context | 14

CHAPTER THREE
The Awakening | 35

CHAPTER FOUR
Soul Talk | 54

CHAPTER FIVE
The Human Condition | 75

PART II: A NEW APOLOGETIC

CHAPTER SIX
The New Apologetic and the Reality of God | 99

CHAPTER SEVEN
Can We Trust Jesus? | 120

CHAPTER EIGHT
An Evangelist's Perspective on Biblical Scholarship | 138

CHAPTER NINE
Before the Sermon | 165

CHAPTER TEN
Progressive Orthodoxy in Eight Sermons | 192

Bibliography | 233

About the Cover

The beautiful painting of the Annunciation with its dramatic and harmonious colors and its rich yet simple symbolism is a wonderfully contemplative and contemporary work by James He Qi (www.heqiart.com). I am so appreciative of his permission to use it as the cover for this book.

Acknowledgments

I THANK THE REV. Canon Nancy Holland for stirring my imagination with visions of evangelization as spiritual practice, and Christopher Hays, professor of Near Eastern Studies at Fuller Theological Seminary, for so generously helping me to understand what is happening today in Old Testament scholarship and for guiding me in developing a comprehensive reading list covering the "maximists" to "minimalists." I also thank John Shore for allowing me to use an excerpt of his conversion story in *Penguins, Pain and the Whole Shebang: Why I Do the Things I Do, by God (as told to John Shore)*. Again, I thank James He Qi for permission to use his painting of the Annunciation, Phyllis Atha at Imaginative Images for her wonderful way of using the painting for the cover, as always my daughter Carolyn for her technical support with my unruly computer, and finally, of course, all the people at Wipf & Stock who turned the manuscript into a book.

Introduction

My wife Brenda, whose opinion I respect above all others, tells me this is not a book for everyone—that it's not even a book for every Christian. For one thing, she says it doesn't lend itself to the three-minute rule for postmodern attention spans. I told her I am both too incompetent and too lazy to write the whole thing over, but that I would issue a strong and appropriate notice. So, if you would like a book on evangelization, you can quickly browse for a couple of good ideas then this book is sure to disappoint you. I am afraid that's due, well, I won't say what it is due to, but all the pieces fit together and without the whole the parts don't always make sense—or at least don't make the sense intended. But there are other audience limiting factors as well.

For instance, if you tend to hang out at the fundamentalist end of the theological street, whether Protestant or Catholic, you will likely find what you read here rather incomprehensible, and if you like to spend time in the cul de sac at the other end you will probably find it equally unintelligible. This book is written from the perspective of what might be characterized as a liberal or progressive orthodoxy. And so it's more for people from the progressive Catholic and the mainline clan who are serious readers and possess a certain proficiency in the Christian faith. It is for people who may have read Dawkins and Erhman, Crossan and Pagel, and therefore are conversant with the often very real scientific, historical, textual, and hermeneutical problems they pose not only for Scripture but for Christian thought and life itself; and yet, while respecting the validity of many of those difficulties, nevertheless experience the Bible as something more than a helpful metaphor or enlightening fable, and in reading Scripture hear the Holy Trinity, mysterious and living, speaking to them in a language that transcends the written text—hear "deep calling to deep." Those who have found the Way—the *torah*, the *hodos*, or the *tao* as it is known in other tongues—and have experienced its profound beauty in Christ desire to share that discovery, and every act of such sharing is an act of evangelization. So this book is for those who feel that desire. But I need to stop talking like this or I will have talked myself out of any potential audience at all, and what publisher will publish a book with no audience? So, here is what you can expect to find in the following pages.

Part I of this two-part book, "A New Evangelization," is meant as a kind of manual for evangelization in the postmodern world of North America. The evocative expression, "new evangelization," to which Pope John Paul II frequently referred in his writing and speeches, comes from his encyclical *Redemptoris Missio*,[1] and was taken up by Pope Paul VI in his *Evangelization in the Modern World*.[2] The need felt by both Paul VI and John Paul II was for a "great launching" of evangelization in the totality of the church's life. John Paul II insisted, "The moment has come to commit all of the church's energies to a new evangelization and to the mission *ad gentes*. No believer in Christ, no institution of the church, can avoid this supreme duty: to proclaim Christ to all peoples."[3] The concern here, then, is with the development and launching of a "new evangelization" appropriate and adequate to the challenges of the contemporary world.

Chapter 1 is based on the conviction that evangelism is a spiritual practice, and that "what does not live in us cannot live around us." In September 2015 I traveled to the School of the Annunciation for the first round of studies in the new evangelization at Buckfast Abbey in the United Kingdom. For me that time was more like a spiritual retreat than a classroom exploration of evangelism. Over a year earlier, the Rev. Canon Nancy Holland of the Episcopal Diocese of San Diego had engaged me in a reflection on evangelism as spiritual practice, and that set me then on a contemplative research quest that took me to the abbey and beyond.

Watchman Nee said in his book, translated into English as *What Shall This Man Do?*, that "two people may use the same words, but in the one you meet something you cannot get past; in the other—nothing. The difference is in the person. You always know when you are in the presence of spiritual worth."[4] It would seem to follow, then, that a new evangelization necessarily includes much more than a few simple evangelistic techniques. It needs to address the person of the evangelizer and encourage the development of a theology of spiritual presence and of evangelism as a spiritual practice like

---

1. John Paul II, *Redemptoris Missio*, 4.
2. Paul VI, *On Evangelization in the Modern World*, 2–6.
3. John Paul II, *Redemptoris Missio*, 2–29.
4. Nee, *What Shall This Man Do?*, 83–84.

other spiritual practices, such as, meditation, prayer, sacred reading, *lectio divina*, or acts of compassion.

Chapter 2 provides a snapshot, as it were, of the changes taking place in our contemporary world. This chapter is especially for those who may not yet be used to distinguishing between modernity and postmodernity and the significance of those changes for the life and work of the church. Although this chapter discusses a number of the changes occurring separately and individually, it is essential to keep in mind that everything, absolutely everything, is connected—the demise of the church in the West, globalization, pluralism, climate change, politics, language, communications, technology, science, information, values, religion, poverty, population growth, health care, violence, art, literature, and economics. It's all connected.

The statistics are well known by the American clergy and public. And while the numbers are constantly changing, and while the surveys I have quoted in the early chapters will be quite dated by the time you read this, the trajectory nevertheless remains constant. The fastest rising category in religious surveys is the classification of "Nones"—those who indicate they are not affiliated with any religious group. Yet, public opinion polls also show that in the United States, many Americans self-identify as both spiritual and religious. Although 20 percent of Americans responded to one survey by declining to identify with a specific religious institution, 68 percent of the religiously unaffiliated still said they believe in God, and 37 percent described themselves as "spiritual, but not religious." Two-thirds of the religious "Nones" indicate they have metaphysical or paranormal beliefs, such as the existence of nonmaterial energies, angels and demons, or accept the possibility of psychic communication. I would speculate that the self-identification as both "religious" and "spiritual" suggests, as the new evangelization asserts, the existence of a substantial number of people in North America who might be "re-evangelized"—people who long for an experience of the transcendent but find the contemporary church oblivious to that longing and clueless as to how it might be fulfilled. The sea is full of fish for those who love and are willing to learn the art of fishing. This being said, it is absolutely essential to keep in mind at all times that a new evangelization will be new not only quantitatively but qualitatively as well.

The essential thing about this chapter is its finding that not only has the world changed externally, but the way people think, the way consciousness forms in the mind, has also changed. When my mother was ninety years old I asked her what it was like to have grown to adulthood in a world where it was once common to travel by horse drawn wagon, or to live without radio, or television, or indoor plumbing, or penicillin, but after nine decades find herself in the atomic age, in the age of organ transplants, television, the internet, cell phones, and moon walks. I only realized lately none of those things were as significant, or as puzzling to her, as how human thought and its communication had changed. Today, thought and communication are less linear and more impressionistic all the time. At the end of a television commercial I said, "That was a really dumb commercial. What was it advertising?" Our grown children responded simply, "That commercial wasn't for you, Dad. It was for us." Watch, without children present, the television series *True Detective*. It is a story in which the principle characters experience a "conversion," but their conversion has nothing to do with linear discursive reasoning.

Chapter 3 looks at the nature of human consciousness and its formation, and proposes a way of thinking about conversion based on intervention work with alcoholics. Vernon Johnson, the Episcopal priest who was himself an alcoholic and pioneered the art of intervention, thought that as the alcoholic progresses in his or her addiction, the wall of denial protecting against self-insight and the healing light of reality grows ever higher, and thicker, and stronger. Denial does not mean, as many think, disagreement with the assertion of some fact, but rather the inability to recognize the fact's relevance for one's life so that meaningful change is sabotaged. There is something about human nature, Johnson thought, that cannot accept the notion that we are not in control. However, he noted, some alcoholics experience an event which breaks through that wall of denial. In the words of Alcoholics Anonymous, the alcoholic "hits bottom." Bottom can be a tragic car accident, going to jail, or losing a job or one's family. Rather than a serious automobile wreck in which people are injured or killed, it could be a minor fender bender. It is simply an event which has the power to break through that particular individual's denial. Johnson saw intervention as a process that raises the bottom, and thus precipitates change.

In working closely with alcoholics and addicts in the late seventies and through the eighties, I came to see that the disease of alcoholism is something of a microcosm for life. The issues, including the defiance, the grandiosity, and the self-deification that make spiritual surrender problematic for the alcoholic are problematic for us all. It is just that for the alcoholic the consequences are usually far more immediate and lethal than for the rest of us. If this is, as I think, a correct view of the matter, then the question becomes, "By what means does light penetrate the dark wall?" I think the answer is that in the case of Christian conversion it is life itself, it is the human condition sometimes joyfully exultant and sometimes tragically sorrowful, which furnishes the catalytic moment for a spiritual awakening—for enlightenment.

Chapter 4 can be thought of as asking the question: How, then, does the evangelizer work with the human condition in such a way that light penetrates the self-imprisoning wall so that the one within experiences freedom? The premise here is that this happens primarily through story, metaphor, and narrative. Chapter 4 is about working with the narrative of being human in a way that is liberating for everyone in the conversation, and makes individual transformation possible. It's not about techniques or methodology, it is simply listening to and sharing stories—something as natural and as organic as growing tomatoes at home.

Chapter 5 deals with the human condition—with life, which, in the words of blues artist Leon Redbone, "in all of its glories and all of its faults is a bitter sweet waltz." If it is true that the human condition, that life itself, is the catalyst for conversion then it is obviously important to reflect on just what the human condition might actually be. If we know about life, but not life itself, if we have theories and doctrines and formulas to impose on others through much talking, then we will be quite unable to minister life. It is one thing to talk "knowingly" about life and to give advice and direction; it is quite another to have the inner reality—the inner wisdom of life. Nevertheless, contemplating what it means to be human can be a helpful starting place.

What is for certain is that a new evangelization will need to understand postmodern men and women in a way that goes beyond knowledge of how to market religion as a commercial product; that is, it will need to explore the spiritual phenomenology of conversion—how consciousness forms in the human mind so as to result in "a spiritual awakening."

Part II, "The New Apologetic," is based on the assumption that a new evangelization further requires a new apologetic. We must ask how we can state the Christian faith in a way that is comprehensible to the postmodern mind while truly remaining the Gospel; that is, how do we present the power, beauty, and reality of the Christian faith in such a way that it becomes accessible to third millennium men and women without unnecessary obstacles or complications.

The task before us requires not the development of a set "catechesis," but an apologetic capable of satisfying the honest questions raised by modern science, philosophy, theology, biblical studies, psychology, and daily life. Simply put, the new evangelization will be a new apologetic that is simultaneously orthodox and progressive—possessing both intellectual integrity and spiritual depth

Chapter 6, "The New Apologetic and the Reality of God," seeks to set out a spiritual apologetic that transcends the rationalism, materialism, and scientism of the modern world without dismissing the reasonable requirements for a faith that possesses intellectual honesty. It argues for the sort of reflective reasoning advocated in Patricia King and Karen Kitchener's book, *Developing Reflective Judgment*, with its helpful thesis that there are certain questions and issues in life and reality that cannot be framed in such a way as to render definitive "yes" or "no" answers. And yet, life nevertheless requires that we make commitments, stake our souls on what we believe, and act according to the needs of the moment. Reflective reasoning leads us away from the pitfalls of dichotomous, either/or thinking and the perils of absolute certainty to the calmer and safer postmodern place of reasonable probability.

Reflective reasoning, it seems to me, further suggests Paul Ricoeur's concept of the "second naiveté." Ricoeur saw three intertwined intellectual and spiritual stages in regard to what we believe about God, Scripture, and the nature of reality through which we may pass. In the precritical stage, problems, incongruities, and logical difficulties just do not register as being in any way problematic. In the second stage, the critical stage, logical or factual problems are glaring and cannot be ignored. But in the third and final stage, the postcritical stage, intellectual quandaries, factual discrepancies, and logical difficulties are acknowledged and understood; and yet, something transcendent, beautiful, true, mysterious, and living in a text of Scripture or in our own human experience continues to be seen. Surely in the "spooky" age of quantum mechanics an apologetic can be developed that appreciates the "ordinariness," the naturalness, the organic quality of biblical stories, events, and teachings, including the divinity of Jesus, while simultaneously recognizing in them the workings of a deeper, larger consciousness, spirit, reality, whatever you want to call it, but which Christians embrace as the Holy Trinity—what C. S. Lewis saw as the "Three Personal God."

Although technically they belonged to the Age of Modernity, Paul Tillich and John A. T. Robinson were both precursors or harbingers of postmodernity. They both suggested decades ago that an apologetic that argues for God as "a being" whose existence can be proven by our syllogisms is incomprehensible to contemporary men and women.[5] Far more helpful, they said, is to think and speak of God as the mysterious reality, as the *sensus divinitatis*, which exceeds all concepts, explanations, and descriptions. What is written here is an attempt to present, in keeping with this perspective which is actually both ancient and postmodern, a more contemplative apologetic that explores problems of belief, including suffering

---

5. Robinson, *Honest to God*; Robinson, *But That I Can't Believe!*; Tillich, *Dynamics of Faith*; Tillich, *Shaking of the Foundations*; Tillich, *Systematic Theology*.

and the classical proofs for God in a way that is to more likely to form in the consciousness of postmoderns.

Chapter 7 takes up the question: Can we trust Jesus? Again, the question is not whether we can believe as hard fact every detail in the Gospels, but whether we can accept both the oral and written classical tradition of Jesus of Nazareth as sufficiently reliable to trust the man from Galilee as the Christ. Consequently, this chapter explores the eyewitness quality of the Gospels, and asserts that when we reduce things to the simple question, "How did the people of Jesus's day see him?" we will have gone a long way toward answering the question we really want answered; that is, when we examine his miracles, not as acts of magic, but as that which astonishes and as signs pointing us to ultimate reality, when we see and experience that beauty of Jesus that is linked to philosophical and theological truth, when we discover Jesus as a person of power and presence and life, as obviously both his friends and enemies did, we will know what we most want to know.

Chapter 8, "An Evangelist's Perspective on Biblical Scholarship," raises the critical question: "Can biblical scholars do what they claim they can do?" Conservative Christians should take no comfort in that much of what is written here focuses on the failings of the more liberal variety of biblical studies. I hold no brief for the fundamentalism of either kind. My intent here is not to dismiss the usefulness of modern approaches to biblical studies, but to advocate for their more humble and judicious use. After exploring literary and historical criticism, as well as the field of archeology, the conclusion reached is that biblical studies, whether from a "conservative" or "liberal" perspective, whether "secular" or "confessional" in nature, have no warrant for claiming their view represents either scientific conclusions or "hard" history. Biblical scholarship is riddled with conjecture stated as fact, and shows at every turn an overreliance on circumstantial evidence. Biblical studies rarely take into account anywhere near all the relevant variables. Archeology in many ways seems to be more scientific than, say, literary criticism, but even an artifact carefully unearthed, photographed, diagrammed, and cataloged at a well-organized dig still has to be interpreted.

Much of this chapter engages with Phil Davies, the well known secular biblical scholar from the University of Sheffield. Davies sees "confessional" biblical studies as somewhat disreputable. Contra Davies, this chapter ends by asserting that intellectual integrity, including the capacity for changing one's mind when that is demanded by the sheer weight of evidence, resides not in the academic or philosophical methodology employed, but in the person of the scholar. Paul Ricoeur noted that there is no philosophy without presuppositions, the mistake is thinking that we can begin without them.

Chapter 9, "Before the Sermon," and chapter 10, "Progressive Orthodoxy in Eight Sermons," actually form one piece in that chapter 9 represents the research out of which chapter 10 emerged. While serving in a congregation with a well read and highly sophisticated laity, I became aware of how frequently in study groups someone would dismiss or attempt to debunk a biblical text or show themselves unable to penetrate a passage with any depth because they were hung up on some theory they had read or seen on television. Then one summer, as I looked over the lectionary readings for the next couple of months, I realized how much of this anxiety could be addressed in a natural and rather straightforward way in the appointed lessons: Phil Davies' assertion that the Hebrew patriarchs and matriarchs as well as David and Solomon were all fictions, the Hebrew exodus with the crossing of the Red Sea and the emergence of Israel in Palestine, Bauer's hypothesis that what Christians have traditionally thought heresy actually preceded orthodoxy, the meaning of faith and how we know the reality of God, miracles as an obstacle to faith, how much of this stuff one needs to believe to stand within the classical Christian faith, the *sensus divinatatis* as a legitimate faculty for the discovery of truth, and understanding genuine biblical myth as the poetic expression of an objective reality.

My hope is that these two chapters taken together will help people see how Scripture can be read and understood, and apologetics done in a way that is organic, natural, and entirely comprehensible to the postmodern mind.

I should perhaps note that chapter 9 does not include any research for the Koan, the homily from the story of Jesus and the Canaanite woman. This is because the research for that sermon relied on an article I had previously written and published in *The Expository Times*—"The Canaanite Woman: Meeting Jesus as Sage and Lord: Matthew 15:24–28 & Mark 7:24–30." You should still be able to find it online by Googling the title and my name, Lawrence D. Hart. It is also available on my personal website—"Father Larry's Journal of Contemplative Living" (http://journalofcontemplativeliving.com). If you are on the website I would suggest you also read another article, "Fundamentalism of Both Kinds."

When I first begin work on this text I intended to have a part three relating to small churches and church growth. I wanted to deal in particular with the question of whether small and struggling congregations could be turned around. But alas, I already have far too many words, sentences, paragraphs, and pages. So what I had in mind will have to wait until another time. Right now, I will just say the following ever so briefly.

In the very early seventies, about four years after my ordination, I experienced something of a second "calling"—a call to devote myself to the

Introduction

good of small congregations. In that experience one question that formed in my mind was: "Can a small congregation without any significant human or financial resources be turned around?" The answer I arrived at through my own often difficult, sometimes joyful, sometimes sad experience was that yes it is possible. The early Church Growth Movement as founded by Donald McGavran used to put it in the form of a kind of catechetical question: "How do small churches grow?" The expected answer was, "Seldom and reluctantly." So it is possible to grow a small church, but as the Church Growth Movement noted, it takes far less effort to plant a new church than to grow an existing one. Small churches are simply carrying too much heavy baggage to ever make it with any degree of frequency. Better to begin the journey with a new group carrying fewer suitcases, chests, and crates.

But whether old or new it's not just local communities of faith, but the larger ecclesiastical bodies that are problematic. The literature is pretty clear, and my own personal experience confirms that mainline denominations need to make a number of changes, not only if they are to survive, but if they are to have a meaningful existence:[6]

1) Bishops and denominational leaders must renounce their status as CEOs and once again become humble pastors.

2) Leaders in central offices, by whatever name, must give up being permission givers and managers. "Managers will manage an organization right into the ground."

3) Resources of every kind must flow from the top down and from the center out, otherwise the denomination, whatever its brand, becomes totally irrelevant.

4) The church as an institution focused on money, power, status, and self-protection must be renounced in favor of the church as a living organism—the Body of Christ.

5) Secular programs and methodologies must be replaced by spiritual practices.

6) A way must be found of choosing clergy and bishops who lead through service and wisdom rather than political astuteness and neurotic ambition.

Quite frankly I doubt the spirituality, the will, or the inclination for anything this bold exists. Most likely candlesticks will be replaced.

6. Mead, *Once and Future Church*; Gibbs and Bolger, *Emerging Churches*; Gibbs, *Church Next*; Chavez, *American Religion*; Roof and McKinney, *American Mainline Religion*; Tickle, *Great Emergence*.

For progressive Roman Catholics there are both different and similar issues.[7] In mainline denominations like the Episcopal Church, the devout may struggle with how to remain within a denomination that increasingly declares it doesn't believe much of anything in particular. The Roman Church will, it seems to me, need to free the theological imagination from fourth century ontological concepts, such as substance thinking, in order to evangelize twenty-first century North Americas. For Roman Catholics, the question is more often how to remain a loyal adherent to a church where one encounters talk of bleeding wafers, Papal infallibility, and a veneration of Mary that is, at times, indistinguishable from deification. What are devout men and women to do when their conscience on birth control, celibacy of clergy, homosexuality, divorce, or the ordination of women is not simply different from, but in serious conflict with the church hierarchy? Although taken humorously by the media, Pope Francis's remark that he finds neurotic, dysfunctional, and unstable clergy "scary" is a serious assessment of the bishops and leaders of every denomination—and it is indeed the faithful who pay the price. In *The Church is Flat: The Relational Ecclesiology of the Emerging Church Movement*, Tony Jones approvingly explains Jürgen Moltmann:

> Moltmann's early ecclesiology is not without pragmatic suggestions for the life of the church. The church can best be what Christ is calling it to be, Moltmann argues, if it stays small, mobile and fluid, avoiding top-heavy bureaucracies and power-hungry individuals. The church can check itself as to whether it is fulfilling this role by always making sure that it is primarily a fellowship of the "godless and godforsaken." When the church becomes the territory of the elite and powerful, it has *de facto* ceased being the church.[8]

Of course, Moltmann needs to be read for himself, as does Hans Kung, the German Catholic theologian and priest, especially Kung's *On Being a Christian*, which, it seems to me, finds a great deal of commonality between progressive Catholics and mainline Protestants; and, serves as a kind of manifesto for "those who do not want to remain at the childhood stage of their faith,"[9] it points to what is required of the future church and its mission.

In neither Part I nor Part II have I addressed the major shift in racial and ethnic demographics taking place in the United States and what that means for evangelization in postmodern North America. Someone far more

---

7. Ralph, *Why the Catholic Church Must Change*.
8. Jones, *Church is Flat*, 135.
9. Kung, *On Being a Christian*, 32–33.

qualified than I am needs to take up that subject. By 2045 White Caucasians will be in the minority across the entire United States. So the question is not going to go away. It is gratifying, and a hopeful sign, to see denominations like the Ecumenical Catholic Communion where, in the Diocese of California, the bishop and the majority of parishes are Hispanic. Without a doubt we need to be about the business of developing multiracial and multicultural communities of faith. That being said, I hope in spite of such limitations to this book, it might, in some small way, be helpful in our larger, more pluralistic world.

In neither Part I nor Part II will you find lists of talking points. When I was counseling professionally I realized that what people in their desperation often wanted was a short response they could repeat to repair a relationship or "fix" a husband, or wife, or child, or parent. The reason that doesn't work, of course, is that in order for our words to be effective we must own them, understand them thoroughly ourselves, and mean them. In evangelism and in apologetics talking points, clever arguments and formulas will avail nothing—it all has to come out of our own heart and mind. The aim of this book is to help ordinary Christians and simple priests like myself fill the treasure chest within and then to bring out the right piece at the right time to give as a precious gift—for evangelization, real evangelization, is an act of pure grace.

There are a couple of things of which you should be aware. The first is in regard to footnotes. I have an almost pathological aversion to noise, and foototes are, to me, a kind of visual noise. I don't like them. I find them distracting. Nevertheless, they are necessary to give credit where credit is due, and to point readers to further paths of exploration. The footnotes you will find here have value only in those two respects. They are really citations rather than footnotes. With one or two exceptions they contain no additional insights or information—they just tell you where to find stuff. There is a bibliography at the end for those who want to read further. There are no footnotes of any sort for chapter 10. This is because it is of a different genre. Homilies don't contain footnotes—they are meant to be heard more than read. However, with the information given in the text, the citations from chapter 9, and the bibliography, it should be quite easy to locate exact quotes and information.

You might also want to be aware that the ideas and reflections in this text are not presented in a highly systematic manner. They are presented more in the style of postmodern communication with its ever shifting perspectives and flow of consciousness. It probably would have been helpful to have included some sort of topical index—a notion that occurred to me all too late. However, there is no help for it now, you'll just have to read in hope of discovering what you are looking for—or not. But there is a second, larger reason, that while there is a desire to be logical, there is no attempt in these pages to be particularly systematic. And that reason is to be found in something Frederick Denison Maurice, obviously alluding to Matt 7:9–11, once said: "Men and women are hungry for God, but instead we give them philosophical and theological systems." I have no interest in presenting a theological system of evangelism or apologetics to you, but if possible, I would very much like to contribute to your own power to think, and to feel, and to just be in such a way in this world as to expand the awareness of "the mystery of the ages which is the hope of Christ in you" (Col 1:27).

PART I

A New Evangelization

Having had a spiritual awakening . . . we tried to carry this message to others, and to practice these principles in all our affairs.

—Step Twelve

CHAPTER ONE

The Practitioner

When the Christian has discovered not only the truth that gives life purpose, but absorbed it into personality by Rule over some years; evangelism becomes a developed instinct rather than an occasional duty. It is natural to wish to share our joy with others, to introduce them to the love of God, and we are all most rightly elated when we can prove of use in this way. But I would say that it is quite useless to think about lay-evangelists until this necessary grounding in Rule has led to a reasonable maturity of faith.[1]

—Martin Thornton

To proclaim fruitfully the Word of the Gospel one is first asked to have a profound experience of God.[2]

—Benedict XVI

Among the greatest of philosophers, theologians, and Christian saints was the medieval Dominican, Thomas Aquinas. One of the core mottos of the Dominican Order of Preachers, *Contemplare et contemplata aliis tradere*, usually translated as, "To contemplate and to share with others

---

1. Thornton, *Christian Proficiency*, 164.
2. Benedict XVI, *Apostolic Letter*, 7.

the fruits of that contemplation," was taken from Saint Thomas's *Summa Theologiae*. More than once, Thomas left academic positions to preach—left to share the fruits of his contemplation.

The Craft of Contemplation

For Aquinas, contemplation meant the contemplation of truth—Divine Truth. It meant the Truth, the Divine Reality, encountered in contemplation that is then shared through preaching and teaching, and through the whole ministry of evangelization. Saint Thomas particularly understood contemplation as reflection on Scripture. So, the *Dominican Constitutions* insist: "Continuous study nourishes contemplation, encourages fulfillment of the counsels with shining fidelity, constitutes a form of asceticism by its own perseverance and difficulty, and, is an essential element of our whole life, as it is an excellent religious observance." Aquinas, it is said, did much of his scholarly writing on his knees so that his study would indeed be prayer.

In the Middle Ages there was not just one but multiple methods of meditation and prayer practiced by monks and nuns in convents and monasteries and by lay people—most dramatically and powerfully by the Franciscans and the Dominican Order to which Thomas Aquinas belonged. The term "contemplation" has changed considerably since the Middle Ages. The word "contemplation" itself is the Latin translation of the Greek "*theoria*," which means "to see"—it is therefore "that at which someone looks." Among the Greek philosophers it referred to mental perception or insight into the reality of something. When the pagan priests concentrated with fixed attention on something like an inscribed circle in which the will of a god was expected to be made manifest, that was contemplation. Richard Woods, OP, the well known writer on Dominican spirituality, makes three points in regard to Dominican contemplation:

> First, the original place of contemplation in Dominican life was simpler and much less esoteric than later formulations imply. But it was foundational.
>
> Second, although contemplative experiences can be gratuitous, preparation and training, including study, are required to develop and maintain a contemplative spirit. But that is easier than one might think.
>
> Third, despite the serious obstacles to contemplation presented by contemporary culture, ordinary life situations, including active ministry, far from being a barrier to contemplation are,

in fact, the necessary condition for and normal occasion of contemplation.³

Dominic de Guzman, the founder of this order of contemplative friars in the early thirteenth century, practiced the methods of meditation or contemplative prayer that were typical of a thirteenth century monk:

> Bowing by profoundly inclining his head before the altar he would slowly chant: "Glory be to the Father, and to the Son and to the Holy Spirit."
>
> Outstretched on the ground he would recite Luke 18:13 (A prayer used by the Desert Fathers and Mothers), "O God, be merciful to me a sinner."
>
> Deep in prayer, he appeared to be meditating upon the words of God, and he seemed to repeat them to himself in a sweet voice.
>
> He appeared then to be listening carefully as if to hear something spoken from the altar. If one had seen his great devotion as he stood erect and prayed, they would certainly have thought that they were observing a prophet, first speaking with an angel or with God himself, then listening, then silently thinking of those things which had been revealed to him.
>
> After the canonical hours he quickly withdrew to some solitary place, to his cell or elsewhere, and recollected himself in the presence of God. He would sit quietly, and after the sign of the cross, begin to read from a book opened before him.

One of the Order's early friars observed: "The holy custom of our father (Dominic) seems, as it were, to resemble the prophetic mountain of the Lord in as much as he quickly passed upwards from reading to prayer, from prayer to meditation, and from meditation to contemplation."

Saint Dominic himself, then, seems, to have engaged in a number of meditative practices—chanting, music, gazing at the crucifix, reciting Scripture sentences, and *lectio divina*, which carried him into a deeper consciousness of God, into a contemplative state, into wisdom, and sustained him in his apostolic ministry.⁴

---

3. Woods, "Recovering Our Dominican Contemplative Tradition."

4. Broslavick, "St. Dominic's Nine Ways of Prayer." Original by anonymous author between 1260 and 1288. See also, www.domcentral.org, which has wonderful miniatures.

Sharing the Mystery of Contemplation

But contemplation was not, for Saint Dominic, Saint Thomas, or Meister Eckhart, perhaps the Order's ultimate mystic, an end in itself. Contemplation may be regarded, as Richard Woods explains it, as "an unflinching and loving look at reality as divine," or in Meister Eckhart's language a generation after Thomas, "Seeing God in all things and all things in God." In the Dominican understanding of Christian spirituality it is also the Truth, the Reality, the Light, the Love, the Wisdom, the Mystery, encountered in contemplation and handed on to others. It reminds one of the ox-herding pictures of Zen.[5]

The famous ox-herding pictures of Zen depict someone in search of the ox—the sacred animal of the East. Successive drawings show the person lost in illusion until finally the footprints of the ox are discovered and eventually the ox itself, which is then tamed and ridden home. Originally, this picture story of enlightenment reached its climax in the eighth drawing when, after the ox itself had disappeared, the person also disappeared so that nothing remained. This was represented by the drawing of a circle—a symbol of nothingness, of nondiscriminating consciousness. But then in twelfth-century China other pictures were added showing the seeker, now old and enlightened, returning to the market place to save all "sentient beings." *Contemplare et contemplata aliis tradere.*

Now here is something about the founding of the Dominican Order that may be pertinent to our own time. In the spring of 1203, Dominic joined Prior Diego de Acebo on an embassy to Denmark for the monarchy of Spain, to arrange the marriage between the son of King Alfonso VII and a niece of King Valdemar II of Demark. At that time the south of France was the stronghold of the Cathar, or Albigensian, heresy. After they encountered the Albigensians at Toulouse, Dominic saw the need for a response capable of winning members of the Albigensian movement back to mainstream Christian thought. Prior Diego recognized immediately that while the representatives of the Holy Church acted and moved with pomp and extravagance offensive to the poor people of the region, the Cathars lived a simpler and more sacrificial life. Prior Diego therefore suggested that the papal legates begin to live a reformed apostolic life. The legates agreed to change if they could find a strong leader. The prior took up the challenge, and he and Dominic dedicated themselves to the conversion of the Albigensians. What Dominic came to see out of this whole experience was the organic connection between spirituality and evangelization.

---

5. Johnston, *Silent Music*, 81.

Superficiality — the Curse of Our Age

A number of people, like Diana Butler Bass, are convinced that the number of people who somewhat paradoxically identify themselves as both spiritual and religious when responding to surveys, as well as the strong indication that, at least in North America, the word "religion" is negatively associated with institutional religion, may indicate many people in the North American culture are not so much closed to the Christian experience of the Divine Mystery we call God as they are turned off by the utter banality of most churches. The reality is that those who are hungry for the transcendent cannot be evangelized by someone who is oblivious to such longings and experiences in his or her own life. If the tree is barren there is no fruit to give away. "What does not live in you cannot live around you." Does this mean that sharp entrepreneurial priests and pastors can't build whopping big churches? Obviously that is not the case, but while not everyone can become a successful shopkeeper, we can all become transformed and transforming contemplatives.

I have no idea how many times I have now quoted the first three lines of Richard Foster's book *The Celebration of Discipline* since first reading them over thirty years ago: "Superficiality is the curse of our age. The doctrine of instant satisfaction is primarily a spiritual problem. The desperate need today is not for a greater number of intelligent people, or gifted people, but for deeper people."[6] Borrowing Foster's perspective we could say, "Superficial evangelism is a curse of the postmodern church. Reliance on programs rather than practice is a spiritual problem. The desperate need is not for a greater number of intelligent evangelists, or more "religious" evangelists, or more gifted church marketers, or better administrators but for deeper evangelists."

Spirituality and Religion

Before leaving the subject I want to at least attempt ever so briefly to recover the positive dimension of the word "religion," but first will offer a nonacademic definition of the distinction between spirituality and religion. When we appreciate the numinous reality that is both transcendent and inner, and are drawn to its qualitative beauty more than to the material, finite, and quantifiable things of this world, we are on our way to becoming spiritual. In fact, many of our worst problems are created by the earth-bound thinking that finite things can satisfy our deepest longings, which are infinite. To

---

6. Foster, *Celebration of Discipline*, 1.

pay attention to the infinite longing within us puts us on the spiritual path. When we value love, compassion, kindness, generosity, gratitude, wonder, the good, the true, and the beautiful more than money, power, or status we are living spiritually. And this is just as true whether we are considering our identity as individuals or collectively as a community of faith.

The first time I ever heard something described as spiritual rather than religious was in regard to Alcoholics Anonymous. The statement that Alcoholics Anonymous was spiritual rather than religious was meant to clarify that AA was not aligned with the theology of any denomination, faith, or philosophical school, but that it had discovered certain universal principles to be essential to sobriety with serenity—principles which could only be adequately described by their practitioners as "spiritual." This made it possible for everyone, even someone alienated from every religious faith, to find the sanity of sober living.

In actuality, religion is something more than all that cumbersome baggage so often associated with institutionalized religion. The English word "religion" comes from a French word which means "to bind back." Religion is what binds us to spirituality, to life that really is life, to Mystery, to God. Prayer, the reading of sacred Scripture, communal worship, the Eucharist, and every act of kindness binds us intimately to the Holy Trinity so it can be said we live in conscious contact, in communion and in union, with God. It could be further said, then, that evangelization is meant to be a religious practice that binds us to the Spirit of Christ.

Understood in this way it becomes quite difficult to hold religion and spirituality in separate categories. Over and over again the New Testament asserts how this mysterious essence of life was in Christ Jesus and when those who had any life, any awareness, any wakefulness in themselves touched it they knew it was life. The unutterably amazing thing is that this power has continued to manifest itself to this very day. The new evangelists, like the evangelists of every age, carry this life in themselves and it is as contagious as laughter.

It might be helpful at this point to ponder something Karl Barth wrote in discussing both the intrinsic and extrinsic growth of the church. Barth emphasized the absolute essentiality of intrinsic, spiritual growth, but he also connected intrinsic growth to the importance and necessity of evangelization and extrinsic, numerical, growth in writing:

> But . . . we must ask in what this growth consists. The most obvious, although not necessarily the final answer, is not to be summarily rejected—that the communion of saints shows itself to be fruitful in the mere fact that as it exists it enlarges

its own circle and constituency in the world. It produces new saints by whose entry it is enlarged and increased. Of course, we are not told, even by the parable of the seed, that it will become constantly greater in this way so that all living persons may eventually become Christians. What we are told is it has the supreme power to extend in this way, that it does not therefore stand under serious threat of diminution, and that as a subject which grows *per definitionem* it has an astonishing capacity for numerical increase. It is not self-evident that this should be the case; that it should have this capacity; that there should always be Christians raised up like stones to be Abraham's children. The more clearly we see the human frailty of the saints and their fellowship as it is palpable both at the very outset and in every epoch, the more astounding we shall find it that from the very first and right up to our own time it has continually renewed itself in the existence of men and women who have been reached by its feeble witness and have become Christians in consequence. It is no doubt true that its power in this respect has been largely denied through the fault of Christians, or its exercise confined to a limited sphere. But it is also true, and perhaps even more true, that it has always had and demonstrated this capacity. It has propagated itself even where everything seemed to suggest that this was quite impossible. It has continually, and often very suddenly, assumed new forms—sometimes for the better, sometimes not for the better, but without forfeiture of its essential and recognizable essence. For always directly or indirectly awakened and gathered by its existence, there have been Christians, and therefore persons who have come to this fellowship and then lived and acted in it. As these men and women—often in the strangest places, and the very last that one would expect—have arisen and come to it, i.e., have discovered and confirmed the fact, that they belonged to it the community has grown. It does not matter whether the growth has been big or little. The fact remains that it has continually grown. And it still grows. It has the power to do so.[7]

What Barth wrote points to the extrinsic growth of the church as a sign of health and vitality (fruitfulness), and does so in a way that avoids both despair and arrogance. The Church, the Body of Christ, has always grown and will continue growing because God's mysterious power and quickening is always at work in it—at work in the people of God—but that emphasis

---

7. Barth, "Growth of the Community," 263.

must be maintained in the new evangelization; that is, it is a spiritual power which is at work, and in which the evangelist must be immersed.

The Practice of Presence

All Christian ministry, whether emanating from the laity or clergy, is first and last about presence rather than techniques and methods. Presence may be felt but never quite explained. The experience itself is ineffable, and all descriptions are, as T. S. Eliot said, "raids on the inarticulate." To feel at one with God—that sublime power and mystery that infuses all things, that is over all things, around all things, and through all things is to know Presence. To see and know the beauty of a flower, a poem, an idea, a kind gesture, or the moral law within, or the silence of falling snow as it is in itself is presence. To give focused attention to what others are thinking, feeling, and saying is presence. To respond to the requirements of the moment out of that harmonic convergence of spirit with the Spirit is presence.

I did a chaplain residency in which the aim was to learn to use one's own person to help the hospital patients. My friend and colleague Jim West had an amazing ability to still the anxiety and even relieve the physical pain of patients by just being present with them—using no or very few words. Jim was a Roman Catholic lay person who had spent years practicing Christian meditation as well as Zen. Once on retreat in the rainy Pacific Northwest he was given a *koan* to work on. "Where," he was asked, "is the master of the water when it rains?" In response, Jim began gently drumming on the hardwood floor with his fingers. And that was an acceptable answer in that it indicated identification, awareness, an experience of the rain that had everything to do with presence and little or nothing to do with intellectual analysis. I can hardly ever reflect on presence without thinking of those lines from Wadsworth's well-known poem:

> For I have learned
> To look on nature, not as in the hour
> Of thoughtless youth, but hearing oftentimes
> The still, sad music of humanity,
> Nor harsh nor grating, though of ample power
> To chasten and subdue. And I have felt
> A presence that disturbs me with the joy
> Of elevated thoughts; a sense sublime
> Of something far more deeply interfused
> Whose dwelling is the light of setting suns,
> And the round ocean, and the living air,

And the blue sky, and in the mind of man,
A motion and a spirit, that impels
All thinking things, all objects of all thought,
And rolls through all things.[8]

But this presence of the evangelist, with the ability to recognize, embrace, own, and nurture his or her own experience of mystery, and with its facility for assisting others like a spiritual midwife in the birthing of their own unique and sacred realizations, is most certainly not automatic—it is required and necessary but it is not a given.

A Sacred Discipline

David Gortner in *Transforming Evangelism* says it like this: "Evangelism is a spiritual practice: active—and receptive. Just as in prayer, study, and acts of compassion, in evangelism you experience a sense of your own movement not being entirely your own. Receptive to the Holy Spirit's activity within you—and trusting that the Spirit is active in others all around you—you move into action as the Spirit's partner."[9]

Notice Gortner's insistence that evangelization is itself a spiritual practice—a sacred discipline. The Charles Monroe Sheldon novel *In His Steps* was first published in 1896. It is the story of what happens in a town when a minister, after a number of tragic events, convinces his congregation to vow that they will do nothing without first asking themselves in each decisive moment: "What would Jesus do in this case?" The novel is, then, the fictional chronicle of the wonderful changes that take place in the lives of its characters and in the town. Dallas Willard, who was professor and director of the School of Philosophy at the University of Southern California, and a Southern Baptist minister, made this incisive observation on Sheldon's novel and its relation to spiritual life:

> The book is entirely focused upon trying to do what Jesus would do in response to *specific choices*. In the book, there is no suggestion that Jesus ever did anything but make right choices from moment to moment. And more interestingly, there is no suggestion that his power to choose rightly was rooted in the kind of overall life he had adopted in order to maintain his inner balance and his connection with his Father. The book does not state that to follow in his steps is to adopt the total manner of life

---

8. Wadsworth, "Lines Composed," 69.
9. Gortner, *Transforming Evangelism*.

he did. So the idea conveyed is an absolutely fatal one—that to follow him simply means to try to behave as he did when he was on the spot, under pressure or persecution, or in the spotlight. There is no realization that what he did in such cases was, in a large and essential measure, the natural outflow of the life he lived when not on the spot.[10]

Willard goes on to say that asking ourselves "what would Jesus do?" when faced with an important decision or moral choice, is simply not an adequate discipline for anyone who desires the sort of divine mystical intimacy Jesus knew. For the purpose of this inquiry, we could say it is not an adequate practice for anyone hoping to engage in transformative evangelization. Evangelization is a spiritual practice sustained and empowered by all the other classical Christian practices or disciplines.

In *A Long Obedience in the Same Direction: Discipleship in an Instant Society*, Eugene Peterson identifies as particularly harmful to being Christian, and for our purposes here it can be said particularly harmful to the practice of evangelization, "the assumption that anything worthwhile can be acquired at once." Peterson uses as an epigraph a quote from, of all people, Friedrich Nietzsche who said, "The essential thing 'in heaven and earth' is . . . that there should be long obedience in the same direction; that thereby results, and has always resulted in the long run, something which has made life worth living."[11] Neither the skills nor the depth of spirituality, the "soul craft," required to become proficient in evangelization can be attained instantaneously.

The Apostle Paul is perhaps most often admired for two things: his theological brilliance and his missionary work in the early years of the church. But the reality is that all Paul's writing and all of his apostolic work emerge from the most profound mysticism imaginable—from a first-hand encounter with what he refers to as "the mystery of the ages" (Col 1:26), and of a union and a communion so rich and deep Paul can only say, "It is no longer I who live, but Christ who lives in me" (Gal 2:20). In Acts 24:16, Paul offers some spiritual direction along these lines: "And herein do I exercise (*askeo*) myself, to always have a conscience void of offence toward God and men." The English term "asceticism" comes from the New Testament Greek word *askeo* which is used here. The more common term for exercise is *gumnazo* used in 1 Tim 4:7, 2 Pet 2:14, and in Heb 5:14 and 12:11. This is the term from which the English word "gymnasium" is derived. This second word employed as a metaphor for the spiritual life is associated with images

---

10. Willard, *The Spirit of the Disciplines*, 8–10.
11. Peterson, *A Long Obedience in the Same Direction*, 9–17.

of sports and battle. The first word, a*skeo,* means to practice, to exercise, to toil, labor, and work in order to master a certain mental, physical, or spiritual activity. The second, *gumnazo,* has to do with the sort of training into which an athlete must necessarily enter in order to develop his or her body and mind in order to function at the highest possible level.

The sort of discipline or training regimen we discover in the life of Jesus, of Paul, and of all the great saints and sages of the ages may be considered under what Martin Thornton referred to as "Rule" in the epigraph to this chapter. The idea of a Rule of life originally developed in Christian monastic communities, and, in fact, monasteries and convents today still function under a Rule, the best known being that of Saint Benedict, which dates back to the sixth century. A Rule of life serves as a way of living out our spiritual calling, our vocation, and our love for God and for the whole world. To ask, "What is your Rule?" is to ask, "What is your spiritual intention and practice?" Because Rule grounds us in the sustaining "mystery of Christ in us," the new evangelization must begin, for every evangelist, with the articulation, adoption, and practice of Rule.

However, this is not a treatise on mysticism or the contemplative life, nor is it a list of the desirable characteristics for someone interested in becoming an effective evangelist. Spirituality, including, if we want to think in subcategories, the spirituality of evangelism, is "another reality." "The region of awe," is how C. S. Lewis pictured it, where, "in deepest solitude there is a road right out of the self, a commerce with . . . the naked Other, imageless (though our imagination salutes it with a hundred images), unknown, undefined, desired." It is, as Lewis said, "a direct experience of God as immediate as the taste of color."[12] No. This is certainly not meant to define spirituality or to provide a list of necessary qualities for someone who wants to become an "effective" evangelist, but to assert as energetically as possible the perspicacity and wisdom of what we have already learned. "What does not live in us cannot live around us."

---

12. Downing, *Into the Region of Awe,* 12.

CHAPTER TWO

The Context

When I am dreaming quantum dreams, the picture I see is more like a web of relationships—an infinite web, flung across the vastness of space like a luminous net. It is made of energy, not thread. As I look, I can see light moving through it like a pulse moving through veins. I know the light is an illusion, since what I am seeing moves faster than light, but what I see out there is no different from what I feel inside. There is a living hum that might be coming from my neurons but might just as well be coming from the furnace of the stars. When I look up at them there is a small commotion in my bones, as the ashes of dead stars that house my marrow rise up like metal filings toward the magnet of their living kin. . . . Where am I in this picture? All over the place. Up there. Down here. Inside my skin and out. Large compared to a virus and small compared to the sun, with a life that is permeable to them both.[1]

—Barbara Brown Taylor

What forms the context of Christian evangelization? It is a rhetorical question. The answer is everything, absolutely everything, because everything, as in Taylor's vision of the luminous web, is connected. Our God is, as Saint Paul put it, "over all, in all, and through all (Eph 4:6)." When we look at Jesus we see the cosmic Christ in whom everything finds

---

1. Taylor, "Physics and Faith."

its purpose, in whom all things cohere, and who guides and holds the church together like a head does a body (Col 1:16–18).

> Everything comes from God;
> Everything happens through God;
> Everything ends up in God.
> Always glory! Always praise!
> (Rom 11:36 The Message)

Unfortunately, it has been hard for those steeped in modern Occidental thinking to grasp this essential unity of reality.

By enculturation and training the minds of most of us in church leadership have typically been more adept at categorizing, contrasting, comparing, dissecting, and analyzing the parts than in thinking holistically, seeing systems, or in recognizing the "gestalt." Linear, direct cause-and-effect thinking brought the Western world a long way scientifically and technologically, but now increasingly shows more than a little tendency to be unnecessarily limiting, and to exclude what may be of significance from awareness. The context of evangelization is a luminous web in which everything is connected.

Thinking Systemically

Using less poetic imagery we could say that the context of evangelization is a system so that its practice necessitates the ability to engage in systems thinking.[2] Systems thinking is the process of understanding how elements of a system influence one another within a whole. In nature, systems thinking examples include ecosystems in which various elements such as air, water, movement, plants, and animals work together to survive or perish. In organizations, systems consist of people, structures, and processes that work together to make an organization "healthy" or "unhealthy." In systems thinking problems are approached as parts of the total system rather than as isolated events. Systems thinking is based on the belief that the best way of understanding what is happening, good or bad, is by seeing the relationship between all the component elements within a system—their linkages and interactions.

Systems thinking demonstrates how small catalytic events that are separated by distance and time can be the cause of significant changes, and how an improvement in one area of a system can positively affect another area of the system. What follows here is an attempt to understand at least

---

2. Friedman, *Generation to Generation*.

some of the elements of the postmodern cultural context for evangelization in North America. At the same time, we will try to stay connected to that One Greater Mystery in which "we live, move, and have our being"—we will very likely have to work together with some diligence to do this.

The End of White Christian America

By 2045, White Americans will no longer make up the racial majority of the US population; and, the reality is that the death of white Christian America has already occurred. In his fascinating book, *The End of White Christian America*, Robert Jones begins the "obituary" like this:

> After a long life spanning nearly two hundred and forty years, White Christian America—a prominent cultural force in the nation's history—has died. WCA first began to exhibit troubling symptoms in the 1960s when white mainline Protestant denominations began to shrink, but showed signs of rallying with the rise of the Christian Right in the 1980s. Following the 2004 presidential election, however, it became clear that the WCA's powers were failing. Although examiners have not been able to pinpoint the exact time of death, the best evidence suggests that WCA finally succumbed in the latter part of the first decade of the twenty-first century. The cause of death was determined to be a combination of environmental and internal factors—complications stemming from major demographic changes in the country, along with religious disaffiliation as many of its younger members began to doubt WCA's relevance in a shifting cultural environment.[3]

Jones presents as anecdotal evidence the much debated cause for the demise of Robert Schuller's Crystal Cathedral. He contends that the Crystal Cathedral's continuing loss of members and financial resources, culminating in bankruptcy and in selling the campus, is easily discovered in the changing demographics of Orange County.

Schuller's ministry was in the vanguard of the mega-church movement. White American Christians found his emphasis on personal success, political conservatism, and family values appealing. But between 2000 and 2009, the white population in Orange County declined by nine points, while the Asian American population experienced a growth rate of 41 percent. Schuller's white evangelical Protestant vision was overwhelmed by the realities of a radically changing America culture.

3. Jones, *End of White Christian America*, 1.

An Incarnate Presence in Contemporary Culture

Ministry is incarnational and we must understand the culture in which we find ourselves, rather like we must understand our own living bodies. Christians believe Jesus was God become human, and therefore immersed in the system of religion, politics, economics, work, and family life of first century Palestine. It couldn't be any clearer than Paul makes it in 1 Cor 9:19–23 (The Message).

> Even though I am free of the demands and expectations of everyone, I have voluntarily become a servant to any and all in order to reach a wide range of people: religious, nonreligious, meticulous moralists, loose-living immoralists, the defeated, the demoralized—whoever. I didn't take on their way of life. I kept my bearings in Christ—but I entered their world and tried to experience things from their point of view. I've become just about every sort of servant there is in my attempts to lead those I meet into a God-saved life. I did all this because of the Message. I didn't just want to talk about it; I wanted to be *in* on it!

The term "incarnational ministry," like the word "missional" or "emergent church," is used in a wide variety of ways. Sometimes "incarnational ministry" is used to mean ministry that crosses cultural barriers to be an embodied presence of the Sacred to people in need. At other times, it's used to talk about culturally relevant analogies for the gospel. And in other instances it is a way of saying that intellectual assent to the faith is not enough, faith needs to become embodied or "incarnate" in acts of love and service, as in the earthly ministry of Jesus. But with whatever nuance it is used it remains certain that the better we understand the dynamics of any culture the better prepared we are to become the presence of Christ in that living context.

So, what are some of the things to know about postmodern North American culture? I will attempt to outline some of its features here, but first emphasize that it is important to know that a cultural revolution is taking place. And, whether we like or dislike any of these characteristics is not the point, it's just the way things are. Consequently, what follows is simply an attempt to be descriptive of what is, in order to respond appropriately.

1) The End of Christendom

We live in a world obsessed with polls and surveys, constantly and compulsively running the numbers, analyzing the statistics. I suspect this has to do with the belief that if we can gather enough data we can control the future. There are obviously many problems with this assumption, for one thing our knowledge of the future is always partial, ambiguous, uncertain, and inadequate for the purposes to which we would like to apply it. As Leon Redbone sings, "Distant horizons can be quite suprisin' once the journey is through." Yet, there is this innate human craving to know and accurately predict the future. I want to know the future, like I want to know the coffee mug next to me on the breakfast table—study its color and design, see what it is made of, pick it up, turn it around, place it where I please, set it aside, use it, or discard it all together.

Our illusion is that if we can learn enough about anything or anyone, including the future, we can control it. Hence, our obsession with data. If, the logic seems to go, we can amass enough information on how and what people think, feel, desire, fear, like, or dislike we can choreograph the future church here and now. But every poll and every survey appears to only heighten our fear. The more statistical data we seek the more past, present, and future become an ever-accelerating cycle of anxiety. But if we can let go of the anxiety and the need to control, then the data can help us know how to respond appropriately, and with equanimity, to what is required in the moment. Both Christian clergy and lay leaders know the numbers pretty well.[4]

A Pew survey taken in 2008 found that one in ten Americans consider themselves to be ex-Roman Catholic. The Catholic Church in North America was sufficiently disturbed by its drop in numbers that it launched a major campaign urging Catholics to "come home." It is, of course, not just the Catholics who are in decline. It's everyone. Regardless of denominational affiliation, or nonaffiliation, we are all in the same boat—and afraid it is taking on water. At one time, conservative denominations taunted mainline churches with the claim that conservative churches in the United States were growing while mainline churches were in serious decline—a sure indicator, they claimed, of God's delight in their robust theology and keen displeasure with anemic liberalism. That derision is now as silly as a child's taunt. Southern Baptists and Churches of Christ along with Catholics, Methodists, Episcopalians, Lutherans, Presbyterians, the United Church of Christ, and everyone else, to all visible appearances, are in a sinking boat.

In a 1999 survey, 54 percent of the respondents said they were religious but not spiritual. Ten years later only 9 percent of Americans responded that way. Those willing to identify themselves as religious had plummeted, in one decade, by an astonishing 45 percent. What does not bode well for the

---

4. White, *Rise of the Nones*; Hadaway, "Report on Episcopal Churches"; Bader et al., "American Piety in the 21st Century."

future of North American churches is how the word "religion" has become negatively associated with institutional, "organized" religion. The fastest rising category in religious surveys is the classification of "Nones"—those who indicate they are not affiliated with any religious group. In the United States, only 17.3 percent of the population actually attends a church service on any given weekend; or, to see it from a different angle, more than 80 percent of the US population does not attend a Christian worship service on any given Sunday.

A further indication of the general decline of the church in North America is seen in how people view clergy. A 2013 Gallup Poll reported public trust in clergy at an all-time low with only 47 percent of Americans rating clergy high in honesty and ethics (compared to 82 percent saying the same about nurses). Less than one in three young people (32 percent) give clergy high marks in morality and ethics, compared with 50 percent of those 55 and older. This disparity would seem to be yet another indicator of a major cultural shift in the religious thinking and life of North Americans.

For the domestic dioceses of the Episcopal Church, the average Sunday attendance (ASA) in 2002 was 846,640. In 2012, the domestic average Sunday attendance was 640,142—a decline of 206,498, or a staggering 24 percent over ten years.

As I write, the Episcopal Church has 6,825 parishes active in the United States. Of that number, 2,000 have a demographic with the majority age at 60 plus. In addition, more than 2,200 parishes (around one third) have an average Sunday attendance of 40 people or less. The following summary highlights the problem:

- There are 903 Episcopal churches with an ASA of 20 or fewer.
- There are 612 Episcopal churches with an ASA of 20–30.
- There are 704 Episcopal churches with an ASA 31–40.
- There are 552 Episcopal churches with an ASA of 41–50.
- There are 1,826 Episcopal churches with an ASA of 51–100.

The handwriting is on the wall; 2,761 Episcopal churches are at high risk. In fact, the number of total parishes dropped from 6,794 in 2010 to 6,736 in 2011, a decline of 58 congregations.

What is truly significant about the data is not its potential use for better marketing, but its confirmation of the end of Christendom. One of the most helpful things we can do right now is not to use the information we have to figure out how to sell "church" or "salvation" to Boomers, or X-ers, or Millennials, or whatever the latest label may be as if we were marketing smart phones or cool cars, but rather to assess the reality of our culture and to respond adequately to the reality and needs of the present moment. I like something Andy Crouch said in *Culture Making: Recovering Our Creative Calling*: "So hope in a future revolution, or revival, to solve the problems of our contemporary culture are misplaced. And such a hope makes us especially vulnerable to fashion, mistaking shifts in the wind for changes in the climate. Fads sweep across the cultural landscape and believers invest outsized portions of energy and commitment in furthering the fad, mistaking it for real change." Of course, it is not always easy to determine whether we are reacting or responding, engaging in real change or merely being faddish. It requires a good deal of wisdom to make that distinction.

The reality of the moment is that we live in a postmodern, post-Christendom world.

This is something prophets and seers and pundits have been telling us for some time. In his rather feisty and insightful book *The End of Christendom*, published in June 1980, the famous British intellectual Malcolm Muggeridge argued the not very novel idea that the founder of Christianity was Christ, whereas the founder of Christendom was Constantine. Therefore, while the church is in serious decline numerically, politically, and culturally, it is not Christ's Christianity that is floundering, but the Christendom already condemned by Jesus when he announced that his kingdom was not of this world. Christendom, according to Malcolm Muggeridge, is something quite different from Christianity. Christ said his kingdom was not of this world; Christendom, on the other hand, is of this world and, like every other human creation, is subject to decay and eventual desolation. I simply do not know what word is big enough to express this demise of Christendom and the "worldly church" that flourished immediately after World War II but is now falling more and more into ruin. I do take heart in Muggeridge's insistence that we live at the end of Christendom, but not the end of Christ.[5]

2) Our Pluralistic Culture

By the end of 2020, in all major cities in America, and perhaps even in the world, you will find people of different faiths, cultures, ethnicities, races, nationalities, and social backgrounds working, eating, playing, marrying, and doing things together. Exclusive communities are rapidly become a thing of the past. The harmonious balance of competing interests, lifestyles, religions, and cultures becomes more of a compelling necessity for the well-being of the human community, for the whole seven billion of us, every

---

5. Muggeridge, *End of Christendom*.

day. Pluralism is not a set of rules, it is at its most basic stage the attitude of live-and-let-live religiously, politically, culturally, and socially. At its higher level it is a mutual respect and appreciation that seeks the good of all.

Cinco de Mayo (Spanish for "fifth of May") commemorates the Mexican army's unlikely victory over the French at the Battle of Puebla in 1862. It is now widely and enthusiastically celebrated in the United States as a way for Mexican Americans to honor their ethnicity. And young Mexican girls have the *quinceañera*, something like a coming-of-age party for fifteen-year-old girls. The celebration of *Cinco de Mayo* has been, at the very least, puzzling for many older white Americans. "What does the Battle of Puebla have to do with us?" they ask. "We celebrate the fourth of July." Implied in the "us" is the assumption of the "melting pot"—one dominant American monoculture.

A Lutheran pastor told me of how his church had developed two very different worship services. One was a traditional Lutheran service with traditional hymnody. The other was with contemporary music and composed of a rather eclectic group of new Christians. The people in the traditional service were angry because the contemporary worshipers didn't appreciate, and didn't want to join in singing, the old hymns and anthems. "They don't even look like Lutherans," the traditionalists spat out. And they were right—if you expect Lutherans to look like nineteenth and early twentieth expatriate Scandinavians. That church is faced with a choice: Will it limit its membership, its ministry, and its evangelism to those who look and act and think like them; or will it recognize the realities of a pluralistic society and adopt a softer, gentler, more accepting attitude toward those who are other than them. No, it not only needs to be softer and gentler, it must be the enthusiastic acknowledgement of the essential unity in which the universe coheres.

In 2014, waves of children made their way from Honduras and Guatemala and poured across the US border, where they were then captured in large numbers, many of them sent by bus to a detention facility in Murrieta, California, where they were met by furious white protestors. One woman, her face contorted in rage kept screaming for the television cameras, "This is an invasion—call out the National Guard!" I found myself wondering what she wanted done. What more do those who so angrily demand the securing of the border with Mexico want done? Do they want the US Army to stand shoulder to shoulder and gun down anyone (children) who attempts to cross illegally? Be that as it may, my real point is that this woman typifies people who simply do not grasp the fact that our problems are global in nature and therefore require global solutions, and that their concerns with immigration, whether legal or illegal, may be far different from the concerns and hopes of the Hispanic/Latino population of California—which, by the way, constitutes a larger portion of the population than the white minority. A pluralistic society means that the concerns of everyone must be taken into account and that compromises must be made with genuine good will and understanding if the world is going to experience any sort of peace at all. Beyond this, Christianity, from its beginning, recognized human diversity. Part of what the church has to offer to our world, what it proclaims as the "Good News," is the possibility of peace in a world where the challenges of pluralism are frequently reacted to with cruelty and violence.

In the old world of Christendom, professed Christians and churches, whether they were always so or not is another matter, did not need to take into consideration the needs, concerns, or aspirations of other faiths, political ideologies, or ethnicities. But the assumptions of Christendom cannot sustain evangelism in the postmodern world. Mother Teresa imagined joy and love as a fishing net with which to catch souls, but you can only catch the fish that actually swim in the waters into which you cast your net.

3) From Premodern to Postmodern

For the last three hundred years we have been part of an age called *modernity*. The modern age is now giving way to a postmodern age. This means a real difference in how people view the world, how they understand reality and truth, and how they approach the fundamental questions of life. The church, as most of us in North America know it today, has its roots in an ancient premodern Mediterranean worldview. Over time the church eventually accommodated itself to the modern Western world as it emerged. But many now wonder whether it will be able to survive the shift to the postmodern age.

The premodern worldview developed during the time of the ancient temple-state, in which an alliance of king and priesthood joined religion and political power. Religion legitimized the king's rule by providing a moral and religious authority for his reign. In these ancient societies the ruler and the social order was usually thought to reflect the will of God on earth. The premodern worldview was, then, characterized by a rather unquestioning acceptance of authority and a belief in absolute truths. Premodern people normally believed what they were told by authority figures, both religious and secular. They trusted religion to provide the answers to life's mysteries in an unambiguous, simple, and clear way. This is obviously a simplistic explanation in that it neither takes into account exceptions to this paradigm or the human desire for and experience of spiritual transcendence that defies it. Nevertheless, it provides something of a lens through which to view premodern culture—just don't take it too seriously and without nuance.

Where the Bible is concerned one might think along the lines of what Paul Ricouer thought of as a precritical stage of thinking, this stage, regardless of what era it occurs in, is characterized by a naiveté in which whatever conflicts with what is already believed is ignored and so goes unrecognized as a problem in one's thinking. In this stage knowledge is understood as absolute and requires no justification. It is assumed that what is true and what is believed to be true are the same so that contradictions and factual errors are not perceived.

The modern worldview began in the Enlightenment of the eighteenth century. Modernity was founded on the pursuit of objective knowledge and the scientific method. It is characterized by a questioning of authority and tradition. Modernity believes that truth is based on facts. In the modern worldview, people should believe only what they can observe. Modernity trusts the power of reason and critical thinking to solve the world's problems. It looks to science, and not to religion, to provide the answers to life's mysteries. Modern people have often developed an overly optimistic faith in the progress of humanity through knowledge, scientific inquiry, innovation, invention, and rational thought. Indeed, modern thought may be characterized by a precritical orientation just as much the premodern world.

The rise of modernism led to the rise of secularism. Secularism is not necessarily atheistic, although it does, by definition, reject the reality of God as possessing any relevance for the political or social life of the larger community. Secularism maintains that however faith might inform the life of the individual, church and state should be entirely separate entities.

As modernity developed and spread, an intense reaction developed among religious traditionalists firmly entrenched in a premodern worldview, primarily within the religions of Christianity, Judaism, and Islam. Beginning nearly three hundred years ago, European biblical scholars began to question the truth of the biblical accounts, both in the Old and New Testaments. Nothing was considered sacred. The virgin birth of Jesus, his miracles, and his resurrection were all subjected to scrutiny and question. The doubts posed by modern philosophers, biblical scholars, and theologians threatened traditional religious dogma. As a result, in the late nineteenth and early twentieth centuries, reactionary religious movements tried to reinforce what they considered to be the "fundamentals" of the Christian faith. Frequently, this meant asserting the literal truth of biblical stories. Even texts that for centuries had been regarded as metaphorical, now assumed the status of factuality. By the 1920s, the premodern worldview of North American fundamentalists came into increasing conflict with modern secular thought so that now nearly a hundred years later, Christian fundamentalists demand that public schools teach the creation poem of Genesis as "creation science" alongside scientific evolution.

A new historical epoch is now unfolding. It began about the middle of the twentieth century and is continuing to develop today. For lack of a better designation it is being called postmodernism—the successor of modernism. We are not sure how it will play out in the long term, but some initial observations are being made about its nature.

It has been said that postmodern people are essentially disenchanted modernists. They have found human reason and cleverness to be no antidote to the poisoning of the environment, the bloody wars of the twentieth century, or all the continued misery, poverty, and hunger around the globe. Science, far from alleviating human suffering, has only increased it and further raised the level of danger to the human species. But, unlike fundamentalism, postmodernism does not seek to return to an earlier time. Nor does it see a return to authoritarian religion as the answer. Postmodernism is characterized by the belief that both religion and science have failed us. Neither can be trusted to provide the answers to life's mysteries or to solve life's perplexing problems.

In the postmodern world the notion of absolute truth is therefore rejected. Institutions claiming to have a corner on truth are dismissed. There is an uneasiness with facts. The prevailing attitude is that all truth, even to some extent scientific knowledge, is subjective, biased, and socially constructed. There is a sense that feeling is all that counts because, in the end, feeling is all there is. The postmodern attitude is, "If I can't feel it, then it must not be true." Obviously, this has enormous implications for the practice of evangelization.

There is a pervasive cultural pessimism and even cynicism about politics and the ideological showboating of authorities and institutions. People are disillusioned with their inherited faiths, the institutional church, political parties, and the political process in general. Only one's own experience may be trusted.

Neither a modern nor postmodern worldview is in the majority everywhere. On a worldwide basis, Christianity continues to embrace a premodern worldview. In the Global South (the areas that we often call the Third World) huge and growing Christian populations—currently 480 million in Latin America, 360 million in Africa, and 313 million in Asia (compared with 260 million in North America)—now make up what the Catholic scholar Walbert Buhlmann has called the Third Church. Some observers see it as a form of Christianity as distinct as Protestantism or Orthodoxy; however, our concern here is with evangelization in the North American context. This does not mean ignoring the Global South, but it does require that the church of North America and Western Europe think creatively and positively as it relates to the concerns and needs of Global Christianity.

In the twenty-first century, Christians are facing a shrinking population in the "Liberal West" and a growing majority of the "Conservative Rest." During the past half-century the centers of the Christian world have moved decisively to Africa, to Latin America, and to Asia, and from our vantage point of today it seems improbable that the balance will ever shift back. The point is that one can either rail against the postmodern worldview and find satisfaction in angry denunciation, or accept it as simply the way things are in the twenty-first century and explore how to best carry the good message to a world starving for "the hope of the ages."

To some extent these three worldviews—premodern, modern, and postmodern—each continue to exist in the North American culture. This is especially true in churches. Social epochs are not neatly separated. They are not lined up neatly with smooth end perfectly matched to smooth end. It is possible to continue to live in an era that is essentially over. While one era prevails, its successor is already forming, and its predecessor continues to exert influence for a very long time. Nevertheless, we all are inexorably hastening with gathering speed into this postmodern world.

4) Globalization

Globalization is the process of international integration arising from the interchange of world views, products, ideas, and other aspects of culture. Advances in telecommunications, from the telegraph to the internet as well as infrastructure development and transportation, have generated an astonishing economic and cultural interdependence for the peoples and every nation that inhabit this planet. The problems faced in our world, such as the inhabitability of the planet, are global in nature and will require global solutions. Globalization likely will ultimately reduce the importance of nation states. Increasingly, nongovernment organizations will influence public policy across national boundaries, including humanitarian aid as philanthropic organizations with global missions, rather than churches, come more and more to the forefront.

In 1350 the global population was around 370 million. Current projections show a continued increase in population (but a steady decline in the population growth rate), with the global population expected to reach 10.5 billion by 2050. It is estimated that there are sufficient resources in the world to sustain a population of between 11 and 13 billion people—certainly no more than 13 billion. Some scientists estimate that by 2030, population growth, food shortages, and falling fossil energy resources will create a "perfect storm." The world will have to produce at least 70 percent more food. Climate change will mean catastrophic changes for many, and the world is likely to see a mass human migration the like of which has never been witnessed before.

The urbanization that began in the twentieth century has now resulted in the emergence of global cities as centers of enormous influence and economic activity. Mega cities, cities with a population in excess of 10 million, grew in number from three in 1973, to twenty-four by 2013, and should number twenty-seven by 2025.

As I write, the first Ebola cases have appeared in the United States. And the mosquito-borne Zika virus is terrifying mothers everywhere in the Americas. The reality is that health issues in the postmodern world are global—transcending the perspectives and concerns of not only regions but of nations.

The global workforce reflects a new international division of labor that has been emerging since the late 1970s. The global economic factors driving the rise of multinational corporations—namely, cross-border movement of goods, services, technology, and capital—are changing ways of thinking about labor and the structure of the workforce. Companies can now easily find workers without limiting their search locally. Even foreign executives may be given positions once available only to "locals." We have, however, witnessed the inability of production and service workers in advanced economies to compete with much lower-cost workers in developing countries.

Whether globalization is seen as evil or is embraced as a great advancement in human history is, in many ways, immaterial, in that it is simply the new reality and it cannot be undone. Perhaps the real question is who will address the problems and suffering that are intensified, if not directly caused, by globalization: the growing inequality of wealth, the growth in human trafficking, violence at every level, war, poverty, disease, political corruption, political imprisonment. More and more, global injustice and suffering are addressed, not by the church but by NGOs (nongovernmental organizations) rendering the church further irrelevant and superfluous.

5) The Information Age

Our still-evolving information society can be conceptualized as a society in which the creation, distribution, use, integration, and manipulation of information is a significant activity in the economic, political, educational, cultural, and, for us, religious life of that society. Consequently, it is commonplace to now find churches using PowerPoint projections and large screens for worship, streaming video clips of sermons and worship services, using email for congregational communications, blogging spiritual insights and biblical studies, distributing sermons as podcasts, and evangelizing through Facebook. "The world's combined effective capacity to exchange information through two-way telecommunication networks was 281 petabytes of (optimally compressed) information in 1986, 471 petabytes in 1993, 222.2 (optimally compressed) exabytes in 2000, and 65 (optimally compressed) exabytes in 2007, which is the information equivalent of six newspapers per person per day in 2007. The world's technology capacity to compute information with human-guided general-purpose computers grew from 3.0×10^8 MIPS in 1986, to 6.4×10^{12} MIPS in 2007, experiencing the fastest growth rate of over 60 percent per year during the last two decades."[6] Although changes brought about by the digital revolution and the astonishing evolution of media networking boggle the mind, it is perhaps important not to become so mesmerized by the communications revolution that we become incapable of tracing the threads of historical continuity. Nevertheless, it is possible to make the following observations.

The economy is more information-intensive and less and less labor-intensive all the time. Workers are becoming more productive while the value of their labor is at the same time decreasing. The value of capital is also diminished so that investments in human and financial capital are less predictive of new ventures. The defining characteristic of economic growth in the information age is the "weightlessness" of output. Both production and consumption have moved away from objects and toward information and services. Examples of weightless goods and products include computer software, the Internet, entertainment, consulting, telecommunications, and financial products. Such goods are ideal in that they can be replicated at low cost and used by many people at the same time. The polarization of jobs between relatively high-skill jobs with high wages and low-skill, low-wage jobs creates an ever-growing disparity between the incomes of rich and poor. The implications for evangelism and ministry are obvious. Church growth experts have always emphasized the importance of identifying a specific target group for evangelism. So, with the demise of the middle class, which was so effectively targeted at the end of what is now the last century, what fishing waters will the postmodern church identify—or will it become an enclave of

---

6. "Information Society," *Wikipedia*, https://en.wikipedia.org/wiki/information_society.

a small but privileged class. For a deeper and more extensive reflection there is always *The Epistle of Saint James*.

Observations On the Digital Age

George Barna sees three implications emerging for the church out of the information age. First, he notes, people feel modern life is accelerating rapidly in the amount, speed, and complexity of the changes taking place. The increasing digitalization of life, economic pressures, the disintegration of the family, shifting moral moorings, and many other factors all contribute to this shared sense of cultural acceleration. People, says Barna, also want to be culturally informed but are unwilling to invest the time or effort that would actually require and have become accustomed to skimming content. More than seven out of ten adults affirm this self-description. While the church is often accused of being several steps behind the culture at large, Barna's research shows practicing Christians want to keep up with culture and trends just as much as anyone else; 73 percent of practicing Christians say this is of personal importance to them, mirroring the national average. However, Barna believes his research suggests a third significant implication; namely, that people are moving beyond a search for mere facts and information and are looking for a holistic way of integrating faith and life. Information can now be found virtually everywhere, instantly, and for free. "What consumers in an age of over-information are after is a different kind of intellectual currency. They want knowledge that helps them find meaningful ways of living."[7]

We are probably still in the early stages of an electronic culture, and this electronic culture influences the images that come to us and the images of the language we use. It is, of course, more complicated than this in that images, language, and other cultural expressions all work together, systemically, to form meaning. In a print culture, priority is given to objectivity and discursive reasoning—for hundreds of years, at least in the West, that is the way students have been taught to do theology. But in an electronic culture where images are more important, the emphasis is on the subjective, the intuitive, and the psychological, with its constant flow of changing images.[8]

One further observation that needs to be made is this: The digital age has shown an amazing ability to create powerful human networks. This has been especially discernible in its ability to arouse, in nations and peoples, a passion for a more democratic way of life, and in the toppling of

---

7. Barna Group, "3 Trends Redefining the Information Age."
8. Sample, *Spectacle of Worship*, 32–33.

authoritarian and corrupt regimes. Just as the church adapted to changes brought about by the invention of the printing press and creatively used the media of print so well (the printers who read Luther's pamphlets while the ink was still wet were among the first converts to Protestantism), the church of the twenty-first century will, one would think almost inevitably, adapt to and become skillful in the use of electronic communications and networking in evangelization.

6) The Convergence of Science and Religion

Some of the most creative work being done in the postmodern world is asymmetrical in that it is sometimes counterintuitive and finds both utility and beauty through paradox, through the juxtaposition of what seem to be opposites, and by combining elements that appear contradictory. Many years ago my son did a painting I very much wanted for myself but didn't get. He painted a 1930s-looking diner that was situated down on the Pacific Garden Mall of Santa Cruz on California's Monterey Bay. The people outside the diner looked like the "punkers" also seen in downtown Santa Cruz—a city the *New Yorker* once described as "an outdoor asylum." It was the combining of such different eras, of such opposing images and their connotations, that made the painting fascinating as a work of art.

This same sort of creativity can also be found in the convergence of science and religion in the postmodern world. The modern era was a time of conflict and struggle between religion and science—faith and reason. Truth was seen as if it was rather like a window pane—flat and two sided rather than a multifaceted diamond. So there was the question of whether Darwin or Genesis was correct—which was true and which was false. Was the world created by the God of Abraham and Sarah, Isaac and Rebecca, Jacob, Rachel, and Leah, or was it the product of evolution—the god of blind chance and time. But thinking people today, who consider themselves Christian, no longer struggle with that either-or dilemma. Instead, they are more likely to experience God as mysteriously and inexplicably at work in the imponderable processes of the cosmos. In *A Brief History of Time*, Stephen Hawking said, "We are very close to knowing how the universe was made; but, if we knew why we would know the mind of God." Since Hawking does not, he says, believe in God, that was a rather curious thing to say unless we understand it as his own poetic exclamation upon encountering the reality of mystery, whether understood from the perspective of physics or religion. It makes me think of a story told by a philosophy professor. He told how at a conference that included both philosophers and physicists, the philosophers had walked out criticizing the physicists as "a bunch of mystics." The 2004 film *What the Bleep Do We Know!?* used documentary-style interviews and animated graphics to argue not only a connection between spirituality and quantum physics, but also to propose that individual and group consciousness can influence the material world. Although the film seriously misrepresents science and contains a good deal of pseudoscience, it is nevertheless a sign of the trajectory of the postmodern world.

A far more serious work, although certainly not without its scientific critics, is *Quantum Enigma: Physics Encounters Consciousness* by two professors at the University of California, Santa Cruz, Bruce Rosenblum and Fred Kuttner.[9] These two physicists posit a connection between quantum physics and consciousness; indeed, there may be no reality other than consciousness. While Rosenblum and Kuttner, unlike the seventeenth century idealist philosopher George Berkeley, are not arguing for the reality of God—that all things have their existence in the mind of God—their work most certainly represents a convergence of science and religion.

Among the many other books representing this convergence is that of geneticist Dean Hamer, *The God Gene: How Faith Is Hardwired into Our Genes*, which sets me personally to thinking of Thomas Aquinas, Alvin Plantinga, and the *sensus divinitatis*, and whether Augustine was not only spiritually but also scientifically correct in saying, "O Lord, you have made us for yourself, and our hearts are unquiet until they find their rest in you."[10]

Much of our perspective on human nature, on spirituality, and on life in the world has to do with our understanding of the mechanics of the universe. Newtonian physics established a paradigm of thinking in terms of linear cause and effect, and the world thought this way even when it came to the psychological understanding of human behavior. But with quantum physics we see everything as connected. Psychotherapists now regard the behavior of every individual as a manifestation of his or her family system, which is itself a part of a whole array of other interlocking systems. And there is in our postmodern world a new understanding of what it means to be human.

The 1982 cult film *Blade Runner* explores what it means to be human by looking at the fears and loves of genetically engineered replicants. But what it means to be human is not a science fiction question, it goes to the very heart of the human condition as lived by all of us. Recently, a documentary aired featuring a quadriplegic woman who could move a mechanical arm with her thoughts through electrodes attached to her head.

---

9. Rosenblum and Kuttner, *Quantum Enigma*.
10. Hamer, *The God Gene*; Plantinga, *Warranted Christian Belief*.

As we become more "mechanized" for medical reasons, one observer has even suggested that we will eventually all be cyborgs, how will that shape the human condition? Already we are faced with tough ethical questions in medicine: When does death occur? When is it ethical to "harvest" human organs to save someone else's life? Is the experience of grief when those closest and dearest to us die a disorder requiring medication or an opportunity to be embraced for the sake of spiritual transformation and wisdom?

Certainly biological science has changed the way people think of sex and reproductivity. The idea that sex is for the sole purpose of procreation rather than pleasure, an entirely unbiblical view by the way, is now rather quaint. Just physiologically we know, no matter what theological argument may be made to the contrary, that is just not true. When it was thought in the Middle Ages that semen actually contained little microscopic people to be implanted in a womb, it was possible to think of women as little more than "incubators," but science has played an enormous role in demolishing this objectification of women. And, if a little person had actually been projected into the womb, then it made sense to say that human life began at conception. But it's a little difficult for today's educated North Americans to believe that an undifferentiated mass of tissue is a human being. And, quoting poetic Bible verses about the mystery of life, of having been "knitted together" by God in our mother's womb will not, in the long run, suffice as an answer. And the scientific observation that homosexuality is not as simple as being "a lifestyle choice" has set Christians to rereading Scripture in a new light. But I am meandering. The simple point is that scientific biology has already reshaped our understanding of what it means to be human and will continue to do so. Bjørn Grinde, a biologist working as a chief scientist at the Norwegian Institute of Public Health in Oslo, argues in his book *Darwinian Happiness* that many of our human problems have to do with humanity's imprisonment in an environment that is at odds with the way evolution has shaped us to live.[11]

7) Consciousness and the Communications Revolution

Twenty years ago I discovered in the written work of David Buttrick, who was until his retirement professor of homiletics and worship at Vanderbilt Divinity School, the most exciting, insightful, and helpful perspective on preaching I have ever encountered. Buttrick proposed a phenomenological way of understanding and practicing homiletics—which also means a new

---

11. Grinde, *Darwinian Happiness*.

way of understanding and practicing evangelization. I was introduced to Buttrick's work when at a spiritual retreat. I asked Richard Eslinger, who is himself a professor of homiletics, how we could make preaching a contemplative practice. He suggested I read Buttrick, who was concerned with how consciousness forms in the mind and with how preaching can be done in such a way as to facilitate the formation of God consciousness. Buttrick said, "We must find a way to preach in a world that is changing its mind. Note the word 'changing': Our consciousness is changing and is not yet fixed, or even close to taking shape. Rather obviously, we live between the times in the midst of tumbling paradigms."[12]

What Buttrick helped me to understand is that it is not just that certain attitudes or societal values and norms have shifted, or that my grandchildren are already more technologically literate than I am or ever will be, but that the very way in which human consciousness, and for our purposes we can say spiritual consciousness, forms has undergone a seismic shift and cannot be reset to its original position any more than slippage along the San Andreas fault can be reversed.

Like it or not, "we are moving toward a new evangelical enterprise." Consciousness simply forms differently in the postmodern mind than it did in the era of modernity.

> The problem of method is now more complex than we know. Human consciousness is historical. Consciousness is not fixed, the same in the first century as in the twentieth century. No, consciousness changes age to age. Clearly we are speaking to a different human consciousness than addressed by the apostles or by St. Augustine or even by priests and ministers a mere century ago. Look at paintings from the age of reason, they all display the same perspective. They are painted as if by a third person objective viewer; in a way they are a testimony to the style of the age, rationalism. The world is viewed as "out there" in careful detail, ordered by detached reason. But wander any art gallery these days, in New York, London, or Paris, and the canvasses are quite different. In a single painting may be several perspectives, angles of vision superimposed upon one another, acknowledging the truth of human relativity. Moreover, artists these days have a much wider definition of reality than artists who were painting the objective "thereness" of rationalism. Artists now are opening up a world beyond the objective, a world that includes memories, and fantasies, and swirls of feeling and strange compelling social myths. Are not memories, myths,

---

12. Buttrick, *A Captive Voice*, 79–80, 65–73. See also, Buttrick, *Homiletic*.

fantasies, feelings, hopes, and the like all components of human reality at any given moment, even though they do not register on film or record on tape?[13]

Buttrick goes on to talk about how the same sort of change has occurred in fiction. Indeed, language itself since the beginning of the twentieth century has undergone an enormous contraction and expansion, and the old metaphors, such as Saint Anselm's expression of the atonement, simply no longer form in consciousness.

As language changes there is also a corresponding change in the way people think—what we might think of as an "epistemological" shift. The question we face then is: "What practice of evangelization do we need to employ so that men and women may experience the presence of Christ as a mystery both transcendent and immediate—the chief beauty and source of meaning within their very souls?" To quote Buttrick one more time, "The task of our age is to not only speak the gospel, but to also find and form new ways of preaching for an emerging new human consciousness."[14]

Tex Sample, professor of church and society at Saint Paul School of Theology in Kansas City, Missouri, says that the shift of rock and roll to accenting the upbeat rather than the downbeat in the sixties has changed how people move, think, and feel. While Sample does not want to push the point too far, especially in regard to North America, he finds Chukwulozie Anyanwu's study of traditional Africa worth reflecting on. "Sound is the model of reality and the criterion of truth in the African culture. To put it too simply, if something doesn't sound 'right' it will not be true or authentic."[15] Of course, music has always carried profound meaning spoken out of the depths of human experience, but it too in our time has been transformed and is transforming human consciousness.

Conclusion

I end this chapter with an extended quotation of the beloved John R. W. Stott, evangelist, preacher, author, and world Christian leader who was rector of All Souls Church in London for two and a half decades. I have chosen this quotation for the end of this chapter because I think that Stott, as a British Anglican evangelical, lends strong emphasis to the need for the church

---

13. Buttrick, *A Captive Voice*, 77–78.
14. Ibid., 80.
15. Sample, *Spectacle of Worship*, 35.

to understand its radically changed context in order to meet the challenges of a changing world.

> For more than twenty years I have been haunted by a conversation I had on this topic with two brothers, which I have related in full in *I Believe in Preaching*. They were university students, who told me they had repudiated the faith of their parents, in which they had been brought up. One was now an agnostic, the other an atheist. I enquired why. Did they no longer believe in the truth of Christianity? No, that was not their problem, they replied. Their dilemma was not whether Christianity was true, but whether it was relevant. How could it be? Christianity, they went on, was a primitive Palestinian religion. It had arisen in a primitive Palestinian culture. So what on earth did it have to offer people like them who lived in the exciting, modern world of space travel, transplant surgery, and genetic engineering? It was irrelevant!
>
> The feeling of the remoteness, obsolescence, and irrelevance of Christianity is widespread. The world has changed dramatically since Jesus' day, and goes on changing with ever more bewildering speed. People reject the gospel, not necessarily because they think it is false, but because it no longer resonates with them. Can the church survive the challenges of modernity? Or will it suffer the ignominious fate of the dinosaur, equally unable to adapt to a changing environment, and become extinct?[16]

---

16. Stott, *Contemporary Christian*, 16–17.

CHAPTER THREE

The Awakening

Morning is when I am awake and there is a dawn in me. Moral reform is the effort to throw off sleep.... The millions are awake enough for physical labor; but only one in a million is awake enough for effective intellectual exertion, only one in a hundred million to a poetic or divine life. To be awake is to be alive. We must learn to reawaken and keep ourselves awake, not by mechanical aids, but by an infinite expectation of the dawn, which does not forsake us even in our soundest sleep.[1]

—Henry David Thoreau

Consciousness and how it forms is a bafflement to scientists, philosophers, and religious thinkers. "There is," as the physicist David Chalmers says, "nothing we know more intimately than conscious experience, but there is nothing harder to explain."[2] The experience of consciousness, of awareness, in the most mundane and uninteresting events of life as well as in those extraordinary moments for which we grasp for words and phrases, no matter how inadequate, in order to describe the experience—mystical enlightenment, a spiritual awakening, a second birth, a feeling of "at-one-ment," a sense of transcendence, a beatific vision or the "oceanic feeling"—is simply, for most of us, what it means to be alive. It is because

---

1. Thoreau, *Walden*, 73.
2. Chalmers, quoted in Rosenblum and Kuttner, *Quantum Enigma*, 171.

consciousness is at the core of our very being that the words of Henry David Thoreau, although written 160 years ago, resonate within us as the apt expression and deep truth concerning the nature of our existence. Indeed, the language of poetry is strangely expressive of something about consciousness that neither science, nor psychology, nor philosophy is ever able to get close to.

René Descartes—the seventeenth century mathematician responsible for the Cartesian coordinate system, known as the father of modern philosophy and the father of analytical geometry—in thinking through the nature of reality, refused to succumb to the obvious and assumed givens in the thinking of his day. In searching for one thing that could not be doubted as the basis for his philosophy, Descartes came to his famous *cogito ergo sum*. "I think, therefore I am." Or, perhaps better, "I am thinking, therefore I exist." Descartes's thesis has through the centuries been dismissed by many brilliant thinkers, including Kierkegaard, who was a person of immense faith, as an inadequate basis for "proving" the existence of God. The most frequent criticism is that Descartes's formula may "prove" the existence of thinking but not the "I" doing the thinking. Critics have frequently challenged Descartes's argument by stating it in the form of a faulty syllogism:

> "X" thinks
> I am that "X"
> I think
> Therefore I am

Descartes himself responded by asserting that *cogito ergo sum* was not a syllogism. Ultimately, Descartes was simply asserting consciousness as the one thing we can be most certain exists.

In my reading, I have not found an entirely satisfactory definition or description of consciousness. John Locke's *An Essay Concerning Human Understanding*, published in 1690, is often cited as the origin of the modern concept of consciousness. In that essay, Locke defined consciousness as, "The perception of what passes in a person's own Mind." Ned Block, professor of philosophy, psychology, and neural science, proposed a distinction between two types of consciousness, what he called *phenomenal* (P-consciousness) and *access* (A-consciousness).[3] If I walk in the rain and feel the wetness of the rain drops, that is phenomenal consciousness. If I then begin to reflect on the water cycle, and the cycle of life and water as a symbol of life, that is access consciousness. Some believe that Block's two types of consciousness do not extend far enough. William Lycan says in his book, *Consciousness*

---

3. Block, "On a Confusion," 375–413.

and Experience, that there are at least eight clearly distinct types of consciousness—organism consciousness, control consciousness, consciousness *of,* state/event consciousness, reportability, introspective consciousness, subjective consciousness, and self-consciousness—and that there are very likely forms of consciousness not covered by these eight.[4]

There is also the perplexing question of how far in any direction consciousness extends. Are human beings alone conscious, or are other creatures also conscious? My dog Jack, as far as I know, has no awareness or appreciation that he was rescued his last day on "death row." Yet, Jack clearly has some sort of an emotional life. An amoeba will react to light. Is that to be considered, at some level, consciousness? For Pierre Teilhard de Chardin, paleontologist, scientist, Jesuit priest, and Christian mystic, the earth is alive, pulsating with energy, and all matter is charged with life and Spirit. This should not be considered at all odd in light of the New Testament Scriptures: "In God we live, move and have our being" (Acts 17:28), says Saint Paul. Or, "God is over all, in all and through all" (Eph 4:6). Or, consider these well-known verses from the Epistle to the Romans:

> For with anxious longing the creation waits eagerly for the revealing of the sons of God. For the creation was subjected to futility, not willingly, but because of Him who subjected it, in hope that the creation itself also will be set free from its slavery to corruption into the freedom of the glory of the children of God. For we know that the whole creation groans and suffers the pains of childbirth together until now. And not only this, but also we ourselves, having the first fruits of the Spirit, even we ourselves groan within ourselves, waiting eagerly for *our* adoption as sons, the redemption of our body. (Rom 8:19–23, NASB)

In fact, many quantum physicists maintain that all reality is mental.

The cognitive scientist Donald Hoffman asserts, "I believe that consciousness and its contents are all that exist. Space-time, matter, and fields never were the fundamental denizens of the universe but have always been, from their beginning, among the humbler contents of consciousness, dependent for it on their being."[5]

If that sounds too terribly bizarre or somehow un-Christian to us, we might reconsider William Berkeley, philosopher and bishop. Berkeley proposed the philosophy of Idealism; that is, everything that exists is mental, existing in the thoughts of God. In this way, Berkeley meant to rescue philosophy from Newtonian physics, which he thought left little room for

---

4. Lycan, *Consciousness and Experience.*
5. Hoffman, quoted in Rosenblum and Kuttner, *Quantum Enigma,* 181.

God. "To be," said Berkeley, "is to be perceived." Samuel Johnson famously responded to Berkeley by kicking a stone while announcing, "I refute him thus!" The controversy of the time is somewhat, although not completely, true to Berkeley's thinking, reflected by two limericks:

> There was a young fellow name Todd,
> Who said, "It's exceedingly odd
> To think that this tree
> Should continue to be
> When there's no one about the Quad.
>
> There is nothing especially odd;
> I am always about in the Quad.
> And that's why the tree
> Can continue to be
> When observed by
> Yours faithfully, God.[6]

In *Foundations of Christian Faith*, Karl Rahner notes that in classical Thomism the ultimate meaning of being and consciousness are the same thing. What quantum mechanics has demonstrated is that our world has a mysterious universal connectedness that goes well beyond what can be explained by what we think of as physical forces.[7]

Perhaps this is a good point at which to interject the question: Does consciousness have a phenomenal aspect, or can it be reduced, as Francis Crick insisted in *The Astonishing Hypothesis*, to the physical makeup of neurons in the brain? "You, your joys and sorrows," according to Crick, "your memories and your ambitions, your sense of personal identity and free will, are in fact no more than the behavior of a vast assembly of nerve cells and their associated molecules."[8] Of course, if Francis Crick is accurate in his assessment of human consciousness, we must all engage in a conspiracy of illusion, for no one can live and maintain their sanity believing all their hopes, joys, sorrows, and loves are nothing more than an electro-chemical process bereft of any ultimate meaning.

In the medieval period, Saint Thomas Aquinas wrote of the *sensus divinitatis*, the sense of the divine, as a faculty that, like the five senses, or memory, or reason, can lead one to knowledge of truth. More recently, Alvin Plantinga has explored this same concept in *Warranted Christian Belief*. Plantinga recognizes that the *sensus divinitatis*, like any of our other

---

6. Rosenblum and Kuttner, *Quantum Enigma*, 175.
7. Rahner, *Foundations of Christian Faith*, 303.
8. Crick, *Astonishing Hypothesis*, 3.

faculties, may guide us correctly or wrongly and so their "warrant" must always be explored. I do not want to present a one-factory model of consciousness here. What I find myself always returning to is the conviction that whether reality is entirely mental, or both physical and mental at once, the mystery of consciousness, which is central to the enterprise of evangelization, remains.

David Bentley Hart who, in his book *The Experience of God: Being, Consciousness, Bliss*, defines God as "an infinite act of consciousness," is helpful at this point. He writes,

> For to say that God is being, consciousness, and bliss is also to say that he is the one reality in which all our existence, knowledge, and love subsist, from which they come and to which they go, and that therefore he is somehow present in even our simplest experience of the world, and is approachable by way of a contemplative and moral refinement of that experience. That is to say, these three words are not only a metaphysical explanation of God, but also a phenomenological explanation of the human encounter with God. Here before us, or so a great many traditions claim, in certain of our most immediate and primal experiences, lies our first knowledge of the mystery of God, as well as a kind of ubiquitous evidence of the supernatural.[9]

In saying this, Hart gestures toward a core question of this present study: How, in practical terms, does consciousness, or less precisely how does spiritual consciousness, form in the human mind?

Some of the most interesting work in the study of consciousness has been done by the Australian philosopher David Chalmers mentioned earlier. Chalmers distinguishes between what he calls the hard problems and the easy problems of consciousness. The easy problems are things like the reaction to stimuli and the reporting of various mental states. The hard problem is that of accounting for how the biological brain generates the subjective inner world of experience. Wholly opposite of Francis Crick, Chalmers says, "It follows that no mere account of physical process will tell us why experience arises. The emergence of experience goes beyond what can be derived from physical theory"[10] It is the hard problem of why spiritual experiences arise, or how consciousness of Sacred Mystery emerges and takes on religious form through evangelization that concerns us here.

---

9. Hart, *Experience of God*, 9, 42.
10. Chalmers, quoted in Rosenblum and Kuttner, *Quantum Enigma*, 179.

Four Stories of Conversion

The question that has haunted me most of my clerical life is how does spiritual consciousness arise in the individual, where does that spiritual awareness that is transformative come from, how can Christian men and women educe that response of faith that leads to salvation, not only in the North American evangelical sense but in the biblical Hebrew and Greek sense of *yeshua* and *sotereos*—that which is large, spacious, expansive, healing, restorative, life giving, and free from everything that diminishes, narrows, or constricts life. Following are four stories of spiritual awakening. Two of these stories have to do with people suffering from alcoholism who discovered sobriety—who, if you will, experienced liberation, were saved from the oubliette of addiction. The other two, one of them rather long, have to do with Christian conversion. If you want to really understand the conversion process, the sort of transformation of consciousness, as suggested here and applied to the practice of Christian evangelization, then read each story slowly and carefully—maybe more than once. After you have finished reading, set this book aside and just quietly sit with what you have read for a few minutes.

David

I had a "good life." I had a loving family. My wife, a school teacher, was smart and kind and, at least in the big stuff, always supportive. Our grown children were people anyone would be proud to claim as their son or daughter.

I owned my own business, a lumber yard that had done very well. Not long after I turned fifty-six I sold the lumber yard and retired. In retirement I spent more and more time pursuing my favorite hobby—drinking. No one recognized how bad my drinking was, that my problem with alcohol was just getting worse and worse all the time. There was no job for it to interfere with and no financial worries. My wife only taught school because it made her happy. We certainly didn't need the money. There were no family fights and no legal problems, like DUIs. The beer I drank raised no concerns, and no one saw all the shots I downed when I went to get beer out of the refrigerator. The worst thing I did was to fall asleep early every evening in my recliner, but the family thought that's just the way it was with Dad now that he had retired.

One morning after my wife had left for her teaching job, I was getting a good start on my drinking when I threw up—something I had never done before. As I washed my face I looked into the mirror and said to myself: "You know your life is slipping away—just slip-sliding away." I walked over, picked up the phone, and called the recovery program at a local hospital.

Becky

I was thirteen and in the eighth grade the first time I had a drink. Well, I don't really know how many drinks I had that night, but however many it was I loved them, every one. I felt free, and funny, and like I was so special. I wasn't worried about pleasing anyone. One of the things I learned right away was that I felt that way every time I drank, I really looked forward to every party where I could drink with my friends, especially sleepovers.

Pretty soon, I discovered that my parents and their friends drank enough that I could raid the liquor cabinet at home without attracting a whole lot of notice. I frequently went to school drunk. I was so drunk for high school graduation that I was barely able to stagger across the stage for my diploma.

I am not sure how I made it through college. I went to a party school where drinking was considered a form of major entertainment. But I knew even then that drinking was something more for me than just having fun.

After college I married but we were more like two drinking buddies than husband and wife. We were each too consumed with our own self-centered cravings to be there for each other or to care in a way that created any real intimacy. The inevitable divorce followed along with DUIs and lost jobs. I tried teaching out of college, but its hard to teach a bunch of inattentive kids when you are in a fog yourself.

I drank more and more and enjoyed it less and less. In the beginning I drank for that great euphoric feeling. But by this time I was drinking in a desperate attempt to just feel half-way normal. That normal feeling never came back no matter how much I drank. I had not quite reached age thirty and my life was a mess. I was miserable all the time. I was so miserable that there were suicidal thoughts along with several failed attempts.

One Saturday my younger sister showed up at my apartment. We had always been close. I have always loved her more than words can say. I had promised to do something special with her for her birthday. When I didn't show and didn't return her calls or reply to her texts, she came over to check on me. I was sick from all the booze, and it was more than just being hungover. I was a mess. The apartment was in chaos. There were used condoms lying on the floor, but I had no idea who had used them. I had run out of liquor and so had a glass of mouth-wash on the rocks in my hand when she came to the door. My sister freaked out. She said if I didn't get help she couldn't be my sister anymore, that it hurt too bad to see what had become of my life.

I guess that was my "bottom," or "spiritual-awakening," or something. For sure it was the beginning of my recovery from the disease of alcoholism. In that moment I saw not only what I was doing to myself, but I saw how much I was hurting my sister and my parents. I put on a pair of pants and a shirt, slipped my feet into flip-flops, and she drove me to a nonprofit treatment center where I began the journey to recovery.

I got my two-year chip from AA not long ago. I won't tell you that I have a perfect fairy-tale life, but I can tell you for sure that it is better than insanity or dying every day from alcoholism.

Diane

Both my parents were alcoholics. Along with my younger sister and baby brother, I grew up with them always fighting and with the police being called because of the violence. Our house always needed painting and always had broken windows. The lawn was never mowed and it was hard to tell the grass from the knee-high weeds. When I reached my teens I would tell anyone giving me a ride home to drop me off two blocks away from our house. I was just too embarrassed for them to see how we lived.

When I graduated from high school I fell in love with someone several years older. He had just gotten out of the Navy. It wasn't long before I found I was pregnant with our son. We were already living together and so I thought, since he said he loved me, that the natural thing would be for us to get married now that we were having a baby. But while we stayed together as if we were a young married couple there was no wedding, no matter how much I pleaded. Eventually I discovered, after finding a letter from his mother who lived on the East Coast, that he already had a wife and child he had left behind when he went into the Navy. By that time I had given birth to our daughter and so stayed, but it wasn't just for the sake of the baby; I loved him very much.

Life was difficult. His drinking became more and more of a problem and so did the other women. We would get evicted from a house or an apartment, and he would leave until I had managed to get the kids and myself into another place. There was never enough money to buy food or clothes.

One day, the worst day of my life, our four-year-old son was playing in front of the house when the woman from next door who had been drinking heavily backed her car over him, killing him instantly. What can I say? There are no words.

Neither are there words for the death of my sister. For so much of my life she and our younger brother had been all I had for affection and comfort. She was addicted to drugs and became involved with a man who was insanely violent. He beat her to death one day because she went for a walk without asking his permission. I cleaned the blood-spattered apartment and took her two children home to live with me, but my husband insisted I place them in foster care. I felt like I had betrayed my sister by doing that.

One day I drove to the cliffs overlooking the Pacific Ocean, intending to jump to my death and quiet all the pain I felt every day. While I was standing there preparing myself to jump, a funny little man from across the road that ran along the bluffs came out of his house and walked to where I was standing.

"Are you thinking about jumping?" he asked.

"Oh no," I lied, "I am just enjoying the beautiful view."

"No," he said, "I have lived here a long time, and I have seen many people come here. Some want to look at the beautiful ocean, but some are thinking black thoughts. I can tell you are thinking about jumping. Maybe you should try God. Some people think that helps." And he walked away. The moment was ruined and, feeling tired and hopeless, I got in my car and started driving home. As I drove the thought came to me, "Why not try God, nothing else has worked?"

When I got home I started to read the New Testament like I was reading a novel. I started with the Gospel of Matthew and read all the way through to the end of the book of Revelation. On nearly every page I found myself saying over and over again, "This is about me. This is all about my life." I felt like I had been in a deep black pit all of my life, scratching and clawing in futile desperation to get out, but now it was like God had reached in, grabbed hold of me, and pulled me up and out into the marvelous light. I went to church the next Sunday and was baptized soon after. I also started attending Alcoholics Anonymous. All that I can say is that in my letting go and surrendering my heart and mind to the loving will of God as expressed in Christ, I had found peace for the first time in my life. It has been so strange because the peace I now feel is there even though I continue to experience many difficulties. And sometimes I still feel the old sadness but somehow it is very different.

John Shore

In the comment threads of some of my posts here on *Huffington Post*, people have speculated about whether or not I'm "really" a Christian. (I'm used to getting that question from the right; it's new to me from the left.) So, I thought I'd share the story of my conversion.

The split-second before I very suddenly became a Christian, I couldn't possibly have been less of a Christian. If anything, I was *anti*-Christian. The religion struck me as ridiculously immature, a way-too-obvious system designed mostly to capitalize on people's guilt: Big Daddy in the Sky knows you did wrong, but will love you anyway if you'll only admit that he's perfection itself, and that you're a wretched, sickening sack of sin.

Please. I always figured that if I wanted Father Knows Best, I'd watch TV.

And it wasn't like I didn't believe in anything. I did. I very seriously believed in me. I hadn't a doubt in the world about the fact that I was somebody truly worthy of my utmost affection and devotion. I was strong, capable, friendly, competent — I was just a general, all-around good guy. I was thirty-eight years old. I'd been happily married for sixteen years. I had a good job. I had friends. People liked me. I liked me.

That is, I liked myself as much as it seemed reasonable to. I was certainly aware of my own shortcomings (which I won't share with you here, in order to save my friends and former friends the shock of suddenly realizing what happened, that one time, to their stashes of porno and pot). But I didn't need God or anybody else to forgive me for the times I behaved poorly. I was perfectly capable (if not spectacularly efficient) at forgiving myself, thank you very much.

Because I knew that, at my core, I was a good, morally sound person.

On the other hand, I was a human being. And human beings, I knew (boy, did I know) have natural needs, and natural weaknesses.

The paramount imperative, I believed, was to love myself. That's what it was all about: loving, and forgiving, oneself. Those who mastered that mastered life. You had to be your own parents, your own nurturer, your own best friend. Who could argue with that?

Then one day I was sitting at my desk at work during a totally typical weekday, feeling regretful about a particularly immature, semi-destructive thing I'd recently done, when this feeling started coming over me that in about four seconds had my undivided attention. "What the hell?" I thought. The next thing I knew, I was very nearly desperate to be alone somewhere. It felt like warm water was filling me up inside—but downward, starting at just beneath my scalp. Right about when the "water" had moved from my neck to my chest, I knew that whatever was happening to me wasn't going to stop.

And I could tell it was something spiritual, or psychological—or something basically nonphysical.

"I'll be right back," I said to a coworker—and then cut out for an auxiliary supply closet in our office that no one ever used. I flipped on its light, closed its door behind me, and waited. I closed my eyes. The intensity of what was happening made that seem like a good idea. And what happened, rather all at once, was that I saw what a complete *asshole* I was. Isn't that awful? All at once, the truth was before me that instead of being a good guy who's basically always trying to do the right thing, I was a selfish, emotional weakling who was always doing and saying whatever best served my own needs at the time.

I never lied; but I'd fudge the truth here and there if it didn't really hurt anybody and would help things roll my way.

I never cheated; but life is complex, and sometimes one has to make deals that more directly serve a Larger Good.

I wanted to help others; but there were so many good shows on TV, especially after a long, rough day at work.

What suddenly became a fact to me was that I'd been fooling myself for so long I'd forgotten the act. I wasn't the great, honorable person I started out to be, that I'd meant to become—that I actually thought I was. I was just another guy so busy thinking he's constructing the perfect home that he doesn't realize how long ago he stopped using a level.

Man, I hate it when that happens.

I hate it when my whole view of myself is suddenly deconstructed and replaced by a view of myself that is *so* not what I expected.

I hate it when in one second I go from being Batman to being the Penguin.

Actually, though, that wasn't the worst part. By far.

The worst part was that, accompanying that less-than-peachy view of myself was the very real knowledge that I was never, ever, ever going to change.

Ever. Never. Ever.

I was born as I was. I had spent my life as I was. And I would die as I'd always been: small, selfish, and mean as a pissed-off penguin.

And there was absolutely nothing I could do about it.

I'd already spent my whole life trying to. Miserable mediocrity was the *best* I could do. I could achieve *that* only when I'd somehow pulled it together enough not to be a completely craven animal.

On a *good* day I was the Penguin!

And then here's what happened: I saw my death. I mean, I didn't see myself writhing around after I'd been hit by a truck on the freeway or anything—I didn't see *how* I would die. But I did see, in a sort of direct, open tunnel, the disturbingly short distance between where I was, and where I was most certainly going. I saw my mortality. I saw the simple fact that I would die—and that, as surely as one day follows the next, at the moment of my death I wouldn't be any different from how I'd been at any other moment of my life.

I wasn't going to get better. I wasn't going to become stronger, or wiser, or smarter, or more honorable. It just wasn't going to happen. I was thirty-eight. I was who I'd die being. At *best.*

Oh, but that was a bad, bad moment for me.

And then my legs disappeared from underneath me. I actually *fell on my knees.*

In the supply closet.

At my job.

Looking at my miserable, weak future, straight to my miserable, means-nothing death. It was just me and the cold, hard, gray, flat fact of . . . me. Which was never going to change. I just did not have the will or means or character to change who I was, which was exactly who I'd always been.

I saw that my life, in any way that could possibly matter, was over.

Then I did something I never, *ever* do. I started to cry.

Because isn't the whole point of being alive to be someone you'd really *want* to be?

So I'm kneeling there, blinded by my sad, stupid little fate, when, from up and off to my left, I hear a disembodied voice say something. And it says what it says in a clear, distinct cartoon voice. Listen: I grew up glued to cartoons. As a kid, I had absolutely no idea what was happening with adults, who were clearly insane. But Daffy Duck I got. Porky Pig was my kind of guy. Wile E. Coyote? Please—my very alter-ego! To this day, I practically shiver with joy when *The Simpsons* are on.

Anyway, of course I can't exactly describe the cartoon voice I heard. But, you know: goofy, precise, rich, pseudo-edgy. Cartoonish. And what that voice said, from up and off to my left somewhere—from offstage, as it were—was, "Isn't this what Jesus is for?"

And just like that, I stopped crying.

That the story of Jesus is historically true. That it happened. That God, desiring above all else to show the people he'd created that he loved them, became a human, and came to earth, and sacrificed himself, and in every way did everything he possibly could to show people exactly how deeply and terribly he loves them.

That's what my conversion consisted of: a sudden, sure knowledge that the historical story of Christ is true.

It wasn't, like, *wisdom* at all. I wasn't suddenly filled with the Mind of God, or anything like that. My soul didn't light up. Angels didn't sing for me. Nothing like that happened. In a way, it was about as boring as learning the year house paint was invented, or that your bank has slightly altered its Saturday hours. All that had changed was that I was now *sure* that the story of Christ, about which I had always scoffed (if I ever thought of it at all), was true.

Then it was like how, when it starts to rain, you think about the only thing you can think, which is: "Oh. Now everything will get wet." That's about what I thought: "Oh. Now I'm a Christian." So I stood, wiped my eyes, opened the door to the supply closet, and went back to work.

And that was that.[11]

---

11. Shore, *Penguins*, 115–24.

Unsettling Moments

Notice that each story involves a catalytic moment or event that changes everything—even though outwardly, as in John Shore's story, it may appear as if nothing much has changed at all. In the treatment of alcoholism and drug addiction, this moment or event is often experienced as a moment of acute crisis—"hitting bottom." In fact, the frequent occurrence of conversion, of moments of profound insight, of growth and enlightenment in moments of suffering and confusion, prompted Watchman Nee, who died after thirty years of captivity in a Chinese communist prison, to write, "It is at the point of desperation that God gives life."[12] However, we want to be careful not to lean too heavily on crisis and desperation as definitive of every catalytic moment. As David Bentley Hart in *The Experience of God: Being, Consciousness, Bliss* writes, "The beginning of all philosophy, according to both Plato and Aristotle, lies in the experience of wonder. One might go further and say that the beginning of all serious thought—all reflection upon the world that is not merely calculative or appetitive—begins in a moment of unsettling or delightful surprise."[13]

From the perspective of academic psychology, the best book I have read on the dynamics of conversion is by a professor of psychology and religion at the San Francisco Theological Seminary and the Graduate Theological Union in Berkley—Lewis Rambo's *Understanding Religious Conversion*.[14] Rambo sees some form of *crisis*, although not always dramatic or at all obvious, as preceding conversion. "Two basic types of crisis," he says, "are important to the conversion process: crises that call into question one's fundamental orientation to life, and crises that in and of themselves are rather mild but are the proverbial straw that broke the camel's back." But always, crisis is a part of the conversion process. Rambo therefore writes,

> In the more than fifty interviews I have conducted and the countless books and articles I have read, conversions are often stimulated by an extraordinary, and in some cases mystical, experience. The nature of the experience varies, but for most people a mystical experience, especially an unexpected one, is profoundly disturbing. The paradigmatic example is the experience of Saul of Tarsus. The biblical accounts describe the catalyst

---

12. Nee, *What Shall This Man Do?*, 116.
13. Hart, *Experience of God*, 87.
14. Rambo, *Understanding Religious Conversion*.

The Awakening

of his conversion as a mystical experience triggered by divine intervention.[15]

The intensity of the crisis stage may vary considerably and while it may be related to a serious life problem such as an illness, it can also reflect a desire for transcendence or meaning.

Even if you are a lay Christian the chances are that you may be, as I often find in the contemporary church, sophisticated enough in biblical studies to know that the Greek New Testament word *kairos* could be resorted to here. The *kairotic* moment is that moment in which everything comes together harmoniously, works together for a desirable end, and like all of nature, including the farmer, moves through the rhythms of the year to the season of harvest—it is the opportune moment and therefore also the decisive moment. Notice this *kairotic*, catalytic, decisive, opportune moment or event in each story.

Although the field of alcohol and drug treatment does not tell us everything we need to know about the conversion process, it does tell us an awful lot. A little more than a dozen years after my ordination in the Churches of Christ I received a telephone call one Sunday afternoon. It was from a woman who was a prominent member in a church of our denomination about two hundred miles away, near the entrance to Kings National Forest in the Sierras. She said I should expect her much younger brother and his wife and infant daughter, I'll call the couple Mike and Cheryl, to be at our church that night and that Cheryl would be asking for baptism. In the Churches of Christ, baptism by immersion is administered immediately after a confession of faith. Mike and Cheryl did indeed show up and Cheryl was baptized—life for the young couple changed dramatically.

Mike and Cheryl had been on their way to meet friends in the mountains for a weekend of sex and drugs and booze. They decided to stop at the home of Mike's sister, which was on the way. Cheryl was persuaded by Mike's sister to watch a slide presentation produced by the Churches of Christ as an evangelistic tool. As Cheryl, who had no religious background whatsoever, watched this not very artful presentation of the love of Christ she found herself saying, "I never knew. I never could have imagined someone loving me like that."

Mike and Cheryl quit using street drugs after her baptism, but continued to feed their craving with prescription "medication." Their family physician was as much of a connection as any street corner dealer in the narcotics trade. And Mike, who worked in a plant that used acids and corrosives, was adept at having minor "accidents" that required potent pain

---

15. Ibid., 46–48, 50.

medication. Then one day Cheryl called me. "I really need to talk," she said. "I am so depressed I can't do anything. I have been lying on the floor all morning crying because I can't even figure out how to write a check." When I saw Cheryl later that day she confided that she had been drinking and taking Valium. She said in an angry and challenging tone of voice, "My faith has done me absolutely no good. I quit drugs before I was even baptized. God has done nothing for me." I responded in a matter-of-fact manner, "But you haven't quit have you?" She told me later she was so angry that she had wanted to slap me hard enough to knock my head off my shoulders. But it was the beginning of an alliance between me and Mike and Cheryl in a long and desperate struggle.

My joining Mike and Cheryl as an ally in their struggle revolutionized my work as a therapist, as a pastor, as a preacher, and taught me far more about the spiritual life than I could ever possibly put into words. I attended AA meetings so often that the men and women in those meetings thought I was an alcoholic who was just either unable or unwilling to talk. I read the Big Book as part of my daily devotions. A rehab center in town had an extensive library and I read every book on its shelves in addition to my numerous purchases. And, although I had studied addictive disorders in earning a master's degree in counseling psychology, I took additional graduate courses and went to wonderful seminars and workshops with highly respected professionals on the physiological, psychological, and spiritual dynamics and treatment of alcoholism and drug addiction. Cheryl's challenge turned out to be something of a catalytic moment for me.

In an intervention workshop with Vernon Johnson, the Episcopal priest and recovering alcoholic who pioneered the intervention technique, and Howard Clinebell, perhaps at that time the world's foremost authority in pastoral theology and counseling, I experienced a paradigm shift that was so strong that it felt physical—as if my brain had actually shifted from one side to the other. Vernon Johnson's theory was that there is something about us, something about our human nature that cannot abide the notion that we are not in control. Consequently, as the individual loses more and more control over his or her drinking a high, thick, and strong fortress wall of denial is built to defend against the consciousness of this loss of control. The blocks of this wall are composed of rationalizations, some of them quite sophisticated, euphoric recall, and even the alteration of memories. This wall of denial is more than refusal to assent or agree to a bare fact. More than anything, denial is the refusal to admit that something is personally relevant. An individual may therefore agree he or she is an alcoholic but still reject any thought of that fact as personally relevant. The catalytic moment for the alcoholic, then, is that moment of crisis, of hitting bottom, in which reality breaks through and the alcoholic is able to admit: "I am powerless over alcohol and my life has become unmanageable."[16]

Johnson believed that when the people who had the most emotional currency with the alcoholic came together so that their collective emotional influence with the alcoholic was powerfully concentrated in a nonjudgmental, non-anxious confrontation that reaffirmed their love while asserting clear boundaries, it was, although there was no guarantee, possible, so to speak, to raise the "bottom" for that individual. Without intervention, without some such attempt to facilitate a catalytic moment, then the bottom the alcoholic/addict hits may very well be death or insanity.

Stephen Wolinsky in *Trances People Live* proposes that uncomfortable emotional states are actually states of trance and that the way out of our dysfunctional behaviors is to awaken from these trances. Whether viewed from Johnson's perspective or Wolinsky's, the question remains how can an awakening to new life be, for want of a better word, "facilitated?"[17]

It was at this same workshop with Johnson and Clinebell that I was indirectly introduced to the work of Harry Tiebout. At one point Howard Clinebell said as a kind of aside that the best book he had read on the theological and psychological dynamics of alcoholism was an unpublished doctoral dissertation written by one of his PhD students, Robert Herbert Albers. As soon as I returned home I ordered a copy of Albers' "The Theological and Psychological Dynamics of Transformation in the Recovery From the Disease of Alcoholism."[18]

In his dissertation, Albers makes extensive reference to Tiebout's conversion therapy, which furnished the inspiration and basis for Vernon Johnson's intervention technique. Harry Tiebout earned his bachelor's degree from Wesleyan University in 1917 and then went to the John Hopkins University School of Medicine where he earned his degree in medicine and completed a specialization in psychiatry. The psychiatric program at John Hopkins at that time was somewhat eclectic with Freudian psychoanalysis being contributory but not dominant. In 1927, he joined the Institute for Child Guidance in New York as a staff psychiatrist. It was at the institute, an important center for training and research, that Tiebout was immersed in the sort of exhaustive case studies that would serve him so well in investigating alcoholism. In 1935, he became the medical director of Blythewood Sanitarium in Greenwich, Connecticut. Blythewood was primarily for the treatment of the mentally ill but also provided care for alcoholics.

16. Johnson, *I'll Quit Tomorrow*.
17. Wolinsky, *Trances People Live*.
18. Albers, "Theological and Psychological Dynamics."

In 1939, Tiebout received a prepublication copy of *Alcoholics Anonymous*, affectionately known in AA as the Big Book.[19] At the time, he was working with a chronic alcoholic patient, Marty Mann, on whom none of the conventional psychotherapeutic approaches had any effect. In spite of the fact that she had been at Blythewood for a year, Marty's drinking continued unabated. Tiebout gave his copy of *Alcoholics Anonymous* to Marty and asked her to read it and let him know what she thought. At first, Marty read the book with considerable interest. And she was excited to discover that her problem had a name—"alcoholism." But she soon found herself repulsed by its underlying religious or spiritual nature and told Tiebout she could never accept such a program. Tiebout quietly encouraged her to continue reading, which she did. After some months, Marty Mann had an epiphany, a catalytic moment, during an episode of fury and resentment and was "converted"—discovered "sobriety with serenity."[20] Tiebout was utterly astounded not only by Marty Mann's ability to stay sober, but even more by the dramatic change in her character structure. "Her aggression subsided, the sense of being out of synchronization with the world disappeared, and the generally suspicious nature which characterized her disposition towards others virtually vanished."[21]

Utilizing the case study method, Tiebout began a rigorous scientific investigation first of Marty Mann's transformation and then that of other alcoholics working through the AA program. To the consternation of his peers in the psychiatric profession, Tiebout found it most helpful to conceptualize what he witnessed as a "religious" phenomenon. As already noted, he regarded this radical reversal of lifestyle in the case of the alcoholic as a "conversion," and called the method of treatment he proposed "conversion therapy." With the conversion experience, Tiebout believed, the alcoholic's compulsion is divested of its power, and a liberation or deliverance from all the negative forces that have held the alcoholic in bondage takes place. He said,

> When the wall suddenly melts as in a sweeping personality turnabout there develops a peculiar phenomenon which people conversant with religion refer to as "a release of power." . . . Conflict, tension, doubt, anxiety, hostility all dissolve as though they were nothing and the individual discovers him or herself

---

19. W., *Alcoholics Anonymous*.
20. Brown and Brown, *A Biography of Mrs. Marty Mann*.
21. Albers, "Theological and Psychological Dynamics," 92.

on an exalted plane where there is a felt communion with God, humanity, and all the creative forces of the universe.[22]

It is perhaps important to note that although Tiebout recognized that this reorientation and reawakening could be both sudden and dramatic, he also believed that probably 90 percent of such "conversions" represented a less dramatic and more gradual experience.[23]

But key to understanding this present project is the recognition that in religious conversion, as with recovery from alcoholism, a catalytic moment, a crisis, an event whether large and dramatic or small and seemingly of little consequence, is required to flip the conversion switch. And, that where in alcoholism the drinking creates the crisis, in religious conversion the human condition is itself the crisis; or, as Albers put it in his dissertation:

> The reality of the human condition and the need for the power of God may not be acknowledged by human beings. The awareness of this truth is often brought about by crisis.... The need to be lifted out of oneself and fragmentation and to relate to oneself, others and God is at stake. Under the general disease with life, there is the need for an answer which lies outside of oneself. The human predicament is in need of resolution.... Theologically speaking, it is the crisis which occasions the transformation. The crisis is the human condition.[24]

The one thing to take away from this chapter, then, is that the human condition itself is the crisis, is the catalytic event capable of breaking through denial and educing the conversion experience, a consciousness of God as an awareness of Sacred Mystery. The question for us is how the evangelist, as Christ's coworker, might move effortlessly and harmoniously in working with and through the human condition as the event precipitating a spiritual awakening.

---

22. Tiebout, *Conversion*, 4; Albers, "Theological and Psychological Dynamics," 101.
23. Albers, "Theological and Psychological Dynamics."
24. Ibid., 311–12.

CHAPTER FOUR

Soul Talk

Being Christian is not the result of an ethical choice or a lofty idea, but the encounter with an event, a person, which gives life a new horizon and a decisive direction. Likewise, at the root of all evangelization lies not a human plan of expansion, but rather the desire to share the inestimable gift that God has wished to give us, making us sharers in his own life.[1]

—Benedict XVI

But the fellowship which Jesus brings, and the fellowship of people with one another to which he calls, would be described in one-sided terms if another "title" were not added, a title to describe the inner relationship between the divine and the human fellowship... Friendship unites affection with respect.[2]

—Jurgen Moltmann

A WOMAN CALLED ONE day and asked if I would be willing to see her husband, Phil, who was not a Christian. He had, she said, a history of work-related problems, which had now become an issue in their marriage. When I saw Phil, the first thing he said was that he was willing to discuss

---

1. Benedict XVI, *Apostolic Letter*, 8.
2. Moltmann, *The Church in the Power of the Spirit*, 115.

his work life, his family life, and his childhood, but he didn't want to have to listen to a sermon. He had, he said, been baptized as an infant, but had rarely been on the inside of any church since then for any reason other than an occasional wedding. "I don't believe all this nonsense about a benevolent God," he asserted, "and I don't want to have to listen to a lot of crazy God talk." I readily agreed that we would focus on just the matters that he found to be of practical concern. Then one day Phil volunteered that he loved fly-fishing. "That's when I am most relaxed, most at peace," he said. "There is, you know, a rhythm to fly-fishing, and when I am fishing I feel a part of that rhythm, a kind of harmony, that is larger and deeper than the river or any of my problems." I told Phil that I found this really interesting, and that I hoped the next time he went fly-fishing he would tell me more about it. Eventually, as Phil's awareness and experience of the harmony, peace, and rhythm with which he felt at one while fly-fishing deepened, he came to the conclusion that what he was experiencing in the simplicity of all that beauty while fishing on a Colorado river was the reality of God.

I don't want to lose you in wondering what happened with Phil and so will tell you that in time he received the Sacrament of Confirmation and became a much-appreciated leader in his church. However, notice right now how the circumstances of Phil's life, his problems of work and family, and his own unrecognized spiritual experience and longing, constituted the catalytic moment. Notice that all I did was to help Phil pay attention to the "stuff" of his own life—to his own inner experiences and feelings. Stop, if you need to, and reflect on that for a moment or two. You may also want to think about how this vignette fits a postmodern paradigm of evangelization. Up to the point where Phil's awareness of the presence of God emerged, he heard me offer no argument for the existence of God, no requests that he attend church were made nor reasons given as to why he should do so, his own experience and interpretation of life had been acknowledged and respected without denying my own, there was no debate about relativism or absolutes, and no formulas or canned presentations were presented.

So far in this book I have used the word "educe" a number times. To educe means to draw forth or to bring out something potential or latent. It's a good word for the sort of evangelization advocated here. In the postmodern world, as in any genuinely contemplative Christian spirituality, evangelization must not be conceived of as an act of persuasion, as information to be learned, or a doctrine to be inculcated, and certainly not as a sale to be closed. Evangelization as a spiritual practice is never accompanied by the feeling that conversion is something we must make happen—or that we have the power to make happen. The contemplative evangelist "works without doing." It is one friend helping another to attend to what is significant in the other's experience, it is eliciting the other's own stories of faith and hope and love. To evangelize in our time is to educe the spirituality inherent in every human being, and it can even be thought of in terms of classic spiritual direction, which is characterized more by discovery than convincing.

It is not only important to consider Phil's story in its postmodern cultural context, but also to think about it in terms of Christian spirituality. When I was doing graduate work at the University of Santa Clara, I was introduced to the work of E. Stanley Jones by a fellow student who gave me a copy of his book *The Way*. Jones was born toward the end of the nineteenth century and lived most of his adult life in India. He was nominated five times for the Nobel Peace Prize, and was an ardent supporter of the Indian National Congress, counting Gandhi and Nehru among his friends. There is a joke about how he was a bishop of the Methodist Church for twenty-four hours. After being elected bishop, Jones resigned the next day saying, "God didn't call me to be a bishop, but to be a missionary." I tell this story to give you a feel for the kind of person E. Stanley Jones was. In 1925, he wrote the bestselling book *The Christ of the Indian Road*, which maintained that the work of missionaries was not to spread Western culture in India under the rubric of Christianity, but to assist in making Christ indigenous to India. Jones would go into a town or village and work with its religious leaders, Hindu or Muslim or Buddhist, in presenting a forum. He always invited a leader from a faith tradition other than Christianity to lead the forum. The format was simply that participants were to present what they had discovered so far on their spiritual journey. Jones believed that if he had the opportunity to simply say what he had discovered spiritually in Christ it would have a powerfully transforming effect on others.

This new evangelization calls for practitioners whose faith has enough intellectual integrity and spiritual depth to give them a certain poise—assurance of who they are in Christ and confidence in the path they have chosen. I remember a grad student asking her professor, "What if someone in therapy tells you something they can't handle?" The professor simply responded, "You may not be able to handle something a client says, and that could be a problem if the client has to deal with your anxiety, but the client will never say anything they can't handle." The new evangelization assumes your Christian faith has sufficient structural integrity to handle another's self-disclosures, moments of transparency, and even negativity and hostility; that is, it assumes you have no need to say how things are for anyone other than yourself. This integrity and depth is absolutely crucial to an evangelization which is essentially the work of discovery.

Finally, before we leave the story of Phil, which includes the following additional details, notice that the language, which results in the formation of a new consciousness, a spiritual awakening in him, is the language of metaphor and poetry and story—rhythm, harmony, peace, flowing river, the whole image of the solitary fly-fisher. It is for him ultimately an inexplicable experience and cannot be expressed in concrete and literal language. His story begins with baptism as an infant, a family with minimal interest in religion, doubts that are formed in the rigors of a university education and the sometimes hard contingencies of life itself. His experience has not been the experience of someone who has felt the presence of a benevolent God; therefore, there is no arguing with him that reality is other than what he has experienced. There is an unpleasant encounter with a priest when his wife arranges for the baptism of their child. His story includes his present difficulties, but it also includes the rhythm he feels as he casts his line into the river, which, like his own life, is in continuous movement.

All the stories we are told as we grow up join with all our actual personal experiences so as to form our own story-line—paradoxically unique and universal at the same time. "Thus, stories conjoin in consciousness to tell us who we are and where we are."[3]

Stories are told and the telling requires language. As David Buttrick observes, "Martin Heidegger called language 'the house of being.' And Helen Keller, deaf and blind, was unable to imagine the world she inhabited until miraculously she grasped that very first word. By naming," says David Buttrick, "we think the world we live. For not only does language constitute the world-in-consciousness, it enables us to conceive of ourselves as selves-in-a-world."[4] Buttrick then writes,

> Rhetoric has been captive to rational philosophical logic that has moved it away from the kinds of paralogic native to human consciousness—logics, that are, of course, much closer to patterns of biblical thought. The Bible seems to "think" in narratives, in images and analogies, in ritual symbols and communal recollections. The concept of plot enables us to design a movement of thought that is strung together by a logic of consciousness rather than patterns of deductive reasoning. Thus, the "moves" in a sermon's movement assemble by association, by analogy, by contrast and the like; they may form a plotted sequence designed to match typical modes of human consciousness. The concept of plot also allows for disruptions or reversals in thought in a way that usual homiletic design does not. If, for example, some parables "frustrate our expectations" in surprising ways, a system of "moves" permits the intrusion of the unexpected into a

3. Buttrick, *Homiletic*, 10.
4. Ibid., 7.

> sequence of thought.... Sermons in an age such as ours cannot be "vertically" deductive; they must move, journey toward understanding.[5]

What Buttrick says of preaching is equally true of evangelization—after all the *evangel* and *kerygma*, the good news and its announcement, are one.

What is clear is that the language of evangelization, the language in which the good message is communicated, must change if there is to be a dawning in the postmodern mind. It must rely less on syllogistic-like formulas and metaphors that no longer communicate. For example, in a congregation I once served, we used all contemporary music except for a hymn at the recessional—a concession to the seniors who affectionately remembered them. The music director frequently chose "My Faith Looks Up to Thee, O Thou Lamb of Calvary." In today's world we have little experience with animal sacrifice; and, in fact, if we think about animal sacrifice at all we are a little disturbed by that theme. Our precocious and sensitive granddaughter has been a vegetarian since age three. She became a vegetarian at that age when one evening she was eating out with her family. Her parents were discussing a chicken dish listed on the menu and she asked, "Do you mean chicken you eat or a chicken bird?" She was appalled upon learning that they were the same thing and two weeks later announced she was a vegetarian. "You should help animals," she said, "not eat them." For the first part of their lives my parents, like their mothers and fathers, were subsistence farmers, growing a little cotton for cash. Although unlike my older brother and two sisters I never lived on an actual farm. I grew up raising livestock, and I can tell you how to wring a chicken's head off, pluck and clean it, cut it up and fry it in a pan. If you want to tell me about Jesus as the sacrificial lamb that will form in my consciousness as a life-giving image, but for my granddaughter not so much. To refer once again to Buttrick:

> During formative periods, preaching speaks freely in popular language, language close to everyday speech, and reaches out in search of analogies to explain traditional Christian doctrine in a new way. Thus, though there may be biblical metaphors for atonement—sacrifice, ransom, victory in battle—such traditional images may no longer communicate effectively. Yes, terrorism and ransomed prisoners are still front-page news, but animal sacrifice is seldom practiced in local United Methodist churches, and images of warfare probably have been corrupted by the high-tech Pentagon. Anselm's notion of satisfaction, as well as judicial metaphors from the Reformation period may

---

5. Buttrick, "On Doing Homiletics Today," 96–97.

be equally passé. So, as a cultural formation comes together, preachers must seek new, "two-way" metaphors to convey God's mysterious grace; and, at the same time, human experience of sin and liberation. Christian preaching must play on the edges of "language" where metaphor brings out redefinition of human experience.[6]

If you want to underline one sentence underline this one: Evangelization in the postmodern world must be narrative, for it is the fitting together of your story with that of another person's narrative to discover both are at one with the Good Story told in Christian Scripture, and it therefore requires the art and evocative language of all well-told stories. Let's think now more specifically about how we can go about this practice—telling and evoking stories in such a way as to sow the seeds of the catalytic moment.

The Craft

What follows in the remainder of this chapter is based on my training and experience in both secular and pastoral counseling, as well as graduate studies in religion, biblical studies, theology, and five decades of living and breathing parish ministry. In the midst of my graduate work in counseling psychology I had something of an epiphany in which I saw that the answer to life's most difficult and perplexing problems is fundamentally spiritual rather than "psychological" in nature—although modern psychotherapy, like everything else in the universe, is all bound up with spiritual reality and can, therefore, inform our understanding of spirituality and its practice in important and helpful ways. So here, without giving psychology the preeminence it often claims, we will utilize certain insights provided by psychotherapy to inform us as to how we might go about the actual practice of evangelization.

Several times in my life I have experienced the same, or a very similar, "epiphany." The first time I experienced this moment of "enlightenment," came one day in Dr. Mary Ann Wakefield's class. It was a class on child counseling in the family context. It was a three-hour class with the first hour devoted to Dr. Wakefield working with a family as her graduate students observed. On this day as we sat discussing what had happened during the previous hour when she had worked with this particular young family, a student said, "I don't see the difference between what you have just suggested as a logical consequence and a punishment. Mary Ann, who was

---

6. Buttrick, *A Captive Voice*, 66–67.

both a brilliant academician and a down to earth, common sense therapist, stood thinking for a long moment. Finally, she said slowly, "I guess it just all depends on attitude, doesn't it?" It may sound, I don't know, a little silly," but that became something of a guiding principle for me—attitude, mental orientation, disposition is everything. So, we begin.

The new evangelization, as I posited in my dissertation many years ago, is at its core relational, as is all Christian ministry.[7] All theological and biblical lines of thought converge in the realization that reality is ultimately relational. The Christian understanding of the Trinitarian God, what C. S. Lewis imaged as the Three Personal God, the story of Adam who is unfulfilled so long as he is without a human partner, the way in which the covenant of grace extends beyond Abraham and Sarah and their family to all the families of the earth, the fact that when Jesus comes he comes for the salvation of a people and forms the beloved community, Jesus's teaching that the most basic principle by which Christians are to live is love for God and others, the picture of the final judgment in Matthew 25 as a judgment of our relationships, and the ultimate purpose of God as uniting all things in heaven and earth in Christ—all point to the essence of reality as relational, mysteriously personal.

The study of psychotherapy points in the same direction. The days when psychotherapists identified themselves as belonging almost exclusively to one particular psychotherapeutic school of thought is long over. The evidence is now decades old that what successful clinicians have most in common is not a single theoretical orientation, but a set of conditions that are relational in nature.[8] These relational conditions include empathy, respect, genuineness, concreteness, immediacy, self-disclosure, and even a particular type of confrontation. Hopefully, you will be able to see in this that evangelization is not so much a way of doing as it is a way of being—that these conditions are not techniques but descriptions of how to relate to others in a healthy, life-giving manner.

Evangelization is a practice, not a program—it is the practice of friendship. A program tends to be reward- or results-oriented. A practice is done for the fun or the joy of the thing. Recently, I heard a priest assert at a conference on evangelism, "We have to put butts in the pews. We have to be able to keep the lights on and turn up the heat when it gets cold." He was not only looking for a program, but had something of one he had cobbled together he was presenting—something he thought might get positive results. Unlike a program, then, a practice is done out of joy and gratitude, it is corporate

7. Hart, *A Model for Relational Counseling Through Expository* Preaching.
8. Patterson, *Relationship Counseling and Psychotherapy*, ix–xi.

or communal and relational, it has a sense of historical continuity or tradition to it and so is handed down from one practitioner to another, and as it is practiced one's expertise grows. So again, evangelization is a spiritual practice that can also be thought of as the practice of friendship. Although, whether "friendship" is a practice or a program depends, of course, on attitude.

In 1977, Flavil Yeakley in *Why Churches Grow* explored three methods of evangelization in the Churches of Christ: (1) the Information Transmission model, which was the primary method followed by the Churches of Christ at that time is based on the idea that if people are fully informed biblically and theologically, if they are provided with enough of the right information, they will become disciples of Christ; (2) both the Manipulative Monologue and Dialogue are the equivalent to a "sales model." The evangelist builds a prospects list, makes a "sales" presentation, answers objections and seeks to overcome obstacles, and attempts to close the sale by getting the prospect to pray in some way that demonstrates an acceptance of Christ. The Evangelism Explosion program started in 1962 by James Kennedy and the Four Spiritual Laws are examples of this method; (3) the third model, the Non-Manipulative Dialogue, shows a genuine interest in the other person—his or her hopes, dreams, fears, problems, successes, failures, and understanding of life. In the first model the evangelizer can be thought of as a teacher, in the second, as a salesperson, but in the third, if it is genuinely non-manipulative, as a friend.[9] You can read Yeakley's conclusions for yourself if you are interested in the data, but it is enough here to note that he found the Sales Model resulted in the greatest number of converts but had the lowest retention rate, the Teacher Model was impressive in neither number of converts made or its retention rate, and the Friendship Model, while having a low conversion rate, had the highest retention rate. One of this book's aims is to help in raising the number of converts for the Friendship Model of evangelization.

A woman made an appointment to see me for pastoral counseling. Over a year before our meeting she had answered the ringing of her door bell one day and found two very pleasant and cheerful women from the Jehovah's Witnesses standing there. The last of her family had died not long before, she had no friends, and her husband, who provided very little emotional support, kept her isolated from the rest of the world. Lonely, sad, and longing for human warmth, for friendship, she invited these two women in to talk. They began to "study" together each week. They each shared what was going on in their personal lives. Occasionally they met for lunch. But

---

9. Yeakley, *Why Churches Grow*, 58–64.

now with the passage of time it had become more and more clear that either she would have to convert or these two women, whom she now thought of as dear friends, would move on. She didn't know what to do. She didn't want to lose their friendship and she didn't want to become a Jehovah's Witness. When Yeakley writes about the Friendship Model of evangelization he is not suggesting the feigning of friendship as a technique for making converts, but rather pointing to what is already there in Scripture regarding what manner of persons we ought to be. Nor is it implied by "friendship" that the evangelizer must constantly enlarge the inner circle of his or her personal relationships so that more and more people have to constantly be added to dinners, parties, recreational outings, or entertainment events. To think along such lines is, at least for us introverts, to think more in terms of networking—a program aimed at getting results.

The New Testament word often translated as "neighbor" is *plesion*. It is the word used when Jesus is asked to explain, "Who is my neighbor?" A neighbor is simply one who is close to you, such as a friend. For the lawyer interrogating Jesus a neighbor was anyone who was a member of the Jewish nation or commonwealth, and that is the sort of answer he expected from Jesus. The word "neighbor," understood in this way, allows us to practice all kinds of bigotry and unkindness as long as it is not directed at our own family, clan, village, or nation; that is, as long as it defines neighbor or friend in a very narrow sense. But in the story of the Good Samaritan, Jesus turns the question upside down. By the time the story ends the question is no longer, "Who is my neighbor?" but, "Whose neighbor can I be?" A neighbor is someone who is nigh to us, but the question is no longer who is nigh to me, but who can I be close to—to whom can I be a friend? It could be put this way: Jesus said, "The two core commandments are this: Love God and love your friend as you love yourself." But the self-justifying and ever-so-clever lawyer asked, "But just who is my friend?" Jesus then answered by telling the parable of the Good Samaritan. We can paraphrase Jesus's final words to the lawyer this way: "If you think about it, the real question is whose friend can you be?"

As a spiritual practice evangelization is organic, natural, living. As the practice of friendship there is nothing artificial, mechanical, or contrived about it. There is no prospect list to develop, no knocking on doors, no canned "testimony" to memorize, and no haunting of coffee shops, eavesdropping on private conversations in hopes of overhearing something that will afford an opportunity to preach, and no inventing of occasions to get together to prove you are best buddies with someone with whom you will end contact once they have made a "decision."

Attentiveness

Conversations that are social or personal in nature do not normally begin with one person thinking about how to engage another in discussing a particular topic, unless there are ulterior motives, in which case we are talking about something other than the practice of friendship. There is an exception to this which we will get to shortly, but for now focus on how the many conversations you engage in every single day require no preplanned beginning—they just start.

In ancient Palestine a man's spiritual journey takes him literally down stone paved roads and along dusty paths. With a few friends, he passes into territory hostile to him and his kind. After entering a certain village he sits tired and alone beside a public well while his friends go in search of food and drink. A prostitute comes to the well thinking no one will be around to hurt her with their cruel looks or painful innuendos. She ignores the man sitting there—he is a despised Jew. He looks at her, but he does not look at her as men usually do. Then he does the unthinkable, breaks the social taboos and asks her: "Will you give me a drink of water?" But she is a woman who knows how to reply with some impudence. "It's a little strange you should ask me for a drink—we Samaritans don't like having anything to do with you Jews any more than you like having anything to do with us." And so the conversation begins with a request and a comment emerging from deep ethnic and racial problems, but it ends with her running into the village and excitedly saying to anyone who will listen: "I have just met the most amazing person down by Jacob's Well. I am not kidding! I think he may be the Messiah."

Long, long ago a Jewish Christian by the name of Philip was traveling the road that goes from Jerusalem down to Gaza when another man, a government official from Ethiopia, came along riding in a chariot, reading from the Hebrew Bible as he rode. He gives Philip a ride. "What are you reading?" Philip asks. "I'm reading from the Prophet Isaiah," says the Ethiopian, "but I don't quite get who or what he is talking about." "Well here's what I think that passage means," replies Philip. The conversation has begun and it ends with the Ethiopian official saying, "Look, here is some water, I think I would like to be baptized"—quite an ordinary event with extraordinary implications.

A woman goes to work and says to her colleague, "I hate to have to tell you, as busy as we are, that I am not going to be of much help for a while—I have breast cancer." "Oh!" says her coworker. "I am so sorry to hear that. Don't worry too much about things here. We will get by. You know I am a cancer survivor, and I am here to tell you there is always hope—no matter what, there is hope." And the conversation has begun.

My wife and I have been watching a set of DVDs from a television series given to us by our son—*True Detective*. It is not a family friendly series. It is, however, a good example of nearly everything written earlier on the postmodern mind. At the beginning, Marty Hart and Rust Cohle, two Louisiana State Police detectives who have just become partners are riding to a crime scene in their police car.

> "Are you a Christian?" asks Marty.
> "No," replies Cohle.
> "Then why do you wear a cross?"
> "Because," answers Cohle, "it's a form of contemplation. I contemplate the moment in the garden, the idea of allowing your own crucifixion."
> "Well, then," Marty continues to question, "what do you believe in?"
> "I'd consider myself a realist," says Cohle, "alright? But in philosophical terms, I'm what's called a pessimist. . . I think human consciousness is a tragic misstep in evolution. We became too self-aware."

And on goes their conversation, and other conversations, through each episode of season one, climaxing in a powerful catalytic moment and ending with what can only be described as the conversion of each man to light—to warmth and love. It is only a fictional story, but nevertheless, a real exploration of the human condition and the phenomenon of conversion.

All of the above are meant to illustrate the organic, natural, living, uncontrived nature of conversation. To repeat, conversations simply happen. One of the first things required of the evangelizer, then, is that he or she simply exercise some awareness, demonstrate an inviting openness to conversation, and that he or she pays attention. By being attentive we are communicating to another, "I care about you—about what you think and feel." Following are specific skills of attending, but as you reflect on them keep in mind that they are not so much techniques of conversation as they are ways of being caring.

Listening

You don't need me to tell you that there is a difference between attending or listening, and arguing, interrogating, ridiculing, or dismissing. At least you shouldn't need anyone to tell you since hopefully you know what it feels like to be listened to, but perhaps that is not an assumption I should make too quickly. Not long ago I was listening to a student recording of an assigned counseling session meant to provide practice in "active listening." The student was listening to a man not long out of prison who was trying to adjust to freedom. This newly released inmate kept talking about how no one ever really listened to him, and the student kept responding with wordy assurances that he was there to listen but never, in fact, listened. Whenever something holds emotional significance, involves a strong conviction or value, or is in some other way of special importance to the other person, there are certain responses on the part of the listener, the evangelizer, that are highly likely to trigger either the fight or flight response. For example, the person may become argumentative, change the subject, have something else they need to go do, or derail the conversation into a fruitless philosophical or theological discussion.

    I was walking through the large enclosed overpass at the University of Denver when I noticed a student table that I thought might represent Jews for Jesus and it interested me, so I stopped to talk to the rather serious looking young man sitting there. Thinking to make myself clear about the sort of interest I had, I volunteered that I was a priest. In a rather angry tone he asserted, "All that matters is whether you are born again—whether God would let you into his heaven if you were to die tonight." A brief theological argument concerning the nature and meaning of "born again" ensued. Let's assume, grievous sinner that I am, that I did indeed need to be reborn, as he understood the expression, right there on the spot. It is not likely that such a technique of inattentiveness and deafness would ever have succeeded. But notice that I did not listen either. What might we have discovered together had I done so? To genuinely listen is to be more interested in understanding and in winning a friend than an argument. And thinking about what we want to say once given a chance, even if it is not argumentative, is not listening. Listening is listening. Attending to someone, really listening, involves a relaxed awareness expressed by open body posture, tone of voice, appropriate eye contact (according to the culture), respect for personal space (not too close and not too distant), and body movement—good listeners may gesture or move their body, or nod their head in response to the one speaking. All of this must be for you, and be felt by the other person, as something completely natural.

    So much of the spiritual life and practice is about paying attention—being present. "To give focused attention to what others are feeling, thinking, and saying, to be aware of what is happening here and now, is presence. To be present to Presence is to be aware, awake, attentive to the whole mystery of the God "in whom we live, move, and have our being."[10]

Compassionate Understanding

By listening, speaking, and acting with compassionate understanding I mean what is known in the psychotherapeutic world primarily as empathy. Empathy is the ability to look at the world through another's eyes. Rather than a detached, purely objective, external kind of observation, it allows one to enter into the other person's internal frame of reference so that one comes to understand what it is like to think and feel as that individual thinks and feels. At its deeper levels, compassionate understanding not only accurately perceives what has been stated explicitly, but also correctly senses what has been implied, ambiguously expressed, or even left unsaid.

Many years ago, while he was still engaged in his real area of expertise, I heard James Dobson on one of his early radio programs. A woman called in with a question concerning a child, her son, who had a developmental disorder. Dobson gave a thoughtful and professional response, and then as she was about to hang up he said to her, "But there is something else isn't there?" With compassionate understanding he drew from her a story of hurt and desperation. Her husband, as frequently happens in such cases, had abandoned her and their son. As I remember, Dobson told her to stay on the line and someone would help her identify some helpful resources, and then he finished by saying, "The final thing I want to tell you is that I know you feel like you are drowning, but even if the waves are splashing over your head God is with you and will not let you drown."

Part of what made Dobson's response so powerful that night was not only his perception of what lay below this woman's surface account, but the sympathy and the caring in the tone of his voice. Empathy is the ability to think and feel as the other person does without losing oneself. Sympathy, which is also important, is that feeling of sadness for other people—our caring about how it is for someone. The other day a member of the church I serve told of a friend whose teenage son had overdosed on drugs and died. Her empathy was seen in her ability to perceive the world as her friend found it at the moment, her ability to taste the world as her friend tasted it— absurd, cruel, and lethal. Her sympathy was her feeling of sadness for her friend's profound grief. I have used the phrase compassionate understanding where professional counselors would normally use "empathy" because I think the word "empathy" has become a little too clinical, distancing us

10. Hart, *Numinous*, 1–2.

from the other person. The ears with which we hear and the tongue with which we speak must show wisdom, understanding, and deep caring.

Genuineness

Genuineness refers to the ability of the evangelizer to be deeply and truly him or herself so that he or she is not playing the role of evangelist, or helper, or wise or holy person, or even of Christian, but simply being—complete congruence. There is no facade. There are no affectations—no artificial sweetness, no exaggerated seriousness. What one thinks or feels is one with what he or she says. The evidence seems to suggest that the "therapeutic" value of genuineness is in the lack of phoniness or defensiveness itself. Recently I came across this quote by James Black that I used years ago in writing my dissertation. It is as true today as it was then: "Our task today is to show people, especially young people, that religion is human nature in all its natural bigness, glorified and perfected in Jesus Christ, and that Jesus does not limit or starve the manhood or womanhood which is God's gift to us."[11]

Kathy grew up in an emotionally rejecting and psychologically abusive family. In high school she began to drink and became involved with drugs. In her early twenties she married a drug dealer. At one point they were arrested with enough cocaine in their possession to be sentenced to a lengthy prison term, but the police somehow "lost" the evidence. She gave birth to a son whose intestines were outside his body. Before leaving, her husband said to her, "This is because it's the kind of person you are—a monster who has given birth to a monstrosity!" All alone with a child needing lots of care, living on welfare, Kathy just existed day by day in her little apartment. One day she was invited to a small group Bible study another woman in her apartment complex had started. In this study she heard the women talking about the strangest thing she thought she had ever heard. It was something called "grace"—being accepted and loved just because you are. One of the women asked her if she wanted to receive the grace of God. Karthy said, "Yes. If it is free I'll take it." She became involved in the rather evangelical church most of these women attended. The church paid for her books and tuition to enter the nursing program at a community college. The women babysat for her for free, the church bought her a used car, and a church member who was a mechanic kept it up.

One day a woman, another student, came to Kathy's class looking and acting really out of it. Finally, the teacher asked Kathy if she would escort this woman to the nurse's station. As they walked toward the nurse's office,

---

11. Black, *Mystery of Preaching*, 74.

Kathy learned that this woman had just had an abortion that morning. The man she lived with had insisted on it, and had told her as she left that morning not to come back—he couldn't stand her and had no more use for her. Suddenly, the woman collapsed. Kathy yelled for someone to call the paramedics. Kathy cradled her new friend's head in her arms. "All I have ever wanted," the hemorrhaging woman said weakly, "is for someone to love me." "You don't know me very well," said Kathy, "but right now I love you, and I know that God loves you." The woman squeezed Kathy's hand lightly in recognition and gratitude, and died. What made Kathy's words effective was that they were genuine—came out of who Kathy was and from what she knew to be true from her own experience.

Respect

A woman who was kind and generous, but who, because of her poverty and appearance, was often regarded by others as a "born loser," once said of my wife Brenda, "What I like about her is that wherever I am, she knows me." Apparently, this woman had found that for many people, even from church, there were places and situations where they considered it an embarrassment to acknowledge and greet her kindly. But here was someone who made her feel respected by offering courteous recognition no matter what the social setting. All healthy, growth-fostering relationships include large amounts of respect.

Failure to show respect to everyone we encounter is a failure of humility. When we lack humility, we think that we must fill every conversation with our own stories, ideas, opinions, and observations, and that everything is about us, that everything must revolve around us.

We convey respect through common courtesy, when we speak to people out of the conviction that their thoughts and feelings are as significant as our own. To respect another means that we use honest praise as a means of encouragement. I say honest praise because flattery is dishonest praise. A compliment is for the benefit of the other. Flattery is for our benefit.

If we are humble and respectful there will be a tentative quality to our speech. We can be confident in what we say and clear about how we see things without communicating some sort of godlike certainty. Postmodern people will be quick to dismiss anyone who cannot entertain the possibility that they are quite mistaken. Is it possible that my faith is entirely erroneous? Certainly, but I don't think so. In fact, I would hope that, like the innumerable hosts of martyrs before me, I would be willing to give my life as a witness to the love of God, but that does not preclude the possibility of my being mistaken. And so I speak of what I have discovered and of spiritual probabilities on which I am willing to stake my life—but I do not possess infallible knowledge and should not in any way suggest I do.

By communicating respect we encourage people to respect themselves and, emboldened by this self-respect, to move out to meet the challenges of life.

Charity

I have chosen to use the old King James word "charity,"[12] the Christian practice of unlimited love and kindness, to encourage a fresh reflection on love and what it might mean in ordinary practice. I have found Eugene Peterson's translation of Philippians 4:4 in The Message especially meaningful: "Celebrate God all day, every day. I mean, revel in him! Make it as clear as you can to all you meet that you're on their side, working with them and not against them." To celebrate God, to love and show charity, is to make it clear to everyone we meet everywhere and every day, that we have their legitimate best interests at heart. The practice of charity requires wisdom; otherwise, rather than working with others for their legitimate best interest we fall into the sort of neurotic love that either says, "You must love me, and I'll do anything to get you to do so," or, "You must let me love you, and I'll give up being me if you'll let me." Genuine caring requires wisdom.

Simplicity

The Christian way is utterly profound, and yet, the most profound things are also always the simplest. To be simple as a person means to be open, honest, and straightforward. To be simple is to say what we mean and mean what we say. The person who is simple uses language that is direct and specific. Convoluted or involved theological and philosophical statements or theories simply do not communicate to postmodern people and do not readily form in consciousness. There is, of course, a difference between being simple and being simplistic. Simplistic, obtuse formulas of "salvation" will be dismissed as easily as complex and labyrinthine explanations. And please understand this: The evangelizer must never, ever say or respond with something read or heard somewhere that he or she has not embraced and owned. Every therapist has had the experience of clients with relationship problems—actually all problems are essentially relational in nature—clients looking for

---

12. I Corinthians 13:1 (KJV).

the "right" thing to say to someone in their own troubled life, but find the wisdom they have heard from the therapist just doesn't seem to "work." The reason it doesn't "work" is because it doesn't really come from them—is not a part of who they are.

Hope

"Hope," it has been said, is an arduous search for a future good of some kind that is realistically possible but not yet visible. The new evangelization seeks to bring the most profound and real desires of men and women into awareness; it seeks to articulate the yearning and longing for Love and transcendent Presence that lies beneath all other longings. Hope includes the feeling that we need help from the outside and the confidence that such help is available. Without such hope we are vulnerable to the kind of despair that leads to physical disease and mental disorder. Gerald May, psychiatrist, spiritual director, and author, tells of this encounter in his book *Awakened Heart*.

> I asked a young woman what she most deeply wanted. She responded immediately, "I'd like a happy home and family, security, a sense of being worthwhile." Then I asked her to sit in silence for a moment and try to be open to what desires she could *feel*, right in the moment. After a while she looked up with tears in her eyes. "I don't know what to say. What I actually feel is that things are really okay. I don't think I want anything more than what I have at this very moment." I asked her to be still once again, to look more deeply into her present feelings, to seek any desire that might honestly be there. Softly, she said, "It's very hard to put into words. I feel really blessed, and I feel gratitude; I want to say thank you to someone. Is it God? If it is, I want to give God a hug and say thanks. And I wish people could feel this way more, could have some peace."[13]

Now, it is not likely that you will ever employ such an exercise in the practice of evangelization. But all of us have multiple opportunities to share our own experiences of hope, gratitude, and grace.

For example, a friend and I were talking about our dogs the other day. He said, "You know, one thing I can be certain of is that when I get home at the end of the day, no matter what anyone has to say about me or thinks of me, that dog is going to be glad to see me." I responded by saying, "The other night I was sitting on the couch and Jack, our Queensland/Catahoula mix

---

13. May, *Awakened Heart*, 50.

who doesn't need a lot of affection, was laying with his head on my knees. I felt a sense of joy and peace, and then I thought, 'I wish I could do a better job helping people feel as much joy as this dog gives me.'"

And here is a second personal anecdote: A group of people I was visiting with were talking about all the violence and tragedy and seemingly intractable problems reported each day and night. I said, "I did a year-long chaplain residency at a major urban hospital and saw a lot of horror and despair I hope to never see again. Physically and mentally exhausted, like the other chaplains, I found myself asking, 'Where's the hope?' One night, about three o'clock, after I had seen enough blood and gore and human anguish to last me a lifetime, I was coming down the back stairwell, no sound other than the echo of my own footsteps, and in my head I was singing one line over and over from the old hymn "Amazing Grace": 'Through many dangers, toils, and snares / I have already come / 'Tis grace that brought me safe thus far / And grace will lead me home.' Suddenly I realized that I believed as much as I believe anything that this had been true of my own life, and that I needed to respect the dignity of all the people to whom I offered pastoral care by realizing that the things happening to them were their own "dangers, toils, and snares" through which God could bring them and ultimately lead them home. In that moment I felt not an easy, suspected, or explicable hope, but one which I can only describe as a mystical hope for myself and every suffering human being."

As an evangelist you are a conveyor of hope. "But sanctify the Lord God in your hearts: and be ready always to give an answer to everyone that asks you a reason for the hope that is in you" (1 Peter 3:15).

Mirroring

I am thinking here of what therapists refer to as confrontation. I have used the word "mirroring" because the word "confrontation" has so many negative connotations—hostility, conflict, and anger. But therapeutically, "confrontation" refers to mirroring back to another discrepancies perceived by the listener. David, a deacon in the Episcopal Church, works in a ministry primarily to the homeless, alcoholics, and addicts—he is himself a recovering alcoholic. An alcoholic and addict who has come to know David at the center where David serves asked, looking for David's approval, if David didn't think it would be a good idea if he cut down on his drinking. David replied, "If that works for you and helps get your life back, that is great. But I know that if I tried to cut down rather than quitting, I might as well just jump off a bridge. I know I have a good life today only because I got help in not taking that next drink."

Notice that mirroring is never moralistic; that is, there is no appeal to a negative conscience as a means of changing behavior or of forcing or gaining a relationship. It is simply the presentation of two perceptions of reality that leaves the other free to act or to not act. There are several observations that ought to be made here:

1) Mirroring must be done with humility. It must not be with some sort of instinctive certainty that one is right as if the infallible spokesperson of God, but with the belief that one is probably right arrived at through scrupulous self-doubting and self-examination.

2) Mirroring should be concise, concrete, and congruent so that it conveys the evangelizer's true feeling and meaning. Wordiness, lots of qualifiers, and ambiguity always make intentions suspect.

3) The perceived ability of the other person to respond constructively must always be taken into account.

4) Mirroring is most effective when it focuses on the positive and on feelings rather than information.

5) The strength and quality of the relationship determines the level of the mirroring.

Mirroring is just that—reflecting nonjudgmentally what is going on so that someone has the graced opportunity to reflect on their life from another perspective.

Transformative Language

The language of evangelization is, like the language of Scripture itself, the language of metaphor. God is not a thing, God is the mystery of no-thing, and mystery forms in consciousness through spiritual imagination—images, figures of speech, ritual, and symbols that make sense to the postmodern imagination. "We can only reach out into mysteries via language," said David Buttrick. "We explore the 'beyond of our world' only by dancing the edges of language."[14] New meaning emerges as paradoxical connections are made, words played, and stories shared.

One of my favorite episodes of *Star Trek: The Next Generation* is "Darmok." The mission of the Enterprise is to make contact with the Tamarian

---

14. Buttrick, *Homiletic*, 183.

race who only communicate through metaphors. So, although the universal translator device can translate their precise words, Picard and the crew remain baffled because they do not know the stories to which the Tamarians allude, and the Tamarians are frustrated by Picard's literal straightforward language.

The Tamarian captain, Dathon, has himself and Captain Picard transported to the surface of the planet El-Adrel. Dathon keeps repeating the metaphorical phrase "Darmok and Jalad at Tanagra" and tosses Picard a dagger. Picard mistakes this as a challenge to a duel and refuses. As night falls, Picard fails in making a fire and Captain Dathon shares his fire repeating the phrase, "Temba, his arms wide." The next morning, Dathon comes running and Picard realizes that there is a hostile predator in the area stalking them both. Picard finally begins to understand the way this other race communicates as he recites one of the metaphors and sees the meaning underneath it. Dathon and Picard attempt to fight the beast together, but in the battle Dathon is mortally wounded.

Finally, Picard realizes that Darmok and Jalad were two warriors, like Dathon and himself, who met on an island called Tanagra and had to cooperate to defeat a dangerous beast, becoming friends in the process. Dathon tried to recreate this event between himself and Picard on El-Adrel, hoping that their shared adversity, their shared story, would forge a friendship where words had failed. Picard uses this new understanding of Tamarian metaphors to communicate with the Tamarians and end the battle; the Tamarians record the story as "Picard and Dathon at El-Adrel," adding a new phrase to their language and a shared consciousness of friendship with the human species.

The use of biblical metaphors, allusions, and images are not likely to form as spiritual consciousness if people are unfamiliar with the concrete stories that give those metaphors meaning. Without the context of Nicodemus' late-night meeting with Jesus, "born again" becomes at best a superficial catchphrase used to describe a conservative twentieth century religious ideology with no real connection to its radical spiritual implications. In our time the image of one ransomed from terrorists is of sufficient amplitude to form powerfully in spiritual imagination—as animal sacrifice not so much. The point is that metaphors must be grounded in story. The evangelizer must have at least some skill in expressing his or her own experiences, feelings, and thoughts in appropriate figures of speech and of helping others discover those metaphors that are expressive of their own inner experience.

The more vivid, concrete, and appropriate the metaphor, the better. Language is vivid when it paints pictures with words, it is concrete when it avoids generalities and abstractions and specifically names events, behaviors, thoughts, and feelings. And language is appropriate when it describes events and feelings in a way that fits their level of dignity, significance, and intensity.

A Final Note

My simple and final suggestion is that if you have a passion for evangelization, learn everything you can about good interpersonal communications, and then, having absorbed what you have heard and seen and read, forget it all, because in the end it is quite simply about the quality of your spiritual presence. Evangelization is an existential event—one great moment of experience between two seekers and God. However, if you are looking for a basic and highly practical way to begin, I would suggest you form a small "company of the committed" and work your way first through Richard Peace's *Witness*, and then take up his *Holy Conversations: Talking About God in Everyday Life*. Holy conversations in everyday life—that's evangelization.[15]

---

15. Peace, *Holy Conversations*; Peace, *Witness*.

CHAPTER FIVE

The Human Condition

If we wish to know about people, we ask "what is their story—their real, inmost story?"—for each person is a biography, a story. Each of us is a singular narrative, which is constructed, continually, unconsciously, by, through, and in us—through our perceptions, our feelings, our thoughts, our actions; and, not least, our discourse, our spoken narrations. Biologically, physiologically, we are not so different from each other; historically, as narratives—we are each of us unique.[1]

—OLIVER SACKS

TALK OF THE HUMAN condition is essentially a conversation about the fundamental issues of our existence—birth, life, death, infinity. It is about those needs, desires, thoughts and feelings, which whatever unique shape they take within the context of any individual life, are common to the narrative of each of us. In some ways they are better understood through art, literature, music, and film than psychology and philosophy, for our hunger for meaning, our experiences of sorrow, joy, and loneliness, our desire for the warmth of intimacy and the happiness of discovering it, and the *sensus divinitatis* are all part of the indivisible mystery of being human. It should not surprise us at all that the human condition is essentially mystery, for in the words of Genesis we are created in the image of God who is Ultimate

---

1. Sacks, *Man Who Mistook His Wife*, 110–11.

Mystery. Because all mystery is best grasped through the faculties of awe, wonder, gratitude, and intuition, it is difficult to describe in any meaningful way; nevertheless, something obviously needs to be said here regarding the mystery of the human condition, if, as suggested, we are to grasp something of how existence itself contributes to the emergence of the catalytic experience. In his book *Inner Work*, Robert Johnson, the Jungian analyst, offers this clarifying observation:

> In modern Western society we have reached a point at which we try to get by without acknowledging the inner life at all. We act as though there were no unconscious, no realm of the soul, as though we could live full lives by fixating ourselves completely on the external material world. We try to deal with all the issues of life by external means—making more money, getting more power, starting a love affair, or "accomplishing something" in the material world. But we discover to our surprise that the inner world is a reality that we ultimately have to face.[2]

Johnson, following his mentor Carl Jung, thinks that if we fail to pay attention to the energy of the unconscious mind, if we are inattentive to the realm of the soul, we may very well be caught in the powerful currents of neurosis. We encounter, then, two essential questions. First, what are some of the identifiable elements of the human condition? And second, how can they be worked with organically so as to naturally nurture the catalytic moment—become the blossom that flowers as spiritual awakening?

In an Ocean of Longing

Saint Paul seems to indicate that not only human beings but the whole cosmos yearns, longs, aches for some unnameable something more, for the experience of transcendence (going beyond oneself), for a sense of union and communion, for enlightenment, for complete joy, for complete peace, for complete harmony, for complete intimacy. "All around us," he wrote, "we observe a pregnant creation. . . . The Spirit of God is arousing us within. We're also feeling the birth pangs. . . . We, of course, don't see what is enlarging us. But the longer we wait, the larger we become, and the more joyful our expectancy" (Rom 8:19–24 The Message). Edward Abbey's book *Desert Solitaire* has often been compared to Henry David Thoreau's *Walden*. It is based on that part of Abbey's life when, like Thoreau, he worked as a park ranger at Arches National Monument. In it he describes how when he stood

---

2. Johnson, *Inner Work*, 10.

there in the desert, "gaping at the spectacle of rock and cloud and sky and space," he was filled with a desire "to know it all." Abbey wrote of his wilderness sojourn, "I am here not only to evade for a while the clamor and filth and confusion of the cultural apparatus but also to confront, immediately and directly, the bare bones of existence, the elemental and fundamental, the bedrock which sustains us. I want to be able to look at a juniper tree, a piece of quartz, a vulture, a spider, and see it as it is in itself, devoid of all humanly ascribed qualities, anti-Kantian, even in the categories of scientific description."[3]

In his autobiography, C. S. Lewis spoke of his own pre-Christian condition as a longing for joy. In our Western culture this desire is most frequently conceptualized as the hope and desire for love. The psychiatrist, author, and spiritual director Gerald May has provided some of the most helpful insights into love as the deepest and truest longing of the human heart.

> There is a desire within each of us, in the deep center of ourselves that we call our heart. We were born with it, it is never completely satisfied, and it never dies. We are often unaware of it, but it is always awake. It is the human desire for love. Every person on this earth yearns to love, to be loved, to know love. Our true identity, our reason for being, is to be found in this desire.... But for real proof you must look at your own longings and aspirations; you must listen to the deep themes of your own life story. In most of us the desire for love has often been distorted or buried, but if you look at your own life with honest and gentle eyes, you can discern it in yourself as a deep seeking of connectedness, healing, creation, and joy. This is your true identity; it is who you really are and what you exist for. You have your own unique experience of desiring love, but there is something universal about it as well; it connects you with all other human beings and with all of creation.... It is possible to run away from the desire for years, even decades at a time, but we cannot eradicate it entirely. It keeps touching us in little glimpses and hints in our dreams, our hopes, our unguarded moments. We may go to sleep, but our desire for love does not. It is who we are.[4]

May sometimes capitalizes the word "love," making us think of Saint John's gentle teaching that God is love. In fact, May goes on to reflect on God as the source of love—grace has to come from somewhere and has to be given

3. Abbey, *Desert Solitaire*, 5–6.
4. May, *Awakened Heart*, 1–3.

by something or someone. "We can be sure of one thing," he writes, "our understanding of God is not God. God is love, but love is not God."[5]

Saint Augustine reflected on our desire as a kind of restlessness. "O Lord, you have made us for yourself and our hearts are unquiet until they find their rest in you." We thirst for God, said the Psalmist, like a deer in the hot Palestinian summer panting for the water brook, or like the parched desert earth eager to drink falling rain.[6] This longing, however you name it, although ultimately it is beyond all naming, is the most central and truest characteristic not only of humanity, but of all creation, and because in the end it is nothing less than the desire for God, to feel it is more fulfilling than any satisfaction we could possibly name.[7]

Just as in dream work what matters is not the interpretation a therapist may offer but what it means to the dreamer, so in the new evangelization what matters is not an interpretation imposed on the experience of longing by the evangelizer, but the ability to elicit stories of such experiences, to encourage reflection on them, and when appropriate, to share one's own relevant experiences of desire.

A young woman began e-mailing me with questions about baptism. After several weeks she told me that she was thinking about baptism not only for her three-year-old twins, but for herself as well. She said that part of her uncertainty came from her husband saying that the ocean, only three blocks away, was his church. She knew exactly what he meant, she told me—it was the same thing she had felt backpacking in the Sierras. After listening closely to her story, I shared with her my similar experiences in a Redwood grove, its floor covered by green ferns and golden threads of sunlight filtering through trees nearly three hundred feet tall, of standing on a beach in a storm, and of looking out over the Badlands of South Dakota. Finally, I said, "I believe that the human soul is an ocean of longing—longing for beauty, for transcendence, for an unnameable 'something more,' and that all such experiences are experiences of the mystery that is God." Several weeks later she was baptized along with the twins.

In a Sea of Feeling

In his "Allegory of the Cave," Plato, through the character of Socrates, pictures prisoners who have lived chained in a cave facing a blank wall all their lives. There is a fire at the rear of the cave with people moving back and

---

5. Ibid., 55.
6. Psalm 42:1–2; 63:1.
7. Lewis, *Surprised by Joy*.

forth in front of it so that their shadows, and the things they carry or place in front of the fire, are projected on the wall. The shadows, to which they give names, are as close as the prisoners get to viewing reality. Plato then explains how the philosopher is like a prisoner who is freed from the cave and comes to understand that the shadows on the wall do not make up reality at all. Now the true form of things and not merely their shadow can be discerned. What, then, is the nature of reality? Or, to put it another way, "What is the nature of the sea in which we swim?" And, "Does it matter whether it is a sea of consciousness or of materiality?"

Plato's argument is that mind or consciousness is an ultimate aspect of reality and not merely an accident, and it is not reducible to material processes. Historically, few philosophers, even among those who deny the entire Judeo-Christian tradition, have been materialists. For instance, David Hume, the famous Scottish philosopher who so rigorously opposed religious faith and the idea of ultimate mind, did not believe that matter was the sum of reality. Nevertheless, Keith Ward, regius chair of divinity emeritus at Oxford, writes of his own astonishment at the speed with which materialism has been accepted and embraced by professional philosophers in the last forty to fifty years.

> It is easy to forget how very recent and meteoric the rise of materialism has been in philosophy. How could it get from being a joke to being a claimant to obvious truth in forty years? I think there have been two major factors at work. One is the rise of cynicism about any sort of idealistic approach to life, about all human institutions, including religious ones, and about the failures of religious people to prevent violence and hatred, and indeed their tendency to increase violence and hatred in the world. This cynicism has been largely motivated by the Marxist "hermeneutic of suspicion," the accusation that all religious and moral systems are in fact ideologies, no more than sophisticated disguises for egoistic self-seeking on the part of their proponents.[8]

We do not have to agree totally with Ward's assessment to recognize it as at least a partial sketch of postmodernity.

But perhaps the larger picture coming into focus is of the postmodern human condition as one in which men and women live incongruently. In a storm, and already deserted by the crew, it looks like materialism is the only boat left to launch into fifty foot waves, but there is still reluctance to abandon the ship of spirituality. The negative attitudes toward clergy and

---

8. Ward, *God and the Philosophers*, 131.

churches expressed in survey after survey appear to affirm Keith Ward's anecdotal evidence, but the number of people indicating that they are spiritual though unaffiliated with any church or institutionalized religion suggests something else is also at work.

What is at work may be nothing more than the ease with which postmodern North Americans move back and forth between contradictory beliefs, taking a rather eclectic approach to the questions life presents at any given moment. However, even if this is more or less the case, it can still be logically asserted from the Christian perspective that we human beings simply cannot avoid being confronted with the spiritual nature of reality any more than a fish swimming in a blue lake can avoid dealing with water and its wetness. Again and again the human condition itself confronts us with the challenge to actually live our theories and exposes us to the consequences of the failure, or the practical inability, to do so. Can any of us really believe that the essence of someone who has loved us more than they have loved their own life can be reduced to biochemical sparks or three pounds of ashes? Do justice and truth and beauty arise out of inert matter? And in the end can we live as if they do? Keith Ward, in writing of the "discontents of materialism," says,

> A second discontent is that consciousness—thoughts, feelings, sensations, images, and intentions—remain almost wholly inexplicable in purely physical terms. Materialists take out a blank check on the future, and say that we may find a physical explanation one day. But the truth is that no one has the slightest idea even of what such an explanation might be. The contents of consciousness seem to be new, emergent, and irreducible sorts of reality, and even the most reductive physicalist occasionally feels a twinge of unease that there may be more to consciousness than matter.[9]

Quantum physics suggests that consciousness or mind is the basis of physical reality. "To put it bluntly," says Ward, "matter seems to have an inner orientation towards the emergence of mind."[10]

Although for the Christian believer the final answer to this equation is the divine mind that is not our focus just now. For purposes of evangelization the emphasis here is on the nature of reality as something more than clumps of physical stuff—as having its basis in mind, consciousness, soul, spirit. If this is true then it means that "charity," beauty, and justice are not mere illusions, shadows on the cave wall, but forms of life itself. So, if in a

---

9. Ibid., 144.
10. Ibid., 140.

conversation someone were to say to me, "I only believe in what I see, touch, taste, smell, or hear." I might respond in a positive, nonargumentative tone, "I know there are a lot of smart people, a lot of philosophers who believe that only physical stuff is real. For myself, I don't know how to live as if that is actually true. I wouldn't know how to live as if all the love I feel for and from those closest to me was just some sort of a physical process."

Of Freedom and Bondage

We normally think of interstellar space as silent, but it's not. The universe, the physicists tell us, can be heard by those equipped to hear. There is an old hymn that would suggest that when observers listen to their radio telescopes what they hear is "the music of the spheres." The cosmos is always making music. The universe is a symphony of freedom; it is a ballad of liberation, a lament of oppression, and a mournful dirge of bondage. "The universe is open in that the principle of indeterminacy rules out the possibility of any precise prediction of the future. It establishes probability as more fundamental than definite determinacy, and sees the future as open to creative possibility rather than as predestined to travel along unavoidable tram-lines."[11] The deterministic theology of Calvinism, held so tightly to in the past by much of Protestantism, is another one of those philosophical theories that is impossible for anyone today to live as if it is actually true; that is, we can only live our lives from morning to night as if we are free to choose. I have found the modern theologian Paul Tillich helpful on this point. Tillich said, "Providence is not interference; it is creation. It uses all factors, both those given by freedom and those given by destiny, it is creatively directing everything toward fulfillment. The person who believes in Providence believes and asserts with the courage of faith, that no situation whatsoever can frustrate the fulfillment of human destiny, that nothing can separate us from the love of God which is in Christ Jesus (Romans, chap. 8)."[12]

However, there is in us human beings some sort of a "primal" confusion of freedom with mastery, of the freedom to choose with the ability to control the results of our choosing. This is the original sin of Genesis. Eve and Adam are placed in the luxuriant Garden of Eden. They are asked to do one thing—trust in the goodness of God for all things. But they are unwilling to do so. Instead, they attempt to create their own security, to seize total control of their own fate, to lay hold of self-deification as if it were

11. Ibid., 139.
12. Tillich, *Systematic Theology*, 267.

more than a delusion. But rather than becoming more divine, Adam and Eve become more subhuman. And that is the story of us all. Bertrand Russell once wrote, "We would all like to be God if that were only possible, and some of us have no little difficulty admitting the impossibility." Keith Ward, in explaining the philosophy of Friedrich Nietzsche, quotes and paraphrases Nietzsche like this: "A free person will have no 'devout spittle-licking and fawning before the God of Hosts,' but will insist upon being the author of its own way of life and moral principles by its sheer willing."[13] But here, from what alcoholics frequently refer to affectionately as the Big Book, is a perfect real life response to the sort of sheer willpower proposed by Nietzsche's philosophical theory.

> The first requirement is that we be convinced that any life run on self-will can hardly be a success. On that basis we are almost always in collision with somebody or something, even though our motives are good. Most people try to live by self-propulsion. Each person is like an actor who wants to run the whole show; is forever trying to arrange the lights, the ballet, the scenery, and the rest of the players in his own way. If his arrangements would only stay put, if only people would do as he wished, the show would be great. Everybody, including himself would be pleased. Life would be wonderful. In trying to make these arrangements our actor may sometimes be quite virtuous. He may be kind, considerate, patient, generous; even modest and self-sacrificing. On the other hand, he may be mean, egotistical, selfish, and dishonest. But, as with most humans, he is more likely to have varied traits.[14]

Freedom is a paradox, for the essence of freedom is willingness.

In 1939 Harry Tiebout, director of Blythewood Sanitarium in Greenwich, Connecticut, received a prepublication copy of the book, *Alcoholics Anonymous*. After looking it over, he gave it to one of his patients, Marty Mann. She had been at Blythewood for over a year but none of the standard psychiatric interventions employed by Tiebout had been successful. Since nothing else had worked, Tiebout thought Mann would be a good test of whether the book's approach had any efficacy. At first she was repelled by the overbearingly religious message and told Tiebout that she could never accept it. According to Mann's biographers Sally and David Brown, Tiebout quietly encouraged her to keep reading. Eventually, in a crisis of resentment and fury, she experienced an epiphany in which she embraced the

---

13. Ward, *God and the Philosophers*, 117; Nietzsche, *Thus Spoke Zarathustra*, 186.
14. W., *Alcoholics Anonymous*, 60–61.

wisdom of Alcoholics Anonymous and discovered sobriety. As a psychiatrist, Tiebout was astonished that she was not only able to stay sober but that the very structure of her personality changed. Her aggression and hostility subsided, her feelings of being out of synchronization with the whole world disappeared, and her characteristic suspicious nature vanished. Tiebout, using the case study method he had been taught and in which he was well experienced, began to scientifically probe the causality precipitating Marty Mann's profound change.

Tiebout came to the conclusion that the phenomenon was in the category of a religious or spiritual experience. It could be observed by the outsider and experienced by the alcoholic, but neither could really explain it. He theorized that the traits of "defiant individuality" and "grandiosity" were particularly pronounced in the alcoholic. "Inwardly," he said, "the alcoholic brooks no control from man or God. The alcoholic must be master of his or her destiny, and will fight to the end to preserve that position." Conventional religion was problematic for the alcoholic for this very reason; that is, in requiring the acknowledgment of a power greater than oneself it challenged the alcoholic's stance of self-deification. However, Tiebout concluded, "If the alcoholic could acknowledge a Power greater than self, then that step alone, provided it could be done without resentment, could bring freedom from bondage."[15]

In *The Change of Conversion and the Origin of Christendom*, Alan Krieder, who comes out of the tradition of the Radical Reformation, explores as a professor of church history and mission the intersection of conversion and the missional work of the church. Among the "relevant old ideas" that he believes continue to speak to the church's future is freedom. He writes:

> Regarding bondage and addiction, early Christian thinkers and Catechists were particularly sensitive to the way that conventional folkways—doing what everybody did—trapped people in deathly demon-beset cages. Justin was aware of the way that people in Rome, in their addiction to occult practices, to sexual adventure, to ever-increasing wealth and prosperity, to hating and killing people of different tribes, were the demons' "slaves and servants," Cyprian knew that he—always expecting to wear and eat the best—had been trapped in "gilded torments." At the time of his conversion, as throughout his life as a Christian, Augustine was hyper aware of the *imprisoning* "chain of sexual desire." And Chrysostom saw the oath—not just false swearing (perjury) but even truthful swearing—as a "destructive drug." These were missiological insights, for they pointed to areas in

15. Albers, *Dynamics of Transformation*, 91–92.

which the good news of Jesus could set people free. And at least some of the catecheses of early Christianity were aimed at forming communities of free people in which the addictions that blighted pagan society were being addressed and overcome.[16]

The possibility of freedom, even if limited just to choosing our own attitude when no other choices remain, the desire for freedom, the struggle for freedom, is for twentieth century men and women, as it was for first century men and women, so much a daily experience, as opposed to mere theory, in living the human condition which contains within it more than sufficient power to generate the catalytic moment.

In a Quest for Meaning

As I remember, C. S. Lewis said that prior to his becoming Christian his friend and Oxford colleague J. R. R. Tolkien suggested Lewis attempt a real life experiment by simply attempting to actually live his philosophy. Lewis's inability to do so was a factor in his being surprised by joy—getting on a bus his usual self and getting off a Christian. Since the time I was in high school I have been fascinated by the discrepancy between philosophical theories and the actual human condition. I know, for example, of no logical positivist who can live as if what cannot be explained mathematically is nonsense. Atheistic existentialists start off well enough—the universe is literally godless, absurd, totally contingent, and utterly meaningless. But then prattle on about living an authentic human existence and the meaning we give life through our choices. An article by two bright and competent psychotherapists suggests that clients can be effectively helped if the therapist can help them to see that "nothing matters." It seems to me that nothing is pretty inclusive, and here becomes something that matters a good deal. To help a troubled person learn to think along a continuum is one thing, for them to adopt as a philosophical principle the proposition that nothing matters defies what it means to be human.

Far more helpful, I think, is Viktor Frankl's logotherapy. Frankl, a neurologist and psychiatrist in Vienna, Austria, who later earned a PhD in Philosophy, developed logotherapy out of his experience in the Nazi death camps. Logotherapy relies on Kierkegaard's will to meaning as opposed to Adler's Nietzschean will to power or Freud's will to pleasure. Logotherapy is founded on the belief that it is the striving to find a meaning in one's life that is the primary and most powerful motivating and driving force in human

---

16. Kreider, *Change of Conversion*, 101.

beings. In *Man's Search for Meaning*, later renamed *From Death-Camp to Existentialism*, Frankl provides a brief introduction to logotherapy, but for the most part the book is a moving account of how his theories helped him to survive the brutality of the Holocaust. Frankl affirms Nietzsche's saying, "Whoever has a why can endure almost any how."

Frankl's idea of discovering meaning in the midst of extreme suffering is especially discernible in this account of an experience he had while working in the brutal conditions of the death camp.

> We stumbled on in the darkness, over big stones and through large puddles, along the one road leading from the camp. The accompanying guards kept shouting at us and driving us with the butts of their rifles. Anyone with very sore feet supported himself on his neighbor's arm. Hardly a word was spoken; the icy wind did not encourage talk. Hiding his mouth behind his upturned collar, the man marching next to me whispered suddenly: "If our wives could see us now! I do hope they are better off in their camps and don't know what is happening to us."
>
> That brought thoughts of my own wife to mind. And as we stumbled on for miles, slipping on icy spots, supporting each other time and again, dragging one another up and onward, nothing was said, but we both knew: each of us was thinking of his wife. Occasionally I looked at the sky, where the stars were fading and the pink light of the morning was beginning to spread behind a dark bank of clouds. But my mind clung to my wife's image, imagining it with an uncanny acuteness. I heard her answering me, saw her smile, her frank and encouraging look. Real or not, her look was then more luminous than the sun which was beginning to rise.
>
> A thought transfixed me: for the first time in my life I saw the truth as it is set into song by so many poets, proclaimed as the final wisdom by so many thinkers. The truth—that love is the ultimate and the highest goal to which Man can aspire. Then I grasped the meaning of the greatest secret that human poetry and human thought and belief have to impart: *The salvation of Man is through love and in love.* I understood how a man who has nothing left in this world still may know bliss, be it only for a brief moment, in the contemplation of his beloved. In a position of utter desolation, when Man cannot express himself in positive action, when his only achievement may consist in enduring his sufferings in the right way—an honorable way—in such a position Man can, through loving contemplation of the image he carries of his beloved, achieve fulfillment. For the first time in

my life I was able to understand the meaning of the words, "The angels are lost in perpetual contemplation of an infinite glory."[17]

Frankl's concentration camp experiences thus shaped both his therapeutic approach and philosophical outlook, as reflected in his seminal publications.

He often said that even within the narrow boundaries of the concentration camps he found only two races of Men to exist: decent and unprincipled ones. These were to be found in all classes, ethnicities, and groups. Feelings of discontent, boredom, apathy, emptiness, and cynicism; a sense of futility and pointlessness or direction in one's life, Frankl thought, arise out of an existential vacuum—the negative void of meaninglessness.

I used to save comic strips and cartoons in a scrapbook. One I still have shows a skinny old man in a loin cloth at the entrance of a shallow cave near the sharp jagged peak of a high mountain. A younger man in regular street clothes with a rather desperate look on his face has clawed his way up the sheer rock of the mountain side by his fingers. And the old man is saying, "If I knew the meaning of life would I be sitting in a cave wearing a diaper?" Maybe. Maybe not. One thing is for certain, even if the old man knows the meaning of life he cannot give it to the climber in a neat, tidy formula. There are many variations on the musical score of meaning. Each person must discover which is most expressive of the theme for him or herself. Ultimately, Frankl said, we should not ask what the meaning of life is, but rather we must recognize that it is we who are asked. "In a word, each person is questioned by life, and can only answer to life by answering for his or her own life; to life we can respond only by being responsible. Thus, logotherapy sees in responsibleness the very essence of human existence."[18] Assisting another in this search for meaning, in hearing life's question and responding courageously, obviously requires a great deal of skill and spiritual depth. "What does not live in you cannot live around you."

The first chapter of Saint Paul's Epistle to the Ephesians has been of incalculable help to me in my own quest. It is not an easy text to exegete, but, put simply, what I understand Paul to be saying is that God's vast eternal plan, God's kind cosmic intention, is that I live to the praise of God's glory by living love, and so become one with the work of uniting all things in heaven and on earth in the light and life of Christ. But then, I must work out specifically what that means within the realities of my own daily life. When I can encourage another to enter this same process, that is evangelization. Reflect on this excerpt from Alexandr Solzhenitsyn's novel *The First Circle* as used in Robert Raines's *To Kiss the Joy*.

17. Frankl, *Man's Search for Meaning*, 36.
18. Ibid., 111.

> The setting is an elite prison camp at the end of World War II. At one point in the book, two men are talking. Sologdin, middle-aged, has already spent twelve years in this prison. Endless years stretch ahead of him. He has lost his wife, his children, his property—all but his life. Yet strangely, the experience has not embittered him nor destroyed his spirit, but rather distilled his humanity to a deep, rare wisdom.
>
> Nerzhin is the second man—a brilliant young scientist in his early years of imprisonment. He seeks out the older man for insight into his own years of deprivation stretching ahead of him.
>
> Sologdin looked past Nerzhin into the zone, at the thick little clumps of bushes all furry with frost and just touched by the gentle pink of the east. The sun seemed uncertain whether to show itself or not. Sologdin's face drawn and lean, with his reddish-grey, curly little beard and his short mustache, revealed some ancient Russian quality. . . .
>
> "How to face difficulties?" he declared again. "In the realm of the unknown, difficulties must be viewed as *hidden treasure!* Usually, the more difficult, the better. It is not as valuable if your difficulties stem from your own inner struggle. But when difficulties arise out of increasing objective resistance, that's *marvelous!*"
>
> Sologdin continues: "Failures must be considered the cue for further application of effort and concentration of willpower. And if substantial efforts have already been made, the failures are all the more joyous. It means that our crowbar has struck the iron box containing the treasure. Overcoming the increased difficulties is all the more valuable because in failure the *growth of the person performing the task* takes place in proportion to the difficulty encountered!"[19]

At this point you might want to set this book aside and reflect on the character of Sologdin and how it relates to what we have already discussed about evangelization and the person of the practitioner.

Looking from this angle we can say at least one other thing. The quest for meaning is not the same as the pursuit of a literal heaven. Indeed, in the postmodern age, an emphasis on an immortal life in heaven will not form in spiritual consciousness. Marcus Borg, in writing on why the afterlife should not be emphasized as going to heaven, writes,

> Whenever the afterlife is emphasized, it [is] almost inevitable that Christianity becomes a religion of requirements. If there is

---

19. Raines, *To Kiss the Joy*, 21–22.

a heaven, it doesn't seem right that everybody gets to go there regardless, so there must be something that separates those who do get to go from those who don't, namely, something that we believe or do. The second reason is that such an emphasis creates a distinction between an in-group and an out-group: there are those who are saved and those who aren't. The third reason is that emphasizing the afterlife focuses our attention on the next world rather than on the transformation of this world. My critique of what happens when the afterlife is emphasized involves no denial of the afterlife. My point, rather, is to highlight what happens when heaven is made central and when salvation is virtually identified with going to heaven.[20]

For contemporary men and women, a literal paradise is too small and too fantastic to create the sort of catalytic moment capable of igniting human transformation.

Universal Fear

In the novel *Dune*, named for the harsh desert planet God created to "test the faithful," the Bene Gesserit have a mantra, a prayer, they repeat to prepare themselves for times of crisis, of suffering, and of danger: "Fear is the little death." Fear is the little death because it immobilizes us, leads us to react rather than to respond to the challenges of the moment, separates us from integrity, subverts awareness, derails intentionality, and deadens creativity.

There is, of course, that fear which is "the better part of valor" or at least just plain common sense. There is a nature documentary that shows a scene of young monkeys playing in a tree. Suddenly they scatter, screaming wildly—they have discovered a boa constrictor sharing, or hunting on, a large limb in a tree where they are playing. They all keep a fearful distance, except for one little fun-loving guy who keeps running back to the snake chattering happily as it slaps the snake on the head, runs away and then back again several times. However, his game is ended when the boa suddenly catches the monkey in its jaws and swallows the playful little fellow whole. The poor cocky monkey would have been better served by an ounce of fear. But that's not what I am talking about here. Here, I am talking about the fear that is the little death.

Fear is so universal that our contemporary world has been called the age of anxiety. As a society, we have lived with so much fear for so long that we no longer have any idea of how chronically anxious we are—or how

---

20. Borg, *Heart of Christianity*, 172.

abnormal and destructive that is. Postmodern evangelism must, therefore, help people to recognize and confront their fears constructively through love, gratitude, hope, and presence.

"Perfect love banishes fear" (1 John 4:18 NEB). Certain emotional or conscious states of mind are mutually exclusive. The practice of love and reactive fear cannot exist at the same time in the same person—that's the significance to the title of Gerald Jampolsky's terrific little book, *Love is Letting Go of Fear*. Jampolsky tells how, like most medical students, he was afraid of catching a particular disease. His fear was tuberculosis. When he was an intern in Boston he had to spend an entire month on TB service, and he was really scared. He says his fantasy plan was to take one deep breath as he prepared to enter the ward and not breathe again for the whole month. He was an absolute wreck by the end of his first day. That night at 11:30, he received an emergency call saying a fifty-year-old alcoholic woman who had tuberculosis, as well as cirrhosis of the liver, had vomited blood and was without a pulse. Jampolsky rushed to her room, massaged her heart, and cleared the blood from her throat with a suction machine. At first the oxygen machine wouldn't work. As a nurse ran to find another machine, Jampolsky administered mouth-to-mouth resuscitation, the patient's pulse came back and she began to breathe on her own again. When he got back to his quarters, Jampolsky saw himself in a mirror—saw what a bloody mess he was. "All of a sudden," he writes, "it occurred to me that I had not been fearful at any time during the episode. That night I learned that when I was totally absorbed in what I might get, I was immobilized with fear . . . but when I was totally absorbed in giving I felt no fear."[21]

Gratitude banishes fear. To be grateful is to recognize something as a gift and to be happily surprised by it. Gratitude becomes a fixed orientation to reality itself when we live with awareness that everything, the good and the bad, sorrow as well as joy, our very existence, is sheer gift. I look over at Jack, our Queensland/Catahoula mix with his exotic markings, napping as I write, and I feel the joy of gratitude. It is, I suppose, quite a small thing to be grateful for but one which makes this moment worthwhile—makes it a moment of joy and peace. I alone am left of my family of origin. When I think of them here it no longer brings tears to my eyes, but it does bring a sense of gratitude for their love, which continues to give me good guidance, and thankfulness for all those intimate experiences, which have shaped me and make me uniquely me.

---

21. Jampolsky, *Love Is Letting Go of Fear*, 79.

"Our heart's most comprehensive vision shows us that all is gift—blessing. And in response, our heart's most spontaneous action is thanksgiving—blessing."[22]

> That singular command
> I do not understand,
> *Bless what there is for being,*
> Which has to be obeyed, for
> What else am I made for?
> Agreeing, or disagreeing.[23]

Gratitude banishes fear because, well, because we were made to be grateful. Nevertheless, fear is as familiar to us humans as our own face in the mirror.

In an Ocean of Values

What those of us with a serious interest in spirituality and religion and who have a real love for the church are frequently told, I suspect as a means of riveting our attention and selling us something, is that in postmodern thought there are no moral absolutes—no absolute truths. But the more I have worked on this project the more I doubt that statement, or at least its implications. As I write this, the United States is about halfway through the presidential primaries. The news is full of stories and questions of morality and ethics. Weekly surveys report on the perceived integrity and honesty of the candidates. Questions about immigrants and their treatment, gun violence, genocide, police brutality, the treatment of minorities, providing for the poor, economic opportunity and equality, and abortion are among the questions argued with intense feelings and with the passionate belief that some things are right and some things wrong.

My opinion, which I have not worked out in any great detail or precision, is that when people answer surveys in such a way as to indicate they do not believe in absolute truth or moral principles, they may be indicating at least four things: (1) That they will decide for themselves what is moral and ethical; (2) that they believe the situation has a bearing on what is moral or ethical and therefore has to be taken into account—something Jesus himself taught (Matt 23); (3) that advances in human knowledge require a more provisional approach—more of a willingness to be open to change and growth should we learn something new; and (4) that there is, I suspect, also that aversion to the possibility of true truth, of a deeper truth, which

---

22. Steindl-Rast, *Gratefulness*, 80.
23. Auden, "Precious Five," in Steindl-Rast, *Gratefulness*, 81.

comes from not wanting to face the implications of that truth for our own personal lives.

We live in an ocean of values and people do aspire to a transcendent, spiritual, higher morality. But they are turned off by petty and ignorant notions of right and wrong.

With Death at Our Heels

Whether death is seen as hostile or friendly, or simply as what it is, to be human is to exist with the knowledge of nonexistence, it is to live as a witness to our own demise. "The bottom line is that none of us gets out of here alive. And this is the fate of not just me and us, but of everybody we love, including our children and grandchildren. Death will get us all. Moreover, astrophysicists tell us, even the earth and solar system will be destroyed as the sun explodes in its dying gasp."[24] We can of course deny, as Ernest Becker suggested we all do in his Pulitzer Prize–winning book, that death is not at all relevant to us personally. But woe to anyone whose denial project falls apart, who becomes "bogged down" in his or her carefully constructed "hero system," for neurosis or even psychosis may result when the full weight of our mortality and insignificance comes crashing through.[25] Acknowledged or not, death is always at our heels.

> To what purpose, April, do you return again?
> Beauty is not enough.
> You can no longer quiet me with the redness
> Of little leaves opening stickily.
> I know what I know.
> The sun is hot on my neck as I observe
> The spikes of the crocus.
> The smell of the earth is good.
> It is apparent that there is no death.
> But what does that signify?
> Not only under ground are the brains of men
> Eaten by maggots.
> Life in itself
> Is nothing,
> An empty cup, a flight of uncarpeted stairs.
> It is not enough that yearly, down this hill,
> April

24. Borg, *Heart of Christianity*, 34.
25. Becker, *Denial of Death*.

Comes like an idiot, babbling and strewing flowers.[26]

No, try as we do we can never wholly deny death. It is always a thorn stuck somewhere in our consciousness. We may go for long periods of time without thinking about death but always it is quietly or noisily near at hand. Not all the beauty of flowers and sunlight in April can quiet our grieving thoughts.

And how shall we regard this ever-present reality of our existence? Shall we, as Dylan Thomas urged his dying father, "Rage, rage against the dying of the light." Or with those who have experienced the ghastliest suffering, should it be viewed as a blessed relief? Is it as the old saying goes that "when you're dead, like Rover, you're dead all over"? Yet, belief in some sort of life after death is universal.

> The universality of belief in an afterlife is astonishing because life after death is not one of those empirically obvious beliefs that one would expect every society from the dawn of creation of humankind to share. No one is surprised at the universal belief in mountains, rainstorms or animals, because such things are undeniably present to our senses. But it is an entirely different matter when all cultures in history right down to the present jointly proclaim a proposition that seems impossible to confirm through experiences. This is a striking convergence of views that demands explanation.[27]

There are, of course, those like David Hume, who said that he had not taken the idea of immortality seriously since childhood and died calmly and cheerfully. Hume did cheat somewhat in that he thought reincarnation a possibility. But whether someone who does not believe in some form of immortality can die with equanimity is not the issue here, nor is the question concerning the nature of immortality. What is under consideration just now is death as part of the human condition with sufficient amplitude to generate the catalytic moment.

At a recent conference on process theology a very pleasant man, who like me was early for the class, came in and sat down by me. He cheerfully began explaining how he had come to be there. His pastor had told him about the conference and his wife had encouraged him to register. Actually, he went on to say, it was his wife's pastor—he didn't quite believe as she did. He said, "I think when I am toast I'm toast." When he discovered I was a priest he joked about how now he really would be toast. It was a brief,

---

26. Edna St. Vincent Millay, "Spring," in Williams, *The New Pocket Anthology of American Verse*, 324.

27. D'Souza, *Life After Death*, 40.

playful encounter. Had we talked longer and had the conversation taken on a more serious tone I would have wanted to know about his personal feelings, experiences, and insights into death and how all that affected the way he lives. If he had then shown some interest in my own experiences and discoveries, I might have shared how my father's death when I was thirteen sent me into a rage and down a self-destructive path, but how in time I began to recover as I realized I had not been abandoned by God but that God had been present with me all along—that the love of family and the girl who would become my wife, was nothing other than God's love coming to me through them. I would have shared how I simply cannot believe that all the love we give and receive, that all that is best and noblest about us, that the depth of our most intense experiences come to nothing in the end—that consciousness is finally just "burnt toast."

I might have shared how I am not much convinced by the reports of near-death experiences. However, Marcus Borg makes a point well worth considering. Borg says,

> A significant number of reports include details about what was going on that the person could not have witnessed from within his or her body. For me, this is the most impressive part of the near-death experience. All of the other features could be accounted for as regression to our initial birth experience. But if our consciousness and perception can even momentarily be separated from our bodies, then the modern intrinsic linkage between brain and consciousness is called into question, and we have no idea of what is possible beyond death.[28]

I might have shared how when I was a kid I puzzled over questions of how if there is a resurrection someone who had been burned to ashes or buried at sea, eaten, and scattered by a thousand creatures could be put back together at the resurrection of the dead, but how reading the quantum mathematician John Polkinghorne provided me with a helpful and reasonable perspective. Polkinghorne points out that whatever the "real me" is, it must be more than the material composing my body since the atoms composing my body are continually being replaced. The material of my body is changing all the time so that the material body others recognize as me is no longer the same as my body of a number of years ago. "The real me is the immensely complicated 'pattern' in which these ever-changing atoms are organized. It seems an intelligible and coherent hope that God will remember the pattern

---

28. Borg, *Heart of Christianity*, 181.

that is me and recreate it in a new environment of God's choosing, by a great act of final resurrection."[29]

But Polkinghorne is not only a theoretical physicist he is also a priest in the Church of England and so he continues, "Christian belief in a destiny beyond death has always centered on resurrection, not survival. Christ's resurrection is the foretaste and guarantee, within history, of our resurrection, which awaits us beyond history."[30] So ultimately I believe in my own resurrection from the dead because I believe in the resurrection of Jesus Christ—I believe in Jesus' resurrection, although I certainly have no idea how to explain it, because I think it makes rational sense, because I have experienced Christ as a living presence and companion on my way, because I trust the person of Jesus and have found him a reliable guide, and because I have confidence in Scripture.

All of this is meant to be suggestive rather than formulaic. Death is a ubiquitous phenomenon of the human condition. We can hold our awareness of death at some distance by means of intellectualizations or religious theories, or even by suppressing such awareness altogether, but the caring evangelist will see conversations of death not as a tactic or abstract theory, but as an opportunity to be a healing and reconciling presence.

In Mystical Hope

I might have asked my congenial fellow conference participant what he made of John Cobb, the world's foremost exponent of process theology and the key leader in forming this very conference we were attending with such enjoyment and appreciation. In his *Theological Reminiscences*, Cobb, who is an old man now, reflects on his ever-slackening hold on this life, on how before long he will "welcome sister death," and what death may mean for us all.

> If death is the end, I will have no less gratitude for life, no cause to complain, and in any case, no opportunity. But I doubt that there is nothing more. In our dominant culture, serious discussion of what comes next is virtually taboo. There are some good reasons for this. It is part of a healthy reaction to the early modern period in which in both church and culture it was supposed that only belief in rewards and punishment after death would support the needed social virtues here and now. In polite circles the idea of hell is, in fact, much worse than unfashionable. What remains in the liberal church is a vague assurance that all will be

---

29. Polkinghorne, *Quarks, Chaos, and Christianity*, 109–11.
30. Ibid., 111

well. Since no content is ever suggested for the imagination, the assurance is, for many, not very reassuring. The result tends to be that Christians cling to a rather miserable existence here rather than eagerly anticipating a blessedness beyond.... To affirm the goodness of life here and now and deny that God imposes suffering on anyone does not require an end to discussions of life after death.... What has really ended all such discussion in respectable society is the materialist world view.[31]

Cobb goes on to discuss Alfred North Whitehead's notions of "prehensions" and "conceptual feelings" and then concludes, "For one whose satisfactions are overwhelmingly sensual, the loss would be greater than the gain. And for one who does not care for others, who has related to them only as instruments and competitors . . . that might indeed be hellish. Also, there may be for those whose experience is so limited to the physical that there is no continuation at all." But for those whose dominant experience has been the very presence of God, to die, as Christian Scripture asserts, is to become more fully alive to the beatific vision for which they have longed.

Hope is, of course, not entirely about whatever good lies beyond this life. Hope, Christian hope, mystical hope, arises out of an experience of trust—trust that at the center of reality is something, or rather someone, ultimately and infinitely good and trustworthy; and, therefore, all despair is groundless. It is the conviction that though our own resources may be inadequate to our circumstances there is a strength and help available to us that we can neither explain nor prove other than in our living. Indeed, what we know from Viktor Frankl, Alexandr Solzhenitsyn, and many others of the modern era is that even physical existence is unsustainable without some measure of hope. It is an egregious error to think of hope as an attempt to live in the future, for hope is always experienced in the present—energizes us in both our small and large difficulties of the moment, and sustains us in whatever present darkness we may find ourselves.

---

31. Cobb, *Theological Reminiscences*, 302–5.

PART II

A New Apologetic

An anxious father brought his boy to Jesus. The boy went into convulsions and fell to the ground, thrashing around and foaming at the mouth.

"How long has this been happening," asked Jesus.

"Since childhood," said the boy's father. "He falls on the ground and hurts himself. He has fallen into water—and into the fire. But if you can do anything, take pity and help us."

"All things," said Jesus reassuringly, "are possible to one who believes."

The boy's father cried out in a mixture of desperation and hope against hope, "I do believe.... Help my unbelief."

—MARK 9:14–24, PARAPHRASE

CHAPTER SIX

The New Apologetic and the Reality of God

The sense of transcendence is the sense that the visual, tactile, and aural impressions that tell us of the nature of a hidden world of quarks and atoms also tell us of a spiritual reality of beauty and power which those impressions express in fragmentary ways. The impressions are "sacraments," or sensory signs of the reality of Spirit on which they ultimately depend.[1]

—Keith Ward

If evangelization is a spiritual practice, the sharing of the fruit of Christian contemplation, the natural flowering of a meditative style of life, it will then also result in a "new apologetic," which paradoxically is also the oldest apologetic, an apologetic that transcends the secular reasoning of every age and of the scientism and rationalism of the modern era in particular, and forms organically in the spiritual consciousness of postmodern men and women. It is not that such an apologetic will ignore established principles of logic, or reject hard science, or be dismissive of factual data, but that it will see beyond the secular mentality that has lost the capacity for finding God in all things and everywhere, and finds in the world of logic and science and objective facts "a spiritual reality of beauty and power" to which these all point.

1. Ward, *Why There Almost Certainly Is A God*, 129.

Reflective Reasoning and the Second Naiveté

As previously noted, postmodern people are disenchanted modernists. The human race is like a truck stuck on the tracks at a railroad crossing with a freight train of explosives bearing down, and neither philosophical logic nor scientific analysis can move us off. What is it the Grateful Dead sang?

> Trouble with you is the trouble with me,
> Got two good eyes but we still don't see.
> Come round the bend, you know it's the end,
> The fireman screams and the engine just gleams...
>
> Driving that train, high on cocaine,
> Casey Jones you better watch your speed.
> Trouble ahead, trouble behind,
> And you know that notion just crossed my mind.[2]

If we are to make any real sense of our contemporary world, or of biblical faith, or of our own personal spiritual pilgrimage, we must see the postmodern rejection of rationalism as a positive move toward a more "enlightened" way of thinking. I would suggest that reflective thinking as proposed by scholars like Patricia M. King and Karen Strohm Kitchener offers a way of getting unstuck and off the tracks—a new way of thinking apologetically. "In the final analysis, the real challenge . . . is empowering individuals to know that the world is far more complex than it first appears, and that they must make interpretative arguments and decisions—judgments that entail real consequences for which they must take responsibility and from which they may not flee by disclaiming expertise."[3] Knowledge, and we dare to say even some wisdom, emerges from a reasonable inquiry in which solutions to ill-structured problems are constructed on the basis of the evidence available, and evaluated and reevaluated as required in terms of what is probable.[4]

In watching a video of Daniel Wallace and Bart Ehrman's debate, "Can We Trust the Text of the New Testament," I must admit, even though it exposes my bias against Dallas Theological Seminary, I was quite astounded that a professor from Dallas would argue his case from the postmodern perspective of relativity and probability while Ehrmanm trapped in the mind-set of modernity, demanded absolute certainty.[5] Ehrman's repeated

---

2. Grateful Dead, "Casey Jones," *The Very Best of Grateful Dead*, Warner Bros./Rhino, 2003, CD.

3. King and Kitchener, *Developing Reflective Judgment*, 1.

4. Ibid., 71.

5. *Can We Trust the Text of the New Testament?*

assertion was that we just don't know for sure. Wallace's argument was that based on the evidence it looks as if we probably have a trustworthy text—a strangely turning world indeed when the agnostic is the absolutist and the conservative believer a relativist. Be that as it may, the point here is simply that in the postmodern world the argument from relativity and probability will be more convincing than one from absolutism and certainty.

God Signs in a Suffering World

The philosophical problem of how evil and suffering can exist in our world if there is a good and all powerful God furnishes a significant metaphysical issue where we can contrast the development of postmodern reflective judgement and the principle of probability with that of certainty. The well-worn logic of modernity learned in nearly every introductory philosophy course goes like this:

> 1. If suffering and evil exist, then an all-good, all-powerful, all-knowing God does not exist.
> 2. Suffering and evil exist.
> 3. Therefore, an all-good, all-powerful, all-knowing God does not exist.

A new apologetic might note that there are a number of possible responses to this philosophical problem cast as a syllogistic challenge.

The apologist might begin by denying the very premise, which assumes with human infallibility that the reality of a good and compassionate and powerful God is necessarily incompatible with suffering. She or he might note how much suffering we human beings inflict on one another, our personal complicity in the ills of the world, the responsibility for which we are entirely ready to blame on God. In the case of natural disasters, catastrophic accidents, or certain diseases, recourse might be made to what the quantum physicist John Polkinghorne calls the "free process defense."[6] Polkinghorne sees the whole universe as in some sense free to choose itself—to choose what it will be. Pierre Teilhard de Chardin, the Jesuit priest and paleontologist who saw the entire cosmos as evolving, moving toward union with Christ the Omega Point, put it this way:

> Right up to the reflective zones we have seen the world proceeding by means of groping and chance. Under this heading alone—even up to the human level in which chance is most controlled—how many failures have there been for one success,

---

6. Polkinghorne, *Quarks, Chaos, and Christianity*, 60.

> how many days of misery for one hour's joy, how many sins for a solitary saint? To begin with we find physical lack—arrangement or derangement on the material level; then suffering which cuts into the sentient flesh; then, on a still higher level, wickedness and the torture of spirit as it analyses itself and makes choices. Statistically, to every degree of evolution, we find evil always and everywhere forming and reforming implacably in us and around us.[7]

This free-process apologetic goes a long way to explaining the implacable presence of evil in our world. In the end, however, the more contemplative apologist might note that the problem is indeed, in its formal and academic aspects, a philosophical rather than religious or spiritual difficulty, but that either way it is a question which can never be adequately structured so as to render an answer of mathematical certainty.

Ultimately, a new and more contemplative apologetic will focus on suffering as an inscrutable mystery that, regardless of all our logical analysis, can only be resolved for each person spiritually. My friend and mentor Werner Kroeker as a middle aged Mennonite pastor was in a serious automobile accident and broke his neck. For a long time he wore a stainless steel halo screwed into his skull. Even as an older man there was no day in which he was not in some pain. The day the doctors removed the halo he met a woman who had also broken her neck. She asked Werner, "Do you ever ask God: Why me?" Werner replied that he had asked that often. The doctors told him that he needed to walk as much as he could, but that if he ever felt at all dizzy he should lie down immediately—no matter where he was. A few days later he was walking and as he crossed a busy intersection he felt very dizzy and so laid down right there in the crosswalk. Motorists honked their horns, cursed, and yelled at him. "Are you drunk? Get out of the intersection!" "You stupid idiot!" "I'll run over you if you don't move!" "Get out of the way you moron!" Werner started to ask himself as he had many times before, "Why?" And then he found himself saying, "God I don't know why this is happening, but I don't want the experience to be lost on me." For Werner it was a genuine answer, but one that had nothing to do with the philosophical syllogism above.

Werner's answer, like Job's in the Old Testament, emerged from a mystical encounter with God. In the throes of agonizing loss Job laments the very day he was born. If only he could speak face-to-face with God, if only he had the opportunity to argue his case directly and personally, God would have to acknowledge that Job's terrible suffering is unjust. Then God speaks

---

7. Tielhard de Chardin, *Phenomenon of Man*, 311–12.

to Job out of the whirlwind, but offers no philosophical answer, provides no satisfactory explanation of any sort; rather, he simply points to the beautiful mosaic of creation while noting that Job, man of wisdom that he is, had nothing to do with realizing this mystery of being. Job's unexpected and profoundly puzzling response is, "I have heard of Thee by the hearing of the ear; But now my eye sees Thee" (Job 42:5). What kind of an answer and response is that? It is a "non-answer," understandable only to the mystic.

It is the same sort of thing discoverable in Psalm 73, where the poet explains how he listened to religious people chattering about how good God is, but when he observed how things are in "the real world," saw how much good people suffer and how easy the selfish and arrogant and greedy and violent have it, he nearly lost his faith; but, then he went into the holy temple where he encountered God and experienced a catalytic moment. Sounding very much like Job, the Psalmist concludes, "But as for me the nearness of God is my good" (Psalm 73:28). Paradoxically, it is as if in encountering the presence of God the problem, although still observable to the external observer, simply evaporates.

The most perplexing problems, heartaches, challenges, and difficulties of being human, the deepest questions of the heart and mind, cannot be structured in such a way as to render closely defined and absolutely certain answers. Perhaps we should be grateful that postmodern men and women have pointed us back in this direction. In any event, if we wish to communicate effectively in the postmodern world it will require developing our capacity for reflective reasoning.

Before moving on, another footnote of sorts needs to be added. I went to the public library with my wife and casually looked through religious magazines and journals while she searched for the books she wanted. In the February 28, 2015 issue of *Christianity Today* I came across an article in high praise of W. Mark Lanier, a smart and highly successful trial lawyer who in his book *Christianity on Trial: A Lawyer Examines the Christian Faith*, writes about the plausibility of the Christian faith from a legal perspective. The article described Lanier's apologetic approach as one based on probability—much like the proceedings in a court case in which evidence is weighed, sifted, and considered before reaching a decision. Since this sounded very much like what I have been suggesting here I ordered and read *Christianity on Trial* right away. But something struck me as quite different between what I am suggesting and what Lanier writes, and I think it is this:

1. The feeling I had in reading Lanier's book was that although it speaks of "probabilities" it might as well have used the word "certainty."

2. Rather than cultivating a spiritual awakening, it relies on the relentless pounding of "forensic" logic.

3. It appears to be based on the assumption that only Christian faith as defined by American Evangelicals and Fundamentalists can be genuinely orthodox.

For the consideration of Christian concepts as concepts, Lanier's book can be helpful, but as a way of doing apologetics in the twenty-first century, its reliance on enlightenment era logic simply will not form in human consciousness as spiritual reality. Furthermore, what is more important for Christian faith than the principle of probability is the recognition that the most crucial and intense questions of our existence cannot be solved by mathematical logic—not even the mathematics of probability.

Reflective Thinking and the Second Naiveté

Reflective thinking will, I believe, lead us toward what Paul Ricoeur referred to as "postcritical" thinking and "the second naiveté."[8] What we need, Ricoeur said, is a criticism that can call us out of the desert to the verdant promise of a second naiveté. This second naiveté is actually the third phase of a journey beyond the desert that is taken in three stages—the precritical, the critical, and the postcritical.[9] In our reflections on God, Ricoeur thought, "we wish to be called again beyond the desert of criticism."[10]

The precritical stage is characterized by a certain naiveté—a trusting innocence. What conflicts with what is already believed is simply ignored or not even recognized as problematic. There is a good deal of reliance on the explanations offered by accepted and trusted authorities. Interpretations tend to be rather one-dimensional, concrete, and literal, and more as the individual might see events and situations in his or her own mind than in terms of what, say a text of Scripture, may be trying to communicate. Patricia M. King and Karen Kitchener in their book *Developing Reflective Judgment* note that since in its earlier stages knowledge is understood as absolute and concrete, beliefs need no justification. The assumption that there is absolute correspondence between what is true and what is believed to be true means that contradictions and conflicts are simply not perceived.

With the critical stage comes the recognition of knowledge as an abstraction and the discovery that evidence needs to be related to belief.

---

8. Ricoeur, *Symbolism of Evil*, 349–50.
9. Brueggemann, "Where Is the Scribe?," 389–91.
10. Ricoeur, *Symbolism of Evil*, 349.

However, there may still be some difficulty in distinguishing theory and evidence, and in coordinating the two. Here there is an attempt to justify beliefs with reason and evidence, but arguments can also be idiosyncratic in nature, so that evidence that begs the question and fits established beliefs is chosen as proof. One need look no further than the "Jesus Seminar." At some point in the critical stage there may come the recognition that in some areas irrefutable certainty can never be attained. Nevertheless, the attempt to identify and apply rules of evidence continues.

In the postcritical stage there is a willingness to critique one's own beliefs—a humility in which one recognizes his or her own role in "constructing what is known or believed to be true."[11] But there is more. In the postcritical mode there is a dialectical, dialogical quality. Where the Christian Scriptures are concerned the reader questions and is questioned by the text. The text is no longer so much an object to be dissected and analyzed, as something organic—living. Or to use the words of Martin Buber, the text is no longer an "It," but a "Thou" we encounter; or, perhaps better, the Thou that speaks to us in the very human words of the text. One is now aware of the use of metaphorical and imaginative language, of myth, of the occurrences of textual errors, of irregularities and the impossibility of fully harmonizing narratives, and yet there are signs of a transcendence so profound, so real, that we cannot get over it, or around it, or beneath it—the ground of all being, that than which no greater can be conceived, *Yahweh, Elohim*, God, the Mystery of the Ages, which is the hope of Christ in you. And thus one experiences a second birth, a second conversion, a second innocence and naïveté. It is innocent and naïve in that having "wrestled with angels" it has come to that simple trust essential to the "beatific vision."

My good friend Frank Humphries, a very smart reliability engineer, was drawn to a small Baptist Church as a ten-year-old. They seemed to have "information" he wanted very badly. They also had a rather literal interpretation of biblical stories. In time he was not only put off by their literalism, but also by what he saw as inconsistency with the Christian Way as taught in Scripture. On one occasion they sent a young teenage girl home from church because her skirt was "too short." Frank knew that wasn't right—wasn't Christian. And so he left that fellowship. Now in his highly critical phase he could no longer accept their explanations of life, of the Bible, or of Christ. Eventually as an adult a friend gave him a copy of one of Marcus Borg's books. Suddenly, Frank saw that there was another way of understanding the Christian message—another way of looking at Christ, the Bible, and life. It wasn't that he adopted Borg's position as his own; it was

---

11. King and Kitchener. *Developing Reflective Judgment*, 71.

just that he grasped that there were possibilities he had never imagined. This was the beginning of a quest that ended, or began anew, in faith—the Jesus story could be read with intellectual integrity and remain true in more than a purely literary sense. Today, Frank is a rather orthodox Christian, but it is not orthodoxy of the first but the second naiveté.

Let me tell you about another valued friend—Tom Hostetler. Tom went into the Navy right out of high school and served on a nuclear submarine. After his discharge from the Navy he earned his undergraduate degree in philosophy from Stanford University. For many years Tom earned his living supervising the setting up of experimental stations for scientists at the Stanford Linear Accelerator. One night at Mr. Toots, a second-story coffee shop on the beach in Capitola Village by the sea, I asked Tom to tell me about becoming Christian. He said he could remember the moment and what he had said vividly, "Here I come Jesus. I hope I don't stumble." I hope, although Tom's words are written here, that you can hear the simplicity, the innocence, the naiveté with which he spoke them that night. But it was a naiveté fully aware of the questions posed by philosophy, by a religiously pluralistic world, and by modern physics. The new apologetic is an attempt to find the way beyond the first precritical naiveté, through the desert of theological criticism to the second naiveté. Or, as Ricoeur further described it, "A time of restoration that is not a time different from that of criticism; for we are in every way children of criticism, and we seek to go beyond criticism, by a criticism that is no longer reductive but restorative."[12]

Postmodernity and the Quest for God

In retrospect, John A. T. Robinson, the famous New Testament scholar from Cambridge, made bishop of Woolwich, was perhaps the first truly postmodern theologian—seeking to move through the desert of modern reductive criticism to a new criticism that is restorative and leads to the springs of the second naiveté. So, how do we address matters of faith and belief, as both trust and mental assent, how do we share the ancient mystery, "the hope of Christ in you,"[13] in a contemporary environment of suspicion? This is the issue with which Robinson attempted to address in his controversial book, *Honest to God*. As a bishop, Robinson found his concerns shifted from the world of academic discussion to the concrete and pressing questions of pastoral care, and to the spiritual formation of the people of his diocese—people facing, not in theory but in every fact, the joys, sorrows,

---

12. Ricoeur, *Symbolism of Evil*, 350.
13. Col 1:27.

and challenges of daily existence. What Robinson began to ask himself was how he could restate the Christian faith to contemporary men and women, and to himself, in a way that was comprehensible to the modern mind. He thought that the prognosis for the future of the church, given the ever-accelerating complexity, risks, and scientific advancements of our world, was not good—that men and women living in the third millennium would find Christian belief, including belief in God, both irrelevant and unbelievable. Robinson further thought that simply refining and restating Christian belief would not be enough. While acknowledging the good work of many scholars in giving fresh expression to Christian faith, he thought that would not be adequate to the task confronting priest and preacher. He said presenting the case for God as "a being" in new ways was not sufficient, but that the whole Christian understanding for God had to be "recast." He wrote,

> I believe we are being called, over the years ahead, to far more than a restating of traditional orthodoxy in modern terms. Indeed, if our defense of the faith is limited to this, we shall find in all likelihood that we have lost out to all but a tiny religious remnant. A much more radical recasting I would judge is demanded, in the process of which the most fundamental categories of our theology—of God, of the supernatural, and of religion itself—must go into melting.[14]

It wasn't, then, that Robinson thought the evidence for the existence of the being of God needed to be refined and presented in nicer attire and with a more sophisticated image, but that it was counterproductive to think and argue about God as "a being" at all.

In this I think Robinson was absolutely correct, going to the very core of doing apologetics in the twenty-first century. Consequently, Robinson turned to the modern existentialist theologian Paul Tillich who insisted, "God is not a being, but being itself," the "ground of all being," and spoke of God as "ultimate concern."[15] Tillich thought, for instance, that to speak of God's omnipotence, of God being everywhere, and of God's omniscience, of God knowing everything, was as dangerous as it was helpful. Such concepts, he said, "make us picture God as a thing with superhuman qualities," and "transforms an overwhelming religious experience into an abstract, philosophical statement, which can be accepted and rejected, defined, redefined, and replaced . . . out there."[16]

---

14. Robinson, *Honest to God*, 27.

15. Tillich, *Systematic Theology*, 235–39; Tillich, *Dynamics of Faith*, 1, 10–11, 18, 45, 52; Tillich, *Shaking of the Foundations*, 46.

16. Tillich, *Shaking of the Foundations*, 45–46.

The second semester of my first college course in philosophy I was introduced to the work of Tillich by the professor, Dr. Norman Thomas. I am sorry to say that from my ultra conservative orientation I just could not see that Tillich had completely shifted the apologetic field from the fruitless argument of the existence of God as "a being" to God as an experiential reality. Of course, Tillich was not the first to do so. Saint Anselm had famously provided the classical ontological argument in the eleventh century, "God is that than which no greater can be conceived." Anselm's argument, however, wasn't so much a proof of God, as it was a way of regarding the nature of faith. Anselm recognized God as beyond all concepts, images, and thought—defying all definitions and excluding all explanations. The great Jewish scholar and mystic Abraham Joshua Heschel put it beautifully: "There are no concepts," he said, "which we could appoint to designate the greatness of God or represent God to our minds. For God is not a being whose existence can be proved by our syllogisms. God is a reality in the face of which, when becoming alive to it, all concepts become clichés"[17]

What John Robinson wanted to see was an "utterly natural" and "unself-conscious transposition" in the uses of mythological language about God.[18] Yet even Tillich, as noted here, recognized, if not the impossibility, the difficulty in escaping such language. Lewis was certainly aware that the metaphorical character of all God talk is inescapable, and therefore wrote: "Into the region of awe, in deepest solitude, there is a road right out of the self, a commerce with the naked Other, imageless (though our imagination salutes it with a hundred images) unknown, undefined, desired."[19] What both Robinson and Tillich saw was the difficulty of arguing a crudely anthropomorphic God to contemporary men and women—Josh McDowell's books, *Evidence That Demands a Verdict*, *More Evidence That Demands a Verdict*, and *New Evidence That Demands a Verdict*, just will not get it in the third millennium. Unlike C. S. Lewis, what McDowell does not seem to recognize is the necessity of metaphorical or poetic language, which rather than conveying God as cold, abstract, and remote, leaves one with a sense of God's graciousness and with a sense of the possibility and desire for a warm intimacy with God, while at the same time acknowledging the limitations of all concepts, definitions, and descriptions. It seems to me that the great Jewish philosopher and theologian Martin Buber wrote with especially keen insight,

---

17. Heschel, *Quest for God*, 88.
18. Robinson, *Honest to God*, 15.
19. Downing, *Into the Region of Awe*, 68.

The designation of God as a person is indispensable for all who, like myself, do not mean an idea when they say "God," although philosophers like Plato could at times take him for one—all who, like myself, mean by "God" him that, whatever else he may be in addition, enters into a direct relationship to us human beings through creative, revelatory, and redemptive acts, and that makes it possible for us to enter a direct relationship to him. This ground and meaning of our existence establishes a mutuality of the kind that can obtain only between persons. The concept of personhood is, of course, utterly incapable of describing the nature of God, but it is permitted and necessary to say that God is *also* a person.[20]

God is ultimately incomprehensible, indescribable, inexplicable, and most certainly more than "a being" or person, but as C. S. Lewis noted, while God is infinitely more than a person, God is not less than what I mean by personal.

Problem of the Trinity

I now want to make a suggestion for grappling with the problem of the Trinity. I use the word "problem" quite intentionally but without originality, gratefully borrowing it from Arthur Wainwright's *The Trinity in the New Testament*. Although the word "paradox" feels more accurate and descriptive than "problem," thinking about "the problem of the Trinity" may provide a useful beginning point.

What every curious Christian novice learns very early is that the New Testament contains no formal doctrinal statement regarding the Trinity; in fact, the word "Trinity" is not even used in the Christian Scriptures. It is not until the second century that we find the term occurring in the works of Theophilus (*trias*) and Tertullian (*trinitas*), and it is not until the fourth century that it becomes a developed philosophical concept with technical disputes over the meaning of "person" and "essence." It is not until late in the fourth century, then, that we have a philosophical or theological doctrine of the Trinity as one God in three persons. It is, however, a doctrine Christians have been trying to explain ever since as something more than a bit of bad math.

What Wainwright's careful examination of the New Testament texts reveals is that the biblical authors were conscious of the problem. The earliest Christian communities held firmly to the Jewish belief in the unity of

---

20. Buber, *I And Thou*, 180–81.

God, but they also believed Jesus was divine—a belief they demonstrated by attributing divine titles to Jesus and by claiming that he had done, and was doing, what only God alone can do. "How could Father and Son be God, and yet God be one? A further problem was raised because the Spirit was regarded as a person, who had a decisive influence upon the lives of individuals. Was the Spirit also God, and if so, how could God be three and one?"[21]

The writers of the New Testament documents did not look to Greek metaphysics or esoteric philosophy for an answer to the problem, but to their shared experience. Wainwright sees their exploration and discovery as arising out of the development of Christian experience, worship, and thought. "It was rooted in the experience of men and women who were conscious of the power of the Spirit and of the presence and Lordship of the risen Christ. It was rooted in worship, because they worshipped in the Spirit, offered their prayers to God the Father through Christ and sometimes worshipped Christ himself. And it arose out of thought in that the writers first tackled, particularly in the Fourth Gospel, the Christological problem, and then the threefold problem."[22]

There are numerous ways to conceptualize the Trinity. C. S. Lewis pointed out that if you lived in a one-dimensional world all you would be able to work with would be straight lines. In a two-dimensional world you would be able to combine four of those lines so as to create a square—four lines but one square. In a three-dimensional world six of those squares can be combined to form a cube—six squares but only one cube. As you progress from the simpler to the more complex levels you are able to combine things in ways you would never have imagined possible if all you knew were the simpler levels. In our time and space dimension one person is only one being, but in the "heavenly dimension" you find a being who is three persons while remaining "One Being." This, Lewis suggested, is as difficult for us to imagine as it would be to conceive of a cube if you were from a one-dimensional universe.[23]

The famous Catholic theologian Karl Rahner sought to recover the relevance of the Trinity for contemporary Christian life by pointing out that in the Greek, the language in which the creeds were originally formulated, the word for "person" does not mean an independent center of consciousness and freedom, but something more like a "way of being." So Rahner suggested the doctrine of the Trinity might be reformulated as "the One God

---

21. Wainwright, *Trinity in the New Testament*, 3.
22. Ibid., 266–67.
23. Lewis, *Mere Christianity*, 140–45.

who has three ways of being." The early Christians, he noted, experienced God concretely, as incarnate, in Jesus the Son. They experienced God in the depths of their being as the Spirit, and the mystery to which the Son and Spirit pointed, they, as had Jesus, called "Father."

The New Testament writers approach "the Trinity problem" in a more practical than speculative way, focus on understanding it in terms of relationship and how it functions, and on the character of God rather than philosophical precision, fourth century "substance" concepts, or objective dogmatic assertions. It simply was not the aim of the biblical writers to unravel all the metaphysical complexities of the divine nature. One may well wonder whether it would not be wiser to speak humbly of the paradox rather than the problem of the Trinity. "The word 'paradox' does not occur in the New Testament, but there is in the prologue to the Fourth Gospel a clear awareness of the relationship between Father and Son. The man who wrote 'the Word was with God, and the Word was God' certainly knew that his statement contained a paradox."[24]

I have been asked many times, as you can imagine, how to respond to someone who finds the doctrine of the Trinity problematic. My usual answer is that I don't have a "canned" response even for myself, much less for someone else. In general I listen, and frequently commiserate that it is indeed a puzzling piece of Christian theology. I might share that many people find Karl Rhaner's or C. S. Lewis's ideas helpful. One thing this does is to help establish that I am conversant and at ease with the academic aspects of the discussion, and that I know there are rational explanations at hand. But I will also want to point out that what seemed most relevant to the earliest Christians was what the doctrine of the Trinity, or since they didn't use such terminology, what the paradox they saw in the relationship between Father, Son, and Holy Spirit, meant to them in spiritual, relational, and functional terms. In such a conversation I hope it is clear that I am comfortable with ambiguity, paradox, and mystery. I usually say, paraphrasing Thomas à Kempis, "I would rather experience the Holy Trinity than to discuss it learnedly." I might share how I consider powerful feelings of awe and wonder, such as I had as a young boy sleeping beneath a starry sky, as experiences of God the Father. Or, similarly, feelings of being safely held in the loving embrace of an immense and unfathomable power as what some call the *Abba* or *Amma* experience—the Papa or Mama God experience. I can share how I have experienced Jesus as wisdom, beauty, goodness, and as a friend on the way. And the Holy Spirit, I can say, I have experienced as the light that no darkness can overcome—as a strength and hope coming

---

24. Wainwright, *Trinity in the New Testament*, 8.

from beyond myself in times of trouble. The early Church Fathers frequently spoke of the Trinity as *perichoresis*, which can be translated as dancing around. In this way they thought of the Trinity as that mysterious eternal movement, rhythm, or dance of divine love into which we are all invited. For me the doctrine of the Holy Trinity means that at the heart of all reality is what must be described as "relationship"—although that is much too small a word for something so wonderful and mysterious. That is the sort of apologetic as spiritual practice that I would attempt in grappling with the "problem of the Trinity" in the postmodern world.

Classical Proofs

The Medieval Christian mystic and anonymous author of the *Cloud of Unknowing* taught that God may be known through the long, loving gaze of contemplation, but never grasped by the intellect. There are, for example, the classical proofs of God, but in the end none of them individually or collectively provide any sort of mathematical-like certainty, and each is best understood and applied when felt as the Divine Mystery, which enfolds us all.

The cosmological proof states that everything has a cause but you can't engage in an infinite regression because there must be a first cause. The cosmological proof can be presented solely as an academic argument; or, it can be presented out of sheer awe and wonder that anything exits at all.

The teleological proof can be a dispassionate discussion of purpose, of order and disorder in the universe; or, it can be a passion-filled description of one's own experience of physical, emotional, intellectual, and spiritual movement toward the Omega Point and personal coherence in Christ.

The ontological proof can be another explanatory analysis of the nature of God—"God as that than which no greater can be conceived." In that case, when the atheist conceives of God as a figment of the imagination we may reply, "No, that is not God. That is not what I am talking about at all." But, if in our own lives we have personally come "face-to-face" with something or someone that all our thinking and all our reasoning has brought us to, something or someone with which the intellect alone cannot deal, then the Ontological Proof takes on a whole new dimension.

In our conversations we may resort to the moral argument developed by Immanuel Kant who said that all humanity has an astounding sense of morality and that it is self-evident that God is the source of this innate moral quality. "Two things fill me with awe," Kant said, "the starry skies above and the moral law within." Notice how the moral law is, for Kant, not merely legal language written on paper, or even on stone, but a way of being written on and in the heart of humanity—as awesome as the starry skies above.

Making use of the classical proofs in this way is not meant to suggest a suspension of reason or a substitution of ignorance for knowledge. But research suggests that when our emotions are engaged with our cognitive processes we simply think better. Indeed, the more we know the better prepared we are for evangelization, provided we have the wisdom to make spiritual application of such knowledge, "for what does not live in us cannot live around us."

The *Sensus Divinitatis* as Classical Proof

For centuries, Christians like Saint Thomas Aquinas, thinker, scholar, evangelizer, teacher, contemplative, monk, and spiritual guide have spoken and written and witnessed to what is often referred to as the *sensus divinitatis*—the "sense of the divine." Actually, the argument itself goes back at least as far as Plato and perhaps even further back than that. The *sensus divinitatis* or *sensus deitatis* ("sense of deity") is the realization that there exists in the human a natural sense of the Deity. Alvin Plantinga maintains that every human being has this capacity to know God, but that it does not properly function in some due to sin.[25] I am not as interested here in why this sense of the divine seems stronger in some than in others as I am that it exists as a natural human instinct at all. As I write this I glance at my bookshelf and Dean Hamer's book *The God Gene: How Faith is Hardwired into Our Genes*, catches my eye.[26] I find it passingly strange how modern critics of people of faith frequently presented the rather silly argument that since no one had ever discovered anything like a soul in any human being, religious belief was unwarranted. Now that it appears that God is in our very genes, in our biochemistry, which is to be entirely expected if, as Scripture claims, human beings are a psychosomatic unity, the assertion is: "Oh well, it's just all hormonal." Nor am I put off by the argument that this sense of the divine, given the divergent beliefs of world religions and even within denominations of the same faith, cannot possibly be true. What is at stake is not a sense of doctrine but an experience of the reality of God.

The *sensus divinitatis* is, of course, to be understood as a faculty like our faculties of reason, or our five senses, or feelings, or intuition, which are all meant to lead us to a knowledge of the truth. And like each of our other

---

25. Plantinga, *Warranted Christian Belief*.
26. Hamer, *God Gene*.

faculties, our sense of deity is not infallible so that it has to be correlated with our other faculties of discernment.

I think it is out of the *sensus divinitatis* that Augustine spoke when he said, "O Lord, you have made us for yourself and our hearts are unquiet until they find their rest in you." Augustine knew what it was to hunger and thirst for the mysterious presence of God, and as a great apologist he would have thought it exceedingly strange if there was nothing in all of life capable of satisfying that desire, just as it would be absolutely astounding to feel the physical pangs of hunger and for there to be no such thing as food to satisfy that hunger or water to slack one's thirst. I think it is out of the *sensus divinitatis* that Gerald May, psychiatrist, author, and spiritual director, wrote in speaking of our innate desire for Love. In *The Awakened Heart*, May gave this explanatory note, "Our understanding of God is not God. God is love, but love is not God. . . . If love is always more than we can understand, how could we ever expect to comprehend love's source?" Within us, then, is this intense longing that is ultimately a longing and a yearning for God. Then, sounding very much like Augustine, May said,

> There is a desire within each of us, in the deep center of ourselves that we call our heart. We were born with it, it is never completely satisfied, and it never dies. We are often unaware of it, but it is always awake. It is the human desire for love. Every person on this earth yearns to love, to be loved, to know love. Our true identity, our reason for being, is to be found in this desire.[27]

I can say that in all my experience as a preacher I have never explored this phenomenon of the *sensus divinitatis* without people, including people with no particular belief in God, telling me that this was exactly their experience and wanting to talk about it more.

Evangelization at the beginning of this new millennium requires the articulation of this deepest and truest desire of the human heart. I think it is the *sensus divinitatis* within himself that Marcus Borg was conscious of when he said he believed in God because he had experienced God, and it is what the great Carl Jung meant when he responded after being asked, "Do you believe in God?" "I don't need to believe, I know."

Research has shown that, contrary to the older modern idea, the ability to think effectively is enhanced when reason is appropriately engaged with emotion. But what we feel in our guts has even more significance than its impact on our cognitive functioning. William Barry, S.J., sees affective experience as foundational to the knowledge and enjoyment of God. If

27. May, *Awakened Heart*, 1.

belief in God remains nothing more than a notional assent it will not serve, insists Barry, to ground a life in the ineffable reality of Divine Mystery. It is a matter of particular importance, then, for evangelizers to locate in their own lives the foundational experiences of intimacy and love and desire "for the unnameable, the 'All,' the Mystery we call God."

> I was walking by the sea shore on a lovely, clear crisp autumn day. I admired the sun on the leaves and on the blue water. Suddenly there welled up in me a feeling of great well-being and a strong desire for "I know not what," for the "All," for union that made me very happy. I remembered a few other times of such joy and desire and realized why autumn is my favorite season—because it is associated with such experiences. Almost as quickly as it had come it was gone. I was happy afterwards, not downcast even though I no longer had the experience. I would like to have the experience again, but I am not bereft without it. Later that week in a class I recounted the occasion, and many in the class acknowledged having similar experiences. I wonder if these are not experiences of our creation.[28]

The gospel, the good message, is that this higher consciousness, this higher life, this poetic and divine life is a possibility for us all.

It can be further noted that seeing God as Mystery, as Reality, as that Presence which moves in, around and through all things, relieves postmodern evangelization of at least two hard-to-bear intellectual burdens. The first is the felt need to deny the evolutionary process. The nature of nature is evolutionary. Evolution is more than a hypothesis—although there is more to creation than the hypothesis explains. We see evolution, developmental change, manifested in so many ways and at so many levels that it has to be accepted as a fundamental element of reality as we human beings experience reality. What is passed on from one generation to another within any species is much more than genetic coding. Whatever beaver it was that built the first dam introduced a change that all the beavers and non-beavers that followed had to deal with—an evolving environment. As both John Polkinghorne, theoretical physicist and Anglican priest, and Pierre Thielhard de Chardin, paleontologist and Christian mystic, put it, "God doesn't make things. God makes things to make themselves." Polkinghorne, in writing of the interplay of chance, necessity, opportunity, and a general overall purpose that is manifested in a world of "rational beauty," writes, "The picture is of a world endowed with fruitfulness, guided by its Creator, but allowed an

---

28. Barry, *Paying Attention to God*, 16–17.

ability to realize this fruitfulness in its own particular ways. Chance is a sign of freedom, not blind purposelessness."[29]

Second, God as mysterious presence disentangles us from having to explain why some prayers seem to go unheard and unanswered. If God is always and everywhere present, then God is always and everywhere at work—at work in both the best and worst moments of our lives. From this perspective we may pray with confidence that our prayers are indeed efficacious and at times have extraordinary effects without being disappointed when God does not behave as we think God ought to behave—does not appear, as Marcus Borg puts it, to "intervene" as we think appropriate. With this view we are free to live lives of constant gratitude because we discern every triumph of love, beauty, and truth as the unceasing work of the Spirit.

The Meaning of Faith

What we are really talking about, of course, is the nature of faith, or what it means to see everything, absolutely everything, as a person of faith. We are in some important respects back where we began, with the orientation, the perspective, the way of thinking required to do postmodern apologetics. In the *Koine* Greek, the Greek in which the New Testament was written, the words "faith," "believe," and "believed" are usually from the noun "*pistis*" and the verb "*pisteuo*," and carry four interdependent meanings.

Faith or belief can be understood as mental assent—agreement with a propositional statement. In an episode of the old television series *All in the Family*, Edith says to Archie, "Ya gotta have faith." And Archie replies, "Faith is just believin' what nobody in his right mind would believe otherwise." For many people that's about it—faith is believing that something totally irrational is true. In Lewis Carroll's *Through the Looking Glass*, the White Queen tells Alice some things that are difficult to believe and says that in her youth she could "believe six impossible things before breakfast" and urges Alice to acquire this same skill. In the end, irrational disbelief is no better than an uncritical faith, but that is not the real problem. The real problem is that a purely intellectual faith distances us from the kind of spiritual passion that makes life meaningful and intimacy with God possible. Eastern Orthodox Christian monks and mystics of the fourth century, the *hesychasts*, spoke of allowing the mind to descend into the heart. There are certainly things to be believed in any religion, wisdom, or tradition, but what is believed remains manageable and therefore at the deeper levels largely irrelevant to the individual until the mind descends into the heart.

---

29. Polkinghorne, *Quarks, Chaos, and Christianity*, 56–57.

Faith, regardless from whatever angle it is examined, is always about trust—the full realization that the center of all is something, or someone, completely trustworthy. When I was three years old, I had rheumatic fever. After I had recovered, the decision was made to remove my tonsils. And so one afternoon we went into town where Dr. Stockton had his office on a pleasant residential street in Bakersfield. I was on the table wrapped in large white sheets, and they were just about to place the ether mask over my face when my mother, who was standing at the end of the table, saw my silent terror and said, "Larry it's all right. You are going to go to sleep now and when you wake up I will be standing right here." Instantly all my fear was gone. I was completely outwardly and inwardly at peace. Not only that, but I had a rather amazing recovery. When I woke up she was there and we went home where I drank iced tea and asked for and ate my dinner of chicken fried steak. That experience is, for me, something of a metaphor of what it means to trust the Holy Trinity, Father, Son and Holy Spirit or, if you prefer, the more gender inclusive language of Julian of Norwich, Maker, Lover, and Friend.

There is much difficulty, heartache, and even tragedy in our world, and most of us spend much of our time and energy attempting to control the people and events of life with at least enough efficiency to mitigate the damage somewhat. But in the end we usually only succeed in making matters worse. The radical solution of the Christian tradition is "let go and trust God." One of the greatest truths to be found in the Christian Scriptures is that salvation is by faith—trusting that no matter what transpires in any given moment we are being held in the loving embrace of God and all will be well, all is well. Faith as trust opens within us vast vistas of joy and peace and beauty.

Faith is fidelity—loyalty, commitment, faithfulness. I love the epic film *Reds* starring Warren Beatty, as the famous journalist Jack Reed who chronicled the Russian Revolution, and Diane Keaton, as his lover Louise Bryant. What has always fascinated me more than anything else about this movie is how Jack and Louise, a very modern and unconventional couple, repeatedly deny that there are any strings attached, any expectations of sexual loyalty in their relationship, and yet they cannot escape living out fidelity as some sort of inner cosmic law, the movement and flowing rhythm of which can only be ignored to their own hurt. In the end, each is willing to walk across the frozen waste of Siberia to be with the other. But it's right there in Holy Scripture where religious idolatry is equated with sexual adultery. Paul Tillich distinguished between true and idolatrous faith like this: "In true faith the ultimate concern is a concern about the truly ultimate; while in idolatrous faith preliminary, finite realities are elevated to the rank of ultimacy. The inescapable consequence of idolatrous faith is 'existential disappointment,' a disappointment which points to the very existence of humanity."[30] Finite things like money, success, power, sex, status, entertainment, friends, family, substances, or places must inevitably disappoint for the simple reason that our hunger is for the infinite.

Faith is a way of seeing, of understanding, of knowing. How we see reality and our place in it is a fundamental question that, willingly or unwillingly and with or without awareness, we all answer. And so the question is, "Have we discovered in our own contemplation a vision of reality that is true, and good, and beautiful—a vision that is reasonable while transcending the purely rational and which can be shared out of the depths of our own contemplation.

Faith shapes our relationship to everything and everyone. It makes hope and courage and peace possible. Marcus Borg wrote of how faith "enables us to live our lives and face our deaths in a new way." He said, "In this life, a radical centering in God leads to a deepening trust that transforms the way we see and live our lives. Seeing, living, trusting, and centering are all related in complex ways. They are all matters of the heart, and not primarily in the head. And in our deaths, dying means trusting in the buoyancy of God, that the one who has carried us in this life is the one into whom we die."[31]

Conclusion

In his helpful book *Unblind Faith: A New Approach for the Twenty-first Century*, Michael J. Langford proposes a sort of "Christian agnosticism," which distinguishes between the essential truth of biblical myth and literal fact, between the details of events and the historical core essence of Christian faith, between what is essential and nonessential to Christian thought and practice and sees, not doubt but faithlessness as the opposite of faith. "As with Socrates," Langford explains, "Jesus seems to have felt that if we would know a truth, that is really *know* it as opposed to merely being able to give a correct answer we could not go on to explain, then we must discover it for ourselves. Good teachers can sometimes help to draw this truth out from us, but they cannot simply give it to us."[32] What Langford seems to be suggesting is that learning to distinguish between nonessential details of biblical stories and events and their essential historical core in order to assist

---

30. Tillich, *Dynamics of Faith*, 12.
31. Borg, *Heart of Christianity*, 37.
32. Langford, *Unblind Faith*, 9–10, 99–106, 133, 135.

another in discovering the Mystery, that is everything and no-thing, is the work of the new apologist.

CHAPTER SEVEN

Can We Trust Jesus?

Jesus Christ, Jesus Christ
Who are you? What have you sacrificed?
Jesus Christ, Superstar
Do you think you're what they say you are?
Don't get me wrong, Don't get me wrong.
I only want to know.[1]

—From *Jesus Christ Superstar*

My Beloved is the mountains,
the lonely wooded valley,
the strange islands,
the roaring rivers,
the loving whistling winds.

The calm night
at the time of the rising dawn,
the silent music,

---

1. Andrew Lloyd Webber, et al., *Jesus Christ Superstar: A Resurrection.* Daemon Records, 1994, CD.

the sounding solitude,
the supper that delights and inspires love.[2]

—Saint John of the Cross

William Johnston in *Lord Teach Us to Pray* thought of the "Jesus of history" and the "Christ of Faith," or the "Pre-Easter" and "Post-Easter" Jesus, in terms of the Zen metaphor, which pictures enlightenment as the round luminous moon to which all concepts and images are but the fingers of a pointing hand. Anyone becoming too focused on the pointing fingers will miss seeing the silent beautiful moon to which they point.

> Christ is the moon because the people who wrote the Gospel are leading their readers to a vision not only of the historical Jesus (of whom we can assuredly have concepts) but of the risen Christ, the cosmic Christ, the Christ who was at the beginning. And it is he who escapes all images, all thoughts, all ideas, and all pictures. The risen Christ is so far beyond concepts that we find Paul struggling with all kinds of words to express the inexpressible. . . . For Paul, Christ is a "secret" or a "mystery" or whatever you want to call it, and he keeps pointing one finger after another at the moon that no human eye can decry. The poor scholars get all tied up in Paul's fingers; the mystics turn toward the moon.[3]

The point of the new evangelization with its new apologetic is really the same today as in the apostolic age, although in the modern age it was largely lost; that is, it is meant to direct the gaze of men and women to Christ, much as a Zen master might guide a disciple to *satori,* described by Christians as *metanoia*—an unfathomable experience of love, truth, peace, joy, communion, conversion, Trinitarian consciousness, and salvation in its literal sense of what is large, spacious, expansive, healing, and life-giving.

But the hand and fingers are not irrelevant. If the hand is quite shaky we may wonder to what, if anything in the vast expanse of heaven, attention is being called. It is more than legitimate to ask hard questions regarding the man from Galilee—and it is important to be able to say why we feel intellectually justified in trusting Jesus of Nazareth. In first century Palestine

---

2. "The Spiritual Canticle (Second Redaction): Songs between the Soul and the Bridegroom," in John of the Cross, *Saint John of the Cross: From Anabaptist Spirituality,* 62.

3. Johnston, *Lord Teach Us to Pray,* 64–65.

there were those who readily embraced Jesus' words and actions as pointing them to the Holy One of Israel, and others, including his own family, who at one point thought him a mad man. Marcus Borg noted,

> In what is commonly called the story of Jesus' transfiguration, we are told that the inner core of his disciples experienced the presence of the *numinous* in him in a glorified form (Mark 9:2–4; Matt 17:1–8; Luke 9:28–36); Matthew calls the experience a vision. Although most certainly a purely metaphorical narrative and not memory, the story is nevertheless important and illuminating. . . . That there was something "other" about Jesus was recognized even by those who did not think it was from God.[4]

We cannot escape, then, the critical question of whether the deeds and teaching of the Pre-Easter Jesus point us to the Post-Easter (Cosmic) Christ; that is, the evangelist cannot avoid the labor of basic apologetics. However, since all apologetics are essentially personal I can only share my own experience of the pointing hand in hope that what is deeply personal to me will somehow connect with what is personal to you.

Beauty

For me attempting, in spite of my limitations, to be more reflective in my thinking and to follow a more contemplative path has led to seeing the person of Jesus as altogether beautiful. The Hebrew Torah is wise and just, yet shines most brightly when interpreted in the light of Christ. The teaching of Buddha is deep and elegant, but while Siddhārtha Gautama is marvelously intriguing, he is not himself essential to Buddhism or enlightenment. Mohamed too easily made himself an exception to the rule to be beautiful in the way I mean. Taoism as expressed by Lao Tzu in the *Tao Te Ching* is simple, subtle, and attractive but in the end, for me personally, too disconnected from flesh and blood existence and too aligned with militarism to be beautiful in the same way as Jesus; and Joseph Smith is too much of a sociopath to be handsome.[5] But in Jesus of Nazareth I see from every angle unfathomable beauty. Again, you understand I am speaking personally and comparatively.

Even as a child I had an intuitive sense that beauty was somehow of some ultimate significance. As an old man I have discovered, at least for myself, of what this eternal quality of beauty consists. It seems to me that

---

4. Borg, *Jesus*, 127.
5. Brodie, *No Man Knows My History*.

beauty expresses the unfathomable mystery of human existence, awakens us to that which is beyond the ordinary, the mundane, the commonplace, and excites our hunger for that "something more to life" that gnaws in our souls. The other thing is that beauty does not stand alone. Since at least the time of the Greek philosophers it has been recognized that the true, the good, and the beautiful are not three separate things but essentially one. If something is beautiful it is also good, and if it is good and beautiful it is also true. So Einstein thought it more important for something to be beautiful than for it to be true. What he meant, of course, was not that it didn't matter if an equation fit the facts, but that if an equation was elegant, beautiful, it would most likely also prove to be true. If not, the problem was more likely to be in the experiment itself. Seeing beauty is therefore a way of seeing what is also true and good. The Chinese Christian martyr Watchman Nee, using the word "life" rather than" beauty," wrote about it like this:

> Life cannot be explained. When we touch it, we know it is life. But how? Not by thought or feeling or a "sixth sense." Those who know, know. Those who don't know, don't. Those who know life recognize it in others. Those who have death in themselves recognize neither life nor death.[6]

According to *The Gospel of Saint John the Evangelist*, Jesus once said, "What I teach is not mine. I didn't make it up. It comes from the One who sent me. If anyone's will is to do God's will, that person will know whether what I teach comes from God or whether I teach a purely human philosophy" (John 7:17).

I obviously do not know all the millions upon millions of people who have made this discovery for themselves, but I am aware of Madeleine L'Engle, the famous author, and my wife Brenda, who struggled for years with issues of doubt and faith before having this very experience. So, I trust Jesus because he is beautiful and when I touch the Spirit of Christ I know I am touching life itself.

The Witnesses

My experience of the beauty of Jesus takes place in the field of my own prayer, contemplation, Scripture study, in following the Jesus Way, and my own family, church, and culture—that "great cloud of witnesses" of which the author of the book of Hebrews speaks. In a very real sense we are all part of both a complex oral and written tradition. I first learned of "worshipping

---

6. Nee, *What Shall This Man Do*, 121–22.

the Lord in the beauty of holiness," not by reading Psalm 96:9 but from my mother and from a worshipping community. I first learned the Christ story in the same way. I have known people well and even intimately who claimed to have experienced Jesus as a living presence, as their companion on the best and worst of life's ways and whose quality of life gave them immense credibility. The witnesses I have known up close and personal are also the first to pass on to me the written tradition. What, then, of the Four Gospels as written witnesses?

There is much to be said later in these pages about a new apologetic and the biblical documents, but for now the focus is on whether the Gospels are *basically trustworthy* in their portrayal of Jesus of Nazareth. And so we turn to reflect on the four first evangelists, the Gospels of Matthew, Mark, Luke, and John—not necessarily on the individual or individuals who first wrote each one out on papyrus or parchment, but the written Gospels as we possess them. At this point what can be emphasized is that the Gospels are not remote but are immediate "eyewitnesses."[7] This does not mean that the original composers saw or heard any of the things they wrote about, but that what they wrote was obviously based on what people who were there believed they had seen or heard. Notice that the emphasis is not on what actually happened, but on the perceptions and thoughts of those present. As evidence for the sayings and events chronicled in the Gospel being based on eyewitnesses, we can point to the following characteristics of eyewitness testimony:

1) The Gospels are characterized by experiential liveliness. They are filled with all sorts of things one expects from eyewitness accounts—details about people's emotions, gestures, particular times, places, and geographical locations for events.

2) The Gospels are characterized by details that go against self-interest. The inclusion of women at the center of the resurrection story, especially women of questionable reputation, could only have worked against the spread of the Christian faith in the first century.

3) The presence of material that is irrelevant to the developing church is interesting. For example, if the church created stories about what Jesus said and did in order to provide authoritative answers for controversial questions that arose at a later time, and then read or wrote those answers back into the Gospels, then why are such issues as circumcision, charismatic gifts, the role of women in ministry, and what

---

7. Bauckham, *Jesus and the Eyewitnesses*.

foods are kosher, all hot issues in the developing church, not addressed definitively?

4) Jesus and his earliest disciples spoke Aramaic. Many of the sayings of Jesus in the Gospels appear to be Greek translations of Aramaic words; for example, Jesus's saying about straining out a gnat and swallowing a camel. Such Aramaisms support the thesis that the Gospels are correct in crediting the sayings of Jesus to an Aramaic-speaking person rather than to the creative imagination of a Greek-speaking Church.

5) Archeological evidence seems to support the integrity and the eyewitness quality of the Gospels. At one time, critics argued the Gospel of John was incorrect in its reference to the Pool of Bethesda, but now the pool has been identified and confirmed.

6) The Gospels represent a remarkably stable and unified framework. We know from the chronology of the book of Acts and Saint Paul's work that this stability was achieved very early—at most within four years of the death of Jesus. Larry Hurtado, director of the Institute for Christian Origins at the University of Edinburgh, has demonstrated rather conclusively that the story of what Jesus said and did, and the devotion given to him, did not so much evolve over a period of time as it just burst into the world.[8] Apparently, the agnostic Bart Ehrman has now come to a similar conclusion.

7) If Jesus died in 33 CE then the Gospels, indeed the whole New Testament, was completed thirty-five to seventy-five years after his death—by scholarly standards a very early date. Even using the outside date there is far too little time to allow for the sorts of fabrications so often imagined. However, I find John A. T. Robinson's assignment of an early date quite convincing. Robinson, the liberal New Testament scholar, argued that the entire New Testament was completed prior to 70 CE. He thought there simply was no other way to explain why no single book of the New Testament points back to the catastrophic (for both Jews and Christians) fall of Jerusalem and the destruction of the Temple. The probability is that the canonical Gospels do connect us to the beginning of the Jesus story, and provide us, at the very least, with how Jesus was perceived and understood by his family, his closest friends, his enemies, and those among whom he moved.

---

8. Hurtado, *Lord Jesus Christ*; Hurtado, *How On Earth Did Jesus Become a God?*

Miracle Worker and Exorcist

Let's begin with Jesus as miracle worker and exorcist, since that is what is most problematic for many people. The first thing that needs to be said is that there is no reason for the apologist to insist on the miracles and exorcisms credited to Jesus as essential to being Christian. It is possible for one to entirely reject the possibility of miracles, and yet to consecrate his or her heart in love and with complete trust to Christ. Nevertheless, there they are in the Gospels and apologists should not avoid dealing with them. For some, they create huge questions concerning the credibility of Christianity itself and so should be taken seriously. However, for me they are signs, not the most important signs, but signs, pointing to Christ the *Pantocrator*.

I have been using the English word "miracle," although it is not really the best translation. In the New Testament, there are three groups of words often translated as "miracle" or "miraculous"—δυναμις (*dunamis*), σημειον (*semeion*), and τερας (*teras*).

Dunamis comes from the same root as our word "dynamic," and is adequately translated by the word "power." A miracle in the sense of *dunamis*, then, is a powerful act or, as sometimes rendered, "a mighty deed." The Greek *semeion* means "sign." A miracle where *semeion* is used points to someone or something as special and different. When the word *teras* is used in the New Testament, it is paired with *semeion,* and so is roughly the equivalent of *dunamis*. These three words are complementary ways of describing the same events. *Dunamis* and *teras* emphasize God's power, and *semeion* emphasizes the significance.

In the Old Testament, there are also three Hebrew words used for "miracle"—*mowpheth*, *'owth*, and *pala'*. *'Owth* means much the same as *semeion* and is usually translated as "sign." *Mowpheth* means something like "wonder" or "display of God's power." Like the words in the New Testament, these Hebrew words seem to refer to the same things—the same sort of events. *Pala'* means something like "amazingly better than anything else," or things that are amazing because they are so difficult to do. A miracle may therefore be thought of as a manifestation of God that acts as a sign pointing to the nature or qualities of sacred reality. Simply put, miracles are astounding displays of power that point to the compassion, kindness, graciousness, generosity, and the healing and life-giving presence of Christ.

In Scripture, miracles frequently help or save the vulnerable, the sick, the poor, or the oppressed, but they are never self-serving—never for the personal and individual benefit of any prophet, sage, saint, or Jesus—and in this, they point further to the essence of divine reality. Paul Tillich, who saw miracle in this "revelatory" way, said, "The original meaning of miracle, 'that which produces astonishment,' is quite adequate for describing the 'giving side' of a revelatory experience. But this connotation has been swallowed by the bad connotation of a supernatural interference which destroys the natural structure of events."[9] But miracles in the sense of powerful events pointing to divine presence are, as Tillich noted, more likely to be seen as claims of magical occurrences that could never have happened. And so the apologist is expected to affirm or deny the miracles attributed to Jesus.

Because we inhabit a world which perceives, evaluates, and describes reality so differently than the world of twenty-one centuries ago, satisfying answers to the question of miracles and exorcisms are somewhat elusive. And it's important to be clear that the ancient way is not necessarily so much incorrect as simply very different. The Hopi People of the American Southwest thought of time as when what is supposed to happen happens rather than chronologically as determined by watches and calendars—perhaps strange to us but entirely comprehensible and practical to them.

Most scholars today have no real intellectual difficulty with the miracles of healing and exorcisms. We know that a person of hope and confidence and peace may have an extraordinary palliative and even curative impact on disorders of both mind and body. Whether the exorcisms performed by Jesus were purely psychological or the casting out of malevolent nonmaterial, but living entities, does not much matter. Marcus Borg, the Jesus scholar, didn't believe in a "personal evil force," but M. Scott Peck, the humanistic psychiatrist, after researching the clinical nature of evil, thought Satan to be quite real. But whether Jesus confronted and mastered sinister "supernatural" evil or healed the inner chaos of psychological dysfunction, it is equally impressive to be able to heal to any extent without the use of medications or devices. To deliver another human being from inner anguish, from dark and destructive forces, regardless of their nature, can be considered as nothing less than astounding—a powerful and benevolent "miracle"—and either way tells us something important about Jesus.

Turning the water into wine, raising the son of the Widow from Nain, walking on water, stilling the storm, or the feeding of five thousand are among the miracles with which we wrestle a bit more. But even here we may be dealing with historical events remembered by those who surrounded Jesus and then told in a metaphorical way, reflecting their high Christology.

As an old man, my brother Tom told me how he picked his thirteen-year-old daughter Catherine up from school on his motorcycle. As they sped along a major boulevard, a lumber truck pulled out in front of them. There was no way and no time to go around either end of the truck. My brother

---

9. Robinson, *Honest to God*, 115.

tried desperately to lay the motorcycle down on its side so as to slide underneath and avoid fatal impact. But Catherine was fighting as hard as she could to keep it upright. The motorcycle never went down and in an instant they were on the other side of the truck—badly shaken but unscathed and sitting upright. He had no explanation whatsoever, supernatural or natural, to offer as to what had happened that day. Graham H. Twelftree in *Jesus the Miracle Worker: A Historical and Theological Study*, therefore, sees even the more improbable miracle stories as reflecting some actual event in the life of the historical Jesus.[10] Whatever actually happened in any of these events, scientifically speaking, the one fact remains that the people of Jesus' own time and place believed him to be a beautiful, kind, strong, healing, and life-giving presence. Well, that's not entirely correct, his enemies believed he was powerful but that the source of his power must be evil.

Virgin Conception

Perhaps the most difficult question for an apologetic that is both progressive and orthodox concerns the virgin birth; although, the real issue is virginal conception. Many years ago there was a twenty-two-year-old woman in a small group Bible study I was leading. She had a certain sweet and endearing naïve quality about her, but she had seen and experienced much of the sordid side of life and frequently spoke as one far too wise in the ways of the world. We had just started a study of the Gospel according to Matthew and one night as we read, right there it was—the virgin conception. "Uh-uh," she said. "I don't think so, Larry. Nope. Virgins don't have babies." She believed Jesus was the Messiah, she believed Jesus was divine, and by love had somehow "redeemed" her life, but she did not believe in the possibility of a virginal conception.

There is no compelling reason for making a literal virgin birth, or conception, of Jesus a litmus test for Christian orthodoxy. There are, in fact, only two passages in the entire New Testament that can be used in support of the virginal conception—Matt 1:18–25 and Luke 1:34–35. So let's look quickly at Matthew's text:

(Text, Matt 1:18a) "The birth of Jesus Messiah happened like this: When his mother Mary had been betrothed to Joseph, and before they came together,"

(Comment) The word translated as "birth" here is actually "genesis." Matthew's real concern is with the genesis of the Messiah. Joseph and Mary have been betrothed, so they are legally bound to one another in a relationship

---

10. Twelftree, *Jesus the Miracle Worker*, 328–30.

that can only be dissolved by divorce or death. The betrothed woman lives with her parents and is sometimes visited by the groom, but the two do not engage in sexual relations until the woman leaves her parents' home to live in the home of her husband.

(Text, Matt 1:18b) "she was found to be pregnant by the Holy Spirit."

(Comment) Mary was inevitably discovered to be pregnant. "By" or "through" the Holy Spirit is to be understood in the Hebrew sense of the creative intervention of the Holy Spirit and not in the Greek mythological sense of Mary's sexual partner.[11]

(Text, Matt 1:19) "Joseph, her husband, being a man of character, and unwilling to shame her, wished to divorce her secretly."

(Comment) There is no reason to get all ethereal, as in Roman Catholicism, about Joseph thinking he is unworthy to marry the Holy Virgin and so desires a divorce. In time, there is no hiding the fact that Mary is pregnant. Joseph is a working man, a carpenter, and he knows where babies come from. He either knows he is the child's biological father, suspects adultery, or fears rape. But he is kind and generous and does not want to shame Mary and so considers a quiet divorce.

(Text, Matt 1:20) "But as he agonized about this, a divine messenger appeared to him in a dream, and said: 'Joseph, son of David, do not be afraid to take Mary as your wife, for what is conceived in her is through the Holy Spirit.'"

(Comment) I see no reason to argue over whether Matthew himself believed in a literal virginal conception; most scholars seem to think he did. But, there is nothing in this verse itself to demand or require that understanding.

(Text, Matt 1:21) "She will bear a son, and you shall call his name Jesus, because he will save his people from their sins."

(Comment) Although certainly an important part of the story, verse 21 need not concern us right now, other than to emphasize that the Apostles saw, at least in retrospect, Jesus as the promised saving presence of God from the time of his birth.

(Text, Matt 1:22) "All this happened so as to fulfill what the Lord had said through the prophet: 'See the virgin shall conceive and bear a son and they shall call his name Emmanuel (which means God is with us).'"

(Comment) The reference is to the words of the ancient prophet Isaiah in the Old Testament. Judah is faced with an invasion by its northern neighbors

---

11. Luz, *Matthew 1–7*, 95.

Israel and Syria, and the people are afraid, but God instructs the prophet Isaiah to tell King Ahaz that there is nothing to fear, God will destroy Judah's enemies (Isa 7:1–10). Isaiah delivers God's message to Ahaz and tells Ahaz to ask for a sign to confirm that this is a true prophesy (Isa 7:11). Ahaz refuses, saying he will not test God (Isa 7:12). Isaiah replies that Ahaz will have a sign whether he asks for one or not, and the sign will be the birth of a child, and the child's mother will name him Immanuel, meaning "God-with-us" (Isa 7:13–14). By the time the infant is old enough to know right from wrong he will be eating curds and honey, and Israel and Syria will themselves, in that time frame, be destroyed (Isa 7:15–16). The Hebrew word used in Isa 7:14, "*almah*," means nothing more than a young unmarried woman. Matthew, writing in Greek, uses the word "*parthenos*," which generally refers to a young unmarried woman who has not experienced sexual intercourse. But, it should be noted, the Septuagint translation describes Dinah as a *parthenos* even after she has been raped and hence is technically no longer a virgin. The point of the messenger in Joseph's dream is that just as God gave the birth of a child named Immanuel (God-with-us) as a sign of God's presence and sustaining help, so now in this dark hour of Roman oppression and human suffering God has given the same sign—Mary had conceived and would bear a son—Immanuel, God-with-us.

(Text, Matt 1:24–25) "When Joseph had awakened from sleep he did the messenger's bidding and took Mary as his wife. However, he had no marital relations with her until she had borne a son. His name was Jesus."

(Comment) The point of there being no sexual relations until Mary had given birth is that the child is not a different child conceived after the annunciation, but is the very child of promise in her womb before Joseph took Mary into his own home.

William Barclay wrote on this text in Matthew's Gospel like this:

> If we come to this passage with fresh eyes, and read it as if we were reading it for the first time, we will find that what it stresses is not so much that Jesus was born of a woman who was a virgin, as that the birth of Jesus is the work of the Holy Spirit. . . . There is so much more in this chapter than the crude fact that Jesus Christ was born of a virgin mother. The essence of Matthew's story is that in the birth of Jesus the Spirit of God was operative as never before in the world.[12]

---

12. Barclay, *Gospel of Matthew*, 22–23.

If we get what Barclay is saying here then we get the nature of the second naiveté and understand what it means to possess a faith that is both progressive and orthodox.

Sage, Prophet, Teacher, Spirit Person

Numerous scholars have pointed out that Jesus was a sage, prophet, teacher, and, as Marcus Borg called him, spirit person. All of these characterizations are mostly true. I say "mostly" true because sometimes they are colored in a way that caricatures and distorts the picture. For example, Jesus was obviously a sage, but he was certainly not one of the Cynic philosophers of the first century. He was clearly a prophet concerned with social justice in the tradition of the great prophets of Israel, but he was assuredly not a political activist in the tradition of late twentieth century North America. Jesus was all of these things: sage, prophet, teacher, holy person, Jew, and peasant, but none of them are problematic unless they are meant to somehow be dismissive. Beyond these easily identified attributes, Christians believe that Jesus is a living presence. Marcus Borg stated repeatedly that Jesus's earliest followers undoubtedly experienced him as living, and, we could add, so has a countless human host across more than two thousand years. It is entirely true that there have been more than a few charlatans making that claim, but rank upon rank the saints march through the centuries claiming that though Jesus was crucified and buried, they have experienced him as a true companion on the worst and best of life's days, and their lives speak of their veracity.

Living Presence

Nothing is any clearer than that after Jesus's crucifixion, his earliest followers experienced him as a living presence. Furthermore, as they contemplated the rich and extravagant layers of significance found in such expressions as Messiah, Son of Man, Son of God, and King of Israel, as they reflected on all Jesus had said and done in those three years before his death, when they were with him night and day, and as they reflected on their post-Easter experiences of Jesus, they penetrated strata after strata of meaning until they came to understand the depth and full reality of Jesus's divinity. I am utterly convinced that Jesus has been, and is, experienced again and again and again by countless men and women as living, precisely because that is indeed what he is—the cosmic Christ, Life, Light, and Love.

But what about Jesus? Did Jesus think he was divine himself? Conservatives frequently argue for a self-awareness of divinity on Jesus's part that actually becomes a form of the ancient heresy of *docetism*, so that Jesus merely becomes God pretending to be human. The problem is that whether Jesus thought he was the embodiment of God is complicated by the fact that none of the terms like Christ or Son of God originally suggested a divine being. They all have to do with Israel's hope for the coming of a descendant of David who would be the instrument for Israel's full restoration. As the careful New Testament scholar N. T. Wright observes, "Caricatures abound: There is the Jesus who walks around with a faraway look, listening to the music of the angels, remembering the time when he was sitting up in heaven with the other members of the Trinity." Or, says Wright, "what passes for historical scholarship sometimes produces an equal and opposite caricature: the Jesus who wandered around totally unreflective, telling stories without perceiving how they would be heard, announcing God's kingdom, speaking of bringing it about yet failing to ruminate on his own role within the drama"[13] Wright sees Jesus as sharing the common belief of his people that the kingdom of Israel's God was coming and that Israel's enemies, both physical and spiritual, would be vanquished. Where Jesus differed from his contemporaries was in his belief that it was his vocation, his calling, to do what everyone else believed could only be accomplished by God alone—that in his words and actions he embodied the words and actions of Yahweh. For Jesus, the fate of Israel was inextricably bound up with his own. Jesus felt called to defeat evil and complete the victory of God. Wright believes Jesus grasped his divinity through a sense of vocation and with a human mind. He therefore goes on to write,

> Jesus did not, in other words, know that he was God in the same way that one knows one is male or female, hungry or thirsty, or that one ate an orange an hour ago. His "knowledge," was of a more risky, but perhaps more significant sort: like knowing one is loved. One cannot "prove it" except by living it. Jesus's prophetic vocation thus included within it the vocation to attempt certain tasks, which, according to Scripture, YHWH had reserved for himself. He would take upon himself the role of messianic shepherd, knowing that YHWH had claimed that role as his own. Jesus would perform the saving task which YHWH had said he alone could achieve. Jesus would do what no messenger, no angel, but only the "arm of YHWH," the presence of Israel's God could accomplish. As a part of this human vocation grasped in faith, sustained in prayer, tested in confrontation, agonized over in further prayer and doubt, and implemented in action,

---

13. Wright, "Jesus and the Identity of God."

Jesus believed he had to do and be, for Israel and the world, that which according to Scripture only YHWH could do and be.[14]

Similarly, through all their experiences, prayer, and meditation the disciples came to the conclusion that Jesus was who they had believed him to be all along but ultimately in a way so profound it is unfathomable—"God with us."

This whole inquiry leads me to think that it is once we are able to speak authentically of this experience of touching and being touched by the Divine Love of Christ, we are prepared to reflect with others on the reality of the resurrection event. With us, as with the Apostles and earliest disciples and followers of Jesus, first comes the experience and then the explanation.

For some Christians, I would guess the vast majority, the resurrection can only be understood as a literal physical event in which the tomb was found empty and the body of Jesus was brought back to life. And a bodily resurrection does make sense of a good deal of the biblical data, such as why, if the disciples had stolen the body, were they not arrested and the body of Jesus retrieved? Or if a bunch of "tear-blinded women," whose testimony was not acceptable anyway, mistook an empty tomb for that of Joseph of Arimathea where the body had been laid Friday night, or if the authorities had removed the body for safe keeping, why didn't they simply invite everyone to a viewing? It certainly would have saved them an awful lot of trouble. Others also find the empty tomb and the appearances of Jesus to be significant. However, for them the emphasis on a "physical" resurrection is misleading. They believe what should be stressed is Jesus's resurrected body as a spiritual body. A third group believes that while Jesus seemed to have a physical body in his dramatic post-crucifixion encounters with the disciples and closest friends, the physicality of these "appearances," or of Jesus's presence, or even whether the tomb was empty, is not terribly important. For them, the genuineness of the resurrection experience does not depend on the physical. Marcus Borg, for example, suggests that the resurrection appearances might be thought of as visions, and notes that anyone who equates visions with something unreal has obviously never experienced a vision, which may include the sensory perceptions—taste, sight, hearing, smelling, and touch. Borg is worth quoting at length.

> What I am confident of is this. The followers of Jesus had experiences of him after his death that convinced them that he continued to be a figure of the present. Almost certainly some of these experiences were visions; it would be surprising if there weren't any. . . . I also think there were nonvisionary experiences of the risen Jesus. Though not narrated in the New Testament,

14. Wright, *Jesus and the Victory of God*, 652–53.

> they are' implicit. I think his followers felt the continuing presence of Jesus with them, recognizing the same Spirit that they had known in him during his historical life continuing to the present, and knew the power they had known in Jesus continuing to operate—the power of healing, the power to change lives, the power to create new forms of community. For me the truth of the claim "God has raised Jesus" is grounded in these kinds of experiences.... What kind of existence does the risen Jesus have? Does the risen Jesus have a body? If he does it is a very strange kind of body.... If the risen Jesus exists as a body, it is a body so radically different from any meaning we give to the word "body" that it seems misleading to use the term (1 Cor 15:35–50).... Epistemological humility and ontological modesty are called for. And there is one more thing to say about the experiences that are at the heart of Easter. They carried with them the conviction that God had vindicated Jesus. Easter is not simply about people experiencing a person who has died. The Easter stories are not "ghost stories" (see Luke 24:37–43). Rather, they are stories of vindication, of God's "yes" to Jesus. God has exalted, raised him to God's right hand, made him Lord.[15]

Borg helps us to see that, for evangelization, what is crucial is not that we adopt a particular theory of the resurrection of Jesus, but grasp, or are grasped by, the reality of the resurrection event, so that whatever its exact nature may have been, in life and in death we give our hearts into the keeping of Christ.

Always we must keep before us the principle that first comes the experience and then the theory. First comes the event and then its interpretation. "The Easter experiences were prior to the Easter interpretation."[16] I was a young boy living in Bakersfield when it was devastated by the powerful Tehachapi earthquake. It was early in the morning and it was still dark. After the shaking stopped, people began to gather out on the country road along which we all lived. "The power plant must have blown up," said one. "No," said the World War II veteran, "I think we have been bombed!" "The ground is still shaking," said someone else, "maybe it's an earthquake." First, we experienced the earthquake event, and then we looked for an interpretation large enough to explain the event. First comes the experience of the resurrection event, then the feeble theology to explain it.

Indeed, it is impossible to read the resurrection stories without noticing how these experiences caught those closest to Jesus in utter surprise

---

15. Borg, *Jesus*, 288–89.
16. Langford, *Unblind Faith*, 144.

and astonishment. No one in that ancient world thought it possible for any human being to die and rise again from the dead. It is true that some of the religions of the ancient Near East told stories of a god or goddess that died and then arose again every year. These cults reenacted rituals having to do with the death and rebirth of their divinity. In these rites they were attempting to connect with the forces of nature to ensure the fertility of their land, of their animals, and of themselves. Early Christians certainly did not think that Jesus died and rose again every year in synchronization with the farm year. As for some of the later cults like Attis and Mithras the evidence suggest they were influenced by Christianity rather than the other way around. You might want to pursue this further by reading *The Resurrection of the Son of God* by N. T. Wright—hard sloggin' but great material.

A Postmodern Precursor

In the last chapter, I expressed appreciation for John A. T. Robinson as perhaps the first postmodern Bible scholar. But what I resonate with most is Robinson's attempt to communicate the Christian message in such a way as to be comprehensible to contemporary men and women while truly remaining the Christian message. So I would like to invite you to just quietly listen as I quote Robinson directly on Jesus.

Robinson on the Virgin Birth

> In the same way, Christianity stands for a certain commitment to Christ as 'God for us.' It does not bind us to a particular view of where his genes came from or of what happened to the molecules of his corpse.
>
> As I hope to make clear, I accept as strongly as anyone what the New Testament writers are seeking to affirm by the Virgin Birth or Resurrection. But I refuse to have this faith made dependent for me or for anyone else on answers to questions which the New Testament doesn't set out to answer, on which there can never be certainty, and on which Christians should be free to differ.[17]
>
> To say that new life was fathered and quickened in Mary by the Spirit of God is a profound way of expressing an inner truth about Jesus. It is to say that his birth and life cannot simply be thought of as biological events: its significance lies much deeper

---

17. Robinson, *But That I Can't Believe*, 13.

than that. . . . This is not to say that all the traditional stories about Jesus's birth are to be swept away as outgrown fairy tales. On the contrary they speak to us of something marvelously true about him. Nor do I doubt that they are built around memories of actual incidents.[18]

Robinson on the Miracles

The impression made by Jesus's teaching was precisely that he was, as we should say, as good as his word. "What is this? A new kind of teaching! He speaks with authority. When he gives orders, even the unclean spirits submit." This was love not merely in talk but action, changing the stunted, tortured lives of men, women and children. . . . There's the power of love, overcoming resentment, and the physical protest in which it found outlet. And that's why Jesus saw that so often what was needed was a spiritual miracle—the putting right of a person's whole inner outlook on life. And that only love could do, not magic.[19]

Robinson on the Crucifixion

What about the inside story of Jesus's death? What did it mean for him, for his friends and contemporaries, and what, if anything, does it mean for us? . . . He accepted what came, not passively, resignedly, but literally with both arms outstretched to take it. . . . He accepted and absorbed the evil around him. Love was able to take it—and transform it.[20]

Robinson on the Resurrection

Jesus was not a dead memory but a living presence. . . . What was central for Paul and for all the early Christians was the compelling conviction that Christ was alive in them. The empty tomb was simply the external sign of what they knew within. . . . Precisely what happened to the body we shall never know. The New Testament is silent—and we may be silent too. Believing in

18. Ibid., 25.
19. Ibid., 31.
20. Ibid., 35.

the Resurrection doesn't depend on any theory about it. . . . No, the proof of the matter lay for them within. And it was clinched and expressed for them in what we call the appearances. Exactly how physical or how psychological these were, I don't think it matters—and the New Testament accounts differ.[21]

Robinson on the Lord Christ

In these events they felt they had struck rock, they had met what was for them the most real thing in the world, the *ens realissimum*. As they confessed afterwards, "God was in Christ." . . . But for the Christian, Jesus does not simply point away from himself to the Fatherly reality of love. He embodies it. In "the grace of our Lord Jesus Christ," the Christian knows something which speaks supremely in terms of flesh and blood, of who God is. . . . In this human life and death, says the Christian, we see not simply a man living close to God; we see God exposed, God in action as sheer grace, accepting the unacceptable, reconciling the world to himself.[22]

Conclusion

Langford's suggestion as to how the reflective Christian comes to greater and greater confidence in the New Testament stories of Jesus provides something of a summary for this chapter. First, he says, comes an awareness of the extraordinary nature of Jesus of Nazareth. This sense of the beauty of Jesus emerges out of the perfectly plausible Gospel accounts of Jesus's character, his teaching, and his life. Second, there is a belief in God adequately grounded in thoughtfulness and reason, and the conviction that God has conveyed a message through the prophets. Third, a decision that Jesus is the Messiah, the very one, to whom the prophets pointed. And fourth, says Langford, the gospel stories are reread in light of these steps. "In this context, without any gullibility, a reflective person may be unwilling to dismiss outright the historical reality of some events of an extraordinary nature, even though they remain extremely puzzled over exactly what happened."[23]

---

21. Ibid., 38–39.
22. Ibid., 72, 89.
23. Langford, *Unblind Faith*, 144.

CHAPTER EIGHT

An Evangelist's Perspective on Biblical Scholarship

Remember ... unceasingly that the science of this world, which has become a great power, has, especially in the last century, analyzed everything divine handed down to us in the holy books. After this cruel analysis, the learned of this world have nothing left of all that was sacred of old. But they have only analyzed the parts and overlooked the whole, and indeed their blindness is marvellous. Yet the whole still stands steadfast before their eyes, and the gates of hell shall not prevail against it. Has it not lasted nineteen centuries, is it not still a living, a moving power in the individual soul and in the masses of people?[1]

—*The Brothers Karamazov*

Secular Biblical Studies

THE SCHOLAR PHILIP DAVIES is probably correct in making a distinction between secular and sacred biblical studies, or what he calls the "con-

---

1. Dostoyevsky, *Brothers Karamazov*, 156. Father Paissy, fictional Orthodox priest and monk, in Dostoyevsky's novel.

fessional" and "non-confessional," approaches.² For a long time an attempt has been made to distinguish the difference between the two orientations as conservative or liberal, and that hasn't proven at all satisfactory. As Marcus Borg points out, "The familiar labels of 'conservative' and 'liberal' do not work very well, because both are imprecise." The label "conservative," Borg notes, covers everyone from Jerry Falwell to C. S. Lewis, and perhaps even to Karl Barth, while the term "liberal" may include those with "a strong sense of the reality of God and a deep commitment to the Christian tradition," as well as proponents of a nontheistic Christianity. "Thus, 'conservative' and 'liberal' don't tell us very much."³

Because Davies himself represents the secular end of biblical scholarship with such intellectual creativity and vigorous academic ability, he is used as a reference point throughout this chapter and into the next.

Ascientific

Davies, being more than a little disingenuous, says in the preface to his book, *Whose Bible Is It Anyway?*, that the purpose of his writing is not to attack religion,⁴ but "to show how biblical studies might function, in theory and practice, as a secular discipline."⁵ One might have then expected Davies to clearly delineate the tools appropriate to non-confessional biblical studies as well as their correct use. Instead, there is no more than a general endorsement of "the newer literary approaches."⁶ Confessional biblical studies, frequently referred to here as "sacred biblical studies," is seen by Davies as rather disreputable—an embarrassment to serious academicians and unworthy of respect among such scientific disciplines as physics, mathematics, biology, and chemistry.⁷

In "Do We Need Biblical Scholars?" Phil Davies first acknowledges that the field of biblical studies is not a science. Then, commiserating with Carl Sagan's grumbling about the general lack of respect for good science, Davies writes, "I think he is very lucky to be a scientist, he might have been a biblical scholar. Then he would have something to complain about." But in the next paragraph Davies inaccurately laments how fantasy issues such as "new evidence for Noah's Flood" absorbs virtually all the attention of the

2. Davies, *Whose Bible Is It Anyway?*, 3.
3. Borg, *The Heart of Christianity*, 2.
4. Davies, "Do We Need Biblical Scholars?"
5. Davies, *Whose Bible Is It Anyway?*, preface.
6. Ibid., 35.
7. Davies, "Do We Need Biblical Scholars?"

public media. Davies then writes, "It is disappointing that such 'poor science' is foisted on the public."[8]

As much as religion scholars might long for a more precise and systematic methodology, and the status it would bring, the reality is that biblical, theological, and historical studies, whether done from a secular or sacred orientation, are neither good nor poor science—they are simply ascientific. This does not mean they may not involve rigorous study, mental discipline, or considerable intellectual effort, only that they do not meet the criteria of scientific method or render scientific results. As Keith Ward, regius chair of divinity emeritus at Oxford University, explains, "Scientific explanation, in general, works by referring to some initial state (a 'cause') and a general mathematically described law. That law predicts what regularly follows from the initial state, and it does so without any reference to purpose, value, or consciousness."[9] It is precisely this reference to purpose, value, and consciousness that confessional biblical studies may not and cannot relinquish.

Albert Schweitzer, of course, referred in his *Quest of the Historical Jesus* to "the science of historical theology" and to "historical science."[10] But biblical, theological, and historical studies fail to qualify as science in that results cannot be verified through a set of public observations, do not account for significant variables, and cannot meet the test of reliable predictability.[11] The situation might be greatly improved if in biblical research we knew what variables were in play, but the fact is we most often do not know what it is we don't know, and are therefore left with inference and conjecture. Consequently, William R. Herzog II writes in his critique of members of the Jesus Seminar, "They portrayed themselves as doing inductive science because they courted the aura of authority associated with the scientific method. However, they were in fact doing deductive, and at times intuitive, historical work all along."[12]

Literary Criticism as Science

Literary criticism, whether of the older or newer sort to which Davies appeals, represents something more like artistic skill than scientific methodology. Thus, while Edgar V. McKnight sees elements of literary criticism that may help biblical scholars "arrive at satisfying principles and methods," he

8. Ibid., 2.
9. Ward, *Why There Almost Certainly Is a God*, 22.
10. Schweitzer, *Quest of the Historical Jesus*, 5–6.
11. Marshall, *I Believe in the Historical Jesus*, 92.
12. Herzog, *Jesus, Justice, and the Reign of God*, 30, 34–46.

also acknowledges, "Contemporary literary criticism lacks a universally accepted set of principles and methods."[13]

Umberto Cassuto, rabbi and professor of Hebrew and literature, offered a rather devastating, but little noted, critique of literary criticism.[14] And although Perrin brought valuable insight to the work of literary criticism,[15] the newer nevertheless remains rooted in the older—specifically in source criticism. As an aside, it should also be noted that Perrin strangely denied that Mark believed the incidents about which he wrote actually happened; but Mark, nevertheless, misled generations of scholars into believing he was writing an actual historical account.[16] In an essay titled "Methods in Studying the Patriarchal Narratives as Ancient Texts," Alan R. Millard notes, "Even the fresh paths taken in recent years by a few operate with much the same basic criteria."[17]

Cassuto saw literary, or source, criticism as resting on five pillars: a) the use of different names for the Deity; b) variations of language and style; c) contradictions and divergences of view; d) duplications and repetitions; e) signs of composite structure in the sections.[18] Cassuto was quite persuasive in arguing that the grammatical, stylistic, and terminological traits that might be assumed as indicative of separate documents were common in Hebrew literature and language, in both biblical and post-biblical Jewish documents, and in modern Jewish religious writing, the unity of which no one questions, and, also within the context of other cognate Near Eastern literature.[19] However, it is not that Cassuto is entirely correct, or that there were no oral or written sources utilized by the authors of biblical literature (this is not even Casutto's point), the point is that Cassutto's argumentation is of sufficient force to demonstrate that leaning on literary criticism is like leaning on a rickety banister. It is fine to put a light hand on the rail for balance as one descends the stairs, but anything more can be risky. Reading the text with literary sensitivity is more than a little helpful in maintaining balance, anything more and one may topple down several flights.[20]

The premise of secular-oriented scholarship is that it possesses the critical literary tools with which to determine "why and how the biblical

---

13. McKnight, "Contours in Literary Criticism and Methods," 53.
14. Cassuto, *Documentary Hypothesis*.
15. Marshall, *I Believe in the Historical Jesus*, 190.
16. Ibid., 90.
17. Millard, "Methods of Studying the Patriarchal Narratives," 37.
18. Cassuto, *Documentary Hypothesis*, 14.
19. Ibid., 10.
20. Goodacre and Perrin, *Questioning Q*.

literature was composed and how it functioned."[21] Yet this is an entirely subjective process, and one may well find its results as difficult to believe as the announcements of fundamentalists that Noah's Ark has been found on Mount Ararat or Pharaoh's chariot in the Red Sea.

In reading the Synoptic Gospels of Matthew, Mark, and Luke it is easily observed that Matthew and Luke have a good deal of material that they share with each other and with Mark, but there is also much they have in common with one another but do not share with Mark. This has led scholars to the conclusion that Matthew and Luke used Mark as a common source in writing their Gospels, but there must have also been a second source, which is now designated by the letter "Q" for the German word "*quelle*" meaning "source." Academicians now claim that Q was at one time a written document that they can reproduce from Matthew and Luke. Furthermore, they assert, they can identify the various literary strata of Q, as well as determine a good deal about the community in which it was produced. Quite a feat when one considers that no such actual document exists, and may never have existed. Q may indeed have been a common written source used by the authors of Matthew and Luke, but it may also simply have been a shared oral source. It may also be possible, as Mark Goodacre does, to solve the puzzle without resorting to the theoretical Q at all.[22] Goodacre thinks, as do most scholars, that the Gospel of Mark was written first. Matthew may then have written his gospel using Mark as a source, with Luke writing his gospel last, using both Mark and Matthew. This is obviously a much simpler and more elegant solution to the "synoptic problem"; nevertheless, it too is entirely hypothetical. For contemporary bible scholars, the "synoptic problem" is not, as Goodacre's subtitle suggests, so much a puzzle or a labyrinth as it is a maze. What starts out as a reasonable hypothesis, a possibility, becomes as convoluted as something out of an *Indiana Jones* movie or a Dan Brown novel.[23]

Those scholars who sit at the end of Phil Davies' bench have a certain interest in attempting to establish Q as a written document. Q, if it ever existed as ink and parchment, or papyrus, consisted primarily of Jesus's sayings—was what might be called a "sayings gospel." None of this messy business of "mighty deeds," exorcisms, crucifixion, or resurrection. This would mean that before the four gospels there was a tamer gospel of wisdom sayings—an interesting report on the philosophical perspective of a more manageable Jesus. For the same sort of reason, there has been constant

---

21. Davies, *In Search of "Ancient Israel"*, 19–20.
22. Goodacre, *Synoptic Problem*.
23. Goodacre and Perrin, *Questioning Q*.

pressure to give the Gnostic Gospel of Thomas an unwarranted and independent composition.[24] Of course, even if Indiana Jones were to find an authentic copy of Q in a hermetically sealed compartment of the lost Ark it would prove none of these things. It would prove nothing beyond the fact that someone wrote down a copy of Jesus's words without recording much else about him—now wouldn't that be bizarre?

There are numerous types, or emphases, of biblical criticism. Literary criticism focuses on the various literary genres embedded in the text in order to uncover evidence concerning date of composition, authorship, and original function of the various types of writing that constitute the Bible and can, therefore, be quite helpful in exegetical work. Tradition criticism attempts to trace the development of the oral traditions that preceded written texts. Form criticism classifies the written material according to its preliterary forms, such as parable or hymn. Redaction criticism studies how the documents were assembled by their final authors, the whole editorial process they went through before reaching their final form. And historical criticism seeks to interpret biblical writings in the context of their historical settings.

In an attempt to overcome the problems inherent in biblical studies, scholars have sought to invent the tools necessary for reliable historical and textual investigation. However, the fact that their conclusions are so divergent even when applying the same tools and methodology speaks of the inadequacy of such efforts. This is the very question James Charlesworth asks in his "Why Evaluate Twenty-five Years of Jesus Research?"—that is, "How can such divergent views (of Jesus) be possible when all the scholars employ a disinterested methodology?"[25] One quickly comes to realize that in biblical research consensus does not mean scientific or historical verification by other scholars, only that at that particular moment in the chili cook-off more subjective votes have been cast for that scholar's pot of chili than any other. Schweitzer was right—or mostly right. "There really is no common standard by which to judge the works with which we have to do."[26] Schweitzer went on to say that on paper, where ideas do not come into such contrast with reality and where no one is sitting there to contradict, it is possible to write a little more easily, plausibly, convincingly, than what the facts or logic may warrant.

So Bultmann wrote facilely of the criterion of dissimilarity for determining an authentic saying of Jesus, namely that any saying of Jesus that

24. Goodacre, *Thomas and the Gospels*.
25. Charlesworth, "Why Evaluate Twenty-Five Years of Jesus Research?" 1.
26. Schweitzer, *Quest of the Historical Jesus*, 5–6, 9.

could have come from a first century rabbi or the Judaism of that time cannot be counted as an authentic saying, nor can anything that can be attributed to questions that might have arisen in the developing church. For the common sense person this boggles the mind. The criterion of double dissimilarity is virtually worthless, and we could probably delete the word "virtually." (1) It shamelessly begs the question; (2) it disregards how Jesus as a first-century Jew would have shared the ways and thoughts of his people; and (3) it ignores the fact that if the teaching of Jesus was reliably passed on, the questions asked later were very nearly irrelevant. William Herzog says that the criterion of double dissimilarity "produces a very narrow view of the historical Jesus, which could well preclude some of his typical teaching and theological emphasis."[27]

Secular biblical studies have a further problem in that if one regards the biblical text as hopelessly corrupted, as does Bart Erhman, then it is impossible to form any intelligent hypothesis about the historical nature of events it describes, or, for example, to deal decisively with such questions as authorship on the basis of style, vocabulary, or grammar. "One cannot have her cake and eat it too." If most of the sayings and deeds of Jesus as given in the Gospels are inauthentic then any "quest for the historical Jesus" is ludicrous.

Circumstantial Evidence and Conjecture

Biblical, Religious, and Judeo Christian Historical Studies, whether from a progressive or conservative orientation are quite frequently based on rather "iffy" circumstantial evidence, and the word "evidence" more often than not can be replaced by the word "conjecture." For example, the whole business of the Gospels and the "communities," in and for which they were written, is a good case in point. In 1971, Walter Bauer's *Orthodoxy and Heresy in Earliest Christianity*, which was an English translation of a 1934 and 1964 work in German, was published in the United States. Bauer's thesis was that in earliest Christianity orthodoxy and heresy do not stand in relation to one another as primary to secondary. According to Bauer, the evidence shows that in many localities heresy preceded what is now thought of as orthodoxy. In time, the church and its bishops somewhat ruthlessly suppressed "heresy" and in doing so "rewrote" history—there was no one genuine Christian faith in earliest Christianity. According to the Bauer hypothesis, Christianity did not begin with a unified field of teaching. From its very beginning the Christian faith represented a diversity of beliefs, including gnosticism.

27. Herzog, *Jesus, Justice, and the Reign of God*, 39.

Eventually, an ecclesiastical hierarchy coalesced around the views people now think of as orthodox and imposed them on the rest of Christianity.

Richard Horsley in *Christian Origins* asserts Bauer's hypothesis as established fact, and he does so even though no unified hierarchy with that capability existed in the earliest church. He rather pretentiously says, "The movements that formed around Yeshua ben Yosef survived the Roman Crucifixion of their leader as a 'rebel king.' In fact, his martyrdom became a powerful impetus for the expansion and diversification of his movement." Notice that in Horsley's view, Jesus in not the founder of a movement; rather, his death is an "impetus" for the expansion of multiple movements with varied interests. The origins of Christianity, according to Horsley, are not to be found in the person of Jesus as the Christ, but in the large number of "peasants who eagerly responded to the pronouncements of peasant prophets that God was again about to liberate them from oppressive rulers and restore cooperative community life under the traditional divine principles of justice."[28]

Obviously, all history is written with a certain bias, but that doesn't mean it is entirely untruthful. To say that the winners write or rewrite history is a clever response in an age where people enjoy a good debunking; but there is often more wit to the saying than truth, and if one is going to do apologetics it is important to know the difference between what is merely clever and what is valid argument. Truth is ultimately more resilient, harder to suppress, and its history more difficult to rewrite than what conspiracy theorists might surmise. All the time Joseph Stalin and the Soviet Union were telling history their way, and attempting to suppress the magnitude of their inhumanity, Alexandr Solzhenitsyn was quietly writing and documenting the real life stories of the horrors of the Gulag on disparate bits and pieces of paper and hiding them in the lining of his coat.

When one reads how Walter Bauer investigated four ancient geographical sites, or urban areas, in developing his hypothesis that "heresy" actually preceded "orthodoxy" it is easy, especially for the layperson, to imagine Bauer carefully collecting artifacts, gathering hard scientific data, and engaging in rigorous statistical analysis.[29] Such imaginings, however, are just that. Bauer's primary sources were the New Testament documents themselves and the writings of the Church Fathers. Indeed, without his speculation on the New Testament documents Bauer's book would have been a very thin one. Bauer created the illusion that he had reached his conclusion after investigating heresy and orthodoxy from the beginning of

---

28. Horsley, "Jesus Movements and the Renewal of Israel," 11.
29. Bauer, *Orthodoxy and Heresy*.

Christianity. The reality is that using the New Testament and the Church Fathers, he investigated the state of orthodoxy and heresy as it existed several hundred years after the origin of the church and not "earliest" Christianity at all. He insisted without warrant that the process he believed to be in play at a later date must also have been true from the beginning.

Bauer's hypothesis has actually been appropriately weighed and measured and dismissed. For example, Thomas Robinson in *The Bauer Thesis Examined* studied orthodoxy and heresy in the first century using the same approach Bauer had; that is, by attempting to examine the beliefs attested at four major geographical centers of early Christianity. Contrary to Bauer, Robinson found that heresy in Ephesus and in Asia Minor was relatively late and weak—that orthodox believers were both earlier and larger in number than the unorthodox—than the gnostics.[30]

It is also rather interesting that Bauer used his two primary sources of evidence to prove the opposite of what they each claim to be the case. Be that as it may, Bauer established the existence of no community of people in the sense that one might, for example, speak more concretely of the corporal community of Essenes at Qumran. Actually, the earliest known physical artifact is apparently a Christian graffito incised into the plaster of a basement circa 125 CE.[31]

The evidence Bauer offered, then, was at best circumstantial; that is, evidence in which an inference is required to connect it to a conclusion of fact, whereas direct evidence supports the truth of an assertion without any need of additional evidence or the intervening inference. People are convicted of serious crimes, like murder, all the time on the basis of circumstantial evidence. However, it is also true that far too frequently they are later proven innocent by direct scientific evidence such as DNA. The judiciary, of course, instructs jurors in the proper use of circumstantial evidence; nevertheless, the powerful constraints of subjectivity cannot be escaped.

Hultgren and Haggmark, in their useful anthology *The Earliest Christian Heretics*, suggest the discovery of the Nag Hammadi Library may be just the sort of direct evidence Bauer did not have. "This view," they write, "the view that Christianity was the triumph of one form of Christianity over alternative and equally legitimate forms, has been strengthened by the discovery of the Nag Hammadi documents."[32] However, that is pure speculation. Furthermore, as Larry Hurtado notes, the sharp differences in the Christian community, which are so obvious in the canonical docu-

---

30. Robinson, *Bauer Thesis Examined*, 27, 47.
31. Bagnall, *Everyday Writing*, 22–23.
32. Hultgren and Haggmark, *Earliest Christian Heretics*, 6.

ments, demonstrate not only a certain amount of diversity within the early Christian community, but also, unlike the image of the earliest church as authoritarian censor, a willingness to accommodate diversity while sharing an affirmation of the four-fold Gospel.[33] Here is all anyone can definitively say about the Nag Hammadi documents: 1) some fifty tractates dating to the fourth century, including a number of Gnostic religious documents written in Coptic, as well as a copy of Plato's *Republic,* were found buried in a farm field near Nag Hammadi, Egypt, in 1945; 2) one of these Gnostic manuscripts, the nearly complete Gospel of Thomas, is similar enough to fragments of a Greek manuscript found at Oxyrhynchus, Egypt, in 1897 to think it represents a Coptic version of a Greek manuscript, existing now only in fragments, which itself dates to the late second century. Here is what we do not know: 1) we do not know whether the Nag Hammadi collection belonged to one individual, to a group of people, or to a community with distinct religious and philosophical ideas and beliefs; 2) we do not know what person or persons possessed or buried these documents or why; 3) we do not know how or why these documents came to be possessed by this person or persons in the first place.

In fact, well after having written the above, I discovered two important articles along these very lines. The first is Mark Goodacre's "How Reliable Is the Story of the Nag Hammadi Discovery?" in the *Journal for the Study of the New Testament.* The second is Nicola Denzey Lewis and Ariel Blount's "Rethinking the Origins of the Nag Hammadi Codices."[34] Both articles suggest that the codices found at Nag Hammadi were not the Scriptures of some secret sect, but that they were likely circulated among individuals who had a fondness for esoteric literature. Further, they call into question how the codices were discovered. They think that rather than having been buried in order to hide them from "orthodox" bishops, the codices were actually more like "books of the dead," placed in the graves of their owners at the time of their demise, to be later found, taken, and sold by grave robbers—a not uncommon scenario.

Hultgren and Haggmark, though exceptional scholars, further demonstrate the highly conjectural nature of secular biblical studies. "If it is the case," they write stating the very thing to be proved, "that heresy preceded orthodoxy in many areas, it follows," one may ask why it necessarily follows, "that so-called heretical views may well go back to the very beginning, the earliest interpretations of Jesus and his message. And if that is the case, then

---

33. Hurtado, "You've Got to 'Accentuate the Positive,'" 21–29.

34. Goodacre, "How Reliable Is the Story of the Nag Hammadi Discovery?" 303–22; Lewis and Blount, "Rethinking the Origins of the Nag Hammadi Codices," 399–419.

the so-called heretical views may be regarded as alternative, rather than incorrect."[35] This last part of the statement could only be true, of course, if these alternative views were contemporaneous with the apostles, indeed were held by an apostle, and considered of equal authority. But apparently for Hultgren and Haggmark two "ifs" plus two "maybes" might possibly equal a logical conclusion.

As already noted, Thomas A. Robinson, using Bauer's own methodology, rather convincingly refuted Bauer's assertion that heresy preceded orthodoxy.[36] And although Michael Allen Williams is not totally convincing in his characterization of early gnosticism (for example, his insistence that the groups usually labeled as such shared no common set of beliefs may be somewhat overdone), he does make a convincing case that the Nag Hammadi documents are "shards" of failed religious movements—movements that attracted some interest, as the gathering of these fourth century texts indicate, but without sustaining appeal and power.[37] However, even had Bauer's conclusion been correct on some more scientific basis, it would have remained largely irrelevant. It doesn't much matter how many groups existed or how many different ideas about Jesus were in circulation in the days, weeks, months, and years immediately following the crucifixion of Jesus. The defining characteristic of orthodoxy is continuity with Jesus and his teachings through the apostles.

The best evidence suggests that orthodoxy preceded heresy. Indeed, Larry Hurtado, director of the Center for the Study of Christian Origins at the University of Edinburgh, has convincingly demonstrated that devotion to Jesus did not so much evolve as explode into that first century world.[38] Rudolph Bultmann, who built much of his theology on Bauer's theory, argued otherwise. "The diversity of theological interests and ideas is at first great. A norm or authoritative court of appeal for doctrine is still lacking." Bultmann went on to say approvingly of Bauer, "W. Bauer has shown that the doctrine which in the end won out in the ancient church as the 'right' or 'orthodox' doctrine stands at the end of development . . . and that heresy was not, as the ecclesiastical tradition holds, an apostasy, a degeneration, but was already present at the beginning."[39] Bultmann's argument just defies all logic.

---

35. Hultgren and Haggmark, *Earliest Christian Heretics*, 6.
36. Robinson, *Bauer Thesis Examined*.
37. Williams, *Rethinking Gnosticism*, 260–62.
38. Hurtado, *How On Earth Did Jesus Become a God?*
39. Bultmann, *Theology of the New Testament*, 135–37.

There was obviously diversity among the first Christians, and Christianity has certainly continued to evolve, or at least our understanding of it has, but the development in general has been from unity to diversity within the context of a basic orthodoxy. There is an essential historical continuity from earliest Christianity to the well-defined theological orthodoxy we see in the fourth century—an orthodoxy grounded in the person of Christ.

Among the earliest Christians, beginning in first century Jerusalem, the locus of teaching resided in the apostles, and the core of their teaching, their creed, was the person of Jesus and not an esoteric doctrine from Iran. This orthodoxy was clearly not identical to that following the Great Councils, but there was an orthodoxy characterized by the following beliefs: (1) apostolic teaching is orthodox; (2) Jesus is Messiah, Lord, and God's Son; (3) Christ died for humanity's sins (to set right whatever it is that alienates and estranges humanity from God the Divine Mystery), was buried, and was raised from the dead; and (4) the Lord is the God of Israel as the Creator, the Father of Jesus, the Father of Humanity, and as the gift of the Spirit to the Faithful.[40] To say there was no norm defies common sense.

Reading in Poor Light

In reading Scripture we are always, contrary to our mothers' concerns, reading in poor light—reading without knowing all the variables. This also is demonstrated by examining the notion of communities. Less wild than Bauer's theory of the existence of heretical communities from the very origins of Christianity is the idea that there were specific communities from which and to which the Gospels were originally written. One can therefore, it is asserted, speak of a Matthean, Markan, Lukan, or Johannine community- or with the epistles even a Pauline community.

In his extensively documented two-volume commentary on the Gospel of John, Craig S. Keener notes the highly hypothetical nature of Raymond Brown's reconstruction of the Johannine communities. Keener writes, "His stages of the community's development are, as he admits, hypothetical; but while historically plausible, his reconstruction is quite detailed and builds many hypotheses on other hypotheses, a method which seems historiographically questionable."[41] Nevertheless, Keener observes, some have accepted Brown's hypothetical reconstructions as "the decisive historical interpretation."[42]

40. Kostenberger and Kruger, *Heresy of Orthodoxy*, 34–37, 69.
41. Keener, *Gospel of John*, 106.
42. Ibid.

The problem is that scholars, many with impressive academic credentials, postulate not just one but many and varied communities behind each of the canonical gospels. Dwight N. Peterson argues quite effectively that the Markan community is "the product of highly speculative, viciously circular, and an ultimately unpersuasive and inconclusive reading."[43] Many of the conclusions reached by scholars do not take into account the powerful element of pure chance in the ordinary affairs of daily life. It is ultimately impossible to say why any author wrote something. In constructing the community behind Mark, historians have only inference to work with. This is because, for example, there are no sources for constructing a Markan community other than the Gospel of Mark itself. Consequently, scholars must construct the proposed community entirely out of their own imaginations. To paraphrase Peterson, they imagine they can know more than they actually can.[44]

William Johnson's reframing of the relationship of text and community has the possibility of upending biblical studies. "The text," he says, "does not merely reflect or serve its readers . . . but actively seeks to create the 'ideal' reading community to which the writing aspires." Texts are constructed in such a way as to guide speech, thought, and behavior. This would mean communities were not the "source" of biblical texts but the recipients, reading or listening communities, to be shaped by it.[45]

One other brief observation needs to be made in regard to the Gospels and the construction of hypothetical communities. And that has to do with the orality of the Gospels. We have been thinking as if there is only the text but that is, of course, not the case. Although it may be going too far to say, as does Antoinette Clark Wire, that the Gospels are the result of "oral composition" rather than the written product of an author, it is obvious that "oral performance" preceded and played a huge role in the formulation of the written canonical gospels.[46] Since we do not possess digital documentation of the oral tradition, the equation is further complicated; that is, we are once more faced with the problem of unknown and unknowable variables. Constructing communities from which and to which the Gospels were written is at least as difficult as proving Fermat's Last Theorem.

The problem is that this is all too characteristic of biblical studies in general. They are far too speculative, far too dependent on circumstantial evidence, and far too unaware of variables. For men and women simply

---

43. Peterson, *Origins of Mark*, 152, 158.
44. Ibid., 161, 157–63.
45. Johnson, "Constructing Elite Reading Communities," 328–29.
46. Wire, *Case for Mark*.

looking for a stimulating intellectual discussion this represents no great problem, but for those with real spiritual questions it is an issue. A bright, well-educated woman and a person of genuine faith told me that she had been involved in a rather sophisticated Bible study in her mainline denomination. The teacher, who was quite capable and knowledgeable, would constantly throw out "what really happened" and "what does it really mean" comments and would question: "Did you know that there was no one way of understanding the Christian faith, and no one faith, in the early days after the crucifixion of Jesus?" "Did you know that Jesus's hands were probably tied rather than nailed to the cross as this Gospel says?" "Did you know that according to the Jesus Seminar scholars, Jesus didn't really say what we just read; in fact, he probably said less than 20 percent of what the Gospels report him as saying." What had started out for her as a disciplined practice to deepen and enrich her own spirituality became a quagmire of doubt and confusion. As we talked I asked her a number of questions: "What is the quality of your life like when you believe, and what is it like when you don't believe?" "What difference does something like whether Jesus's hands were tied or nailed make?" "When you think about what the most loving, the most spiritual people you know have shared with you about their own journey, do you find yourself drawn to them and the life you touch in them, or do you find someone attempting to debunk a Bible story to be more of the person you want to be?" I spoke some of my own belief that while scholars can be of some help, what they are capable of doing and knowing is far more limited than what they admit, and I spoke of why I find the New Testament documents and the Jesus stories they tell to be basically reliable. I shared with her how a graduate class in research design and statistical analysis reinforced my natural skepticism so that when I hear the conclusions of some study I almost automatically find myself wondering what that would look like on a research design grid. And I told her that for myself I would far rather experience the inner reality of Scripture than discuss it as if I were some great intellectual. I suppose what I was attempting to do was to be a non-anxious presence that could help her find her way through reflective reasoning to the naiveté of the second kind.

Sadly, we human beings seem to find it difficult to believe that God needs neither our ignorance nor our learning. C. S. Lewis, you may remember, told that wonderfully humorous story in *The Great Divorce* about a ghost who takes the bus from hell on an excursion to heaven. The ghost chooses to return to the joyless city, the grey town, rather than to stay in heaven because he cannot give up his intellectual affectations:

"But you've never asked me what my paper is about! I'm taking the text about growing up to the measure of the stature of Christ and working out an idea I feel sure you'll be interested in. I'm going to point out how people always forget that Jesus was a comparatively young man when he died. He would have outgrown some of his earlier views you know, if he'd lived.... I'm going to ask my audience to consider what his mature views would have been ... what a different Christianity we might have had if only the Founder had reached his full stature!"[47]

The humor of Lewis's point in this caricature is somewhat lost today in its uncanny resemblance to reality in the world of academic Jesus studies.

So, what does all this have to do with reading Scripture organically? For one thing, it means even if all the theories, conjectures, speculations, and arguments claiming that in the beginning Christianity was characterized by diversity were true, it wouldn't matter. The only question that really matters is: "Was there a band of men and women, a company of apostles and first disciples, who were willing to stake their lives on what we see as orthodoxy, but what they experienced as a living reality? Secondly, as Frederick Denison Maurice, the great nineteenth century theologian, once wrote, "That which is a tendency and habit of the heart, is not cured by detecting fallacies in the mode in which it is embodied and presented to the intellect."[48] Reading the sacred page is ultimately not about proving any theory, rather it is about allowing, in the words of Eastern Christian thought, "the mind to descend into the heart." Until that descent takes place we will read only with the resources of the intellect. We may think that we have achieved, or become, something important by our level of sophistication in discussing the Bauer hypothesis, or what the mature views of Jesus might have been. But there is no direct knowledge of God, or of Scripture, until the heart and the mind become one so that we read with both intellectual integrity and an exceedingly great love—read Scripture as that which holds cherished significance and liveliness

History and Histories

Philip Davies, in one of his interesting twists of words, makes a distinction between "religion" and "religions." Following his lead, a distinction might be made between "history" and "histories." There is no such thing as a history, there are only histories written from many different personal slants and

---

47. Lewis, *Great Divorce*, 46.
48. Maurice, *Theological Essays*, 32.

making inferences from data that cannot interpret itself. At most, historians can do no more than formulate hypotheses that fall along a continuum of lesser to greater degrees of probability. But the continuum does not have certainty as one of its poles—there is, in historiography, no axis of absolute certitude.

Imagine in three thousand years, with a global nuclear catastrophe somewhere in the middle, archaeologists find fragmentary artifacts relating to President Obama. What might they conclude about whether Barack Obama was a Muslim, or whether in the early twenty-first century United States it would have even been possible for him to become president? With the limited information it would be possible to formulate numerous hypotheses—many of them quite wide of the mark and at total odds with one another but with each claiming to be based on historical evidence.

When it comes to such matters as the quest for the historical Jesus, Schweitzer was correct, "we have not the material" to write a complete life of Jesus.[49] What we do have are enough lines with wide spacing ("yawning gaps") to write many "scholarly" conjectures between them, but to write a life of Jesus would require material we simply do not have.[50] Of course, rather than abiding by this discovery Schweitzer went on to develop his own hypothetical understanding of Jesus. Indeed, Schweitzer did not end the historical quest for Jesus, as often asserted, he merely continued and fueled it with new academic questions—and then went off to Equatorial Africa to live a life of compassion. We cannot, from the documents we possess, say more than what certain people at a particular time thought about Jesus; that is, our greatest degree of certainty has to do with how Jesus was experienced by a few friends. We may find them believable or unbelievable but their account of what they heard, saw, and felt is almost all the data we really have. The hard historicity of events and sayings cannot be definitively established one way or the other.

So, whether scholars give us the Jesus who was a cynic sage, a political activist, the husband of Mary Magdalene, a father, the dead messiah in a ditch who never meant for things to get so out of hand, or, with N. T. Wright, the bodily resurrected Lord of glory, it all remains hypothetical. Whether from a confessing or non-confessing perspective, biblical studies are neither true science nor hard history.

I repeat once more, when it comes to biblical studies much of what passes for historical and scientific biblical research and most of what we read or see on television is based on conjecture and circumstantial evidence—or

49. Schweitzer, *Quest of the Historical Jesus*, 6.
50. Ibid., 7.

is merely entertainment. It's not that we shouldn't take it seriously, but that we shouldn't take it too seriously. And that's the attitude we need to take in doing evangelism—convey in our person that we are conversant with biblical scholarship and appreciate it, while remaining consecrated to a deeper mystery.

C. E. Hill speaks to the issue. Hill quotes the wild exaggerations and erroneous statements of secular scholars like William Petersen and Edith Pagels in regard to the number and popularity of apocryphal gospels in the early centuries of Christianity, specifically that there was "a sea of multiple gospels" and "gospels were breeding like rabbits." They also expressed astonishment that professors had "file cabinets of other gospels." Actually, only nine apocryphal gospels that we know of (and it would not change matters if a few more were found) were written by 175 CE.[51] Read Hill's *Who Chose the Gospels? Probing the Great Gospel Conspiracy* to see more of a statistical analysis. As Hill also notes, the notion that the choosing of the four gospels as orthodox and canonical is the result of a Roman plot that fits well with the conspiratorial myths of our age. Kostenberger and Kruger further see the Bauer hypothesis, and the new life given it by Pagels and Ehrman, as characteristic of the value placed on diversity by modern Western culture.[52] When Richard A. Horsley writes of the diversification of movements that formed around, and were given impetus by, the crucifixion of Yeshua ben Yosef, he really does so with a voice no older than the pop culture of the late twentieth century.[53] No scholar, regardless of his or her orientation, who has not struggled with the demon of his or her own presuppositions, can be trusted. Herzog, therefore, writes of the fundamental dishonesty of the Jesus Seminar in claiming that its members were coming together to do real Jesus research when individually they had already formed intractable conclusions.[54] But if we can also see the humor in all of it then that will aid us in doing evangelism and apologetics in a more relaxed and therefore effective mode.

Archaeology as Direct Evidence

Archaeology, with its systematic explorations, ordered excavations and careful cataloging of physical artifacts, and more precise methods of dating, including radio carbon dating, is obviously much closer to "hard science."

51. Hill, *Who Chose the Gospels?*, 32–33.
52. Kostenberger and Kruger, *Heresy of Orthodoxy*.
53. Horsley, "Jesus Movements and the Renewal of Israel," 11.
54. Herzog, *Jesus, Justice, and the Reign of God*, 30.

An Evangelist's Perspective on Biblical Scholarship 155

But artifacts do not interpret themselves.[55] The meaning of words, symbols, context, and the significance of any particular find are frequently debated in minute detail and in a convoluted manner that confounds reason. Thomas Thompson correctly acknowledges the flawed methodology often used in interpreting the Nuzi documents, but notes that there is nevertheless substantial reason for accepting the customs and names of the patriarchal narratives found in the Old Testament.[56] Matters are further confused and heated up by the way television documentaries sensationalize, exaggerate, and commercialize scholarly work—corrupting both scholar and research.

One of the most intense debates today is between the "minimalists" and "maximalists." As a minimalist, Philip Davies believes there was no Abraham and Sarah, no family of Jacob and Leah and Rachel, no Moses or exodus, and no Davidic monarchy. For minimalists, the Old Testament documents are purely a "literary construct." Where archaeology speaks they hear not even a whisper, and where archaeology is silent they hear disproof;[57] indeed, silence is regarded as evidence of their theories. However, silence only proves silence, and when one considers the size of this nomadic clan, the nature of the relationship between city dwellers and nomadic herders, as well as other factors, the silences regarding Abraham and Sarah's family are not terribly surprising.[58]

Although not without its flaws, Kenneth A. Kitchen's *On the Reliability of the Old Testament* is a comprehensive offering of the sort of relevant extra-biblical evidence frequently asked for by the minimalists.[59] However, there are two counter responses to be found in Davies that actually anticipate Kitchen: First, Davies says arguments that the presence of historical persons, events, and places suggests the historicity of literary works are silly. "Authentic geographical settings and genuine chronological settings do not of themselves," he says, "guarantee the historicity of anything described."[60] One can certainly ask, "Isn't Davies applying this, or a very similar, criterion in his own analysis?" That is, if inscriptions and the names of people and places are scarce does he not use that as evidence that the event is not historical? Second, says Davies, "because most of the Bible's contents are beyond reasonable verification or falsification, the assessment of probability

---

55. Coogan, *Old Testament*, 58–59.
56. Bauckham, "Bauckham on the Talpiyot Tomb Inscription."
57. Thompson, *Mythic Past*, xii, 9–15, 23. See also, Millard and Wiseman, *Essays on the Patriarchal Narratives*.
58. Miller and Haye, *History of Ancient Israel and Judah*, 54–79. See also, Provan, Long, and Longman, *Biblical History of Israel*, 107–92.
59. Kitchen, *On the Reliability of the Old Testament*.
60. Davies, *In Search of "Ancient Israel"*, 32.

in individual cases is, if not futile, then at least only calculable in a very general sense."[61] Again, isn't this what everyone, including Davies, has to do constantly—arrive at decisions, reach conclusions, make commitments, and take action on the basis of assessed probability? Davies, in fact, asks his readers to listen to his arguments and draw conclusions after carefully considering their reasonableness.

Fetters of Time and Culture

"All story is fiction," insists Davies, "and that must include historiography. The historian might like to invest truth in these stories, but should never avoid the question 'why is this story being told?' The answer can never be 'because what it describes happened,' for not only is that untrue, since stories do not neatly reproduce what 'happened,' but the fact of something happening does not itself produce an adequate reason for telling it."[62] But Davies does not appear to recognize that by his definition his own work is "fictional," or that there is a significant difference, as John Knox put it, "between a story that came into existence to express the inner meaning of a known fact, and a story which invents the fact itself."[63] Thomas Merton did not write his *Seven Story Mountain* merely to tell the events of his life, but to express the inner meaning of those events—a meaning he correctly perceived might have some universal significance.

Merton's story, biblical stories, every story arises out of the passion, out of the search for "the first truth, and, more radically still, in search of a point of departure." At least, that's how the French philosopher Paul Ricoeur saw it. He said, "The illusion is not in looking for a point of departure, but in looking for it without presuppositions. There is no philosophy without presuppositions."[64] Every academic, every preacher, doctor, lawyer, cobbler, and baker, every single human being without exception is fettered by emotional, psychological, philosophical, political, and a million mundane presuppositions that are not only individual and personal, but social and cultural as well. Umberto Cassuto, in discussing the sometimes-uncanny parallel developments between biblical and Homeric studies wrote,

> What now are we to deduce from this parallelism that continues from one generation to the other? In part, of course, it is to be

---

61. Davies, "Beyond Labels."
62. Davies, *In Search of "Ancient Israel"*, 13.
63. Knox, *Myth and Truth*, 69.
64. Ricoeur, *Symbolism of Evil*, 348.

explained as the result of reciprocal influence, and in part also as due to general progress in the methods and techniques of research, which is common to humanistic studies, and in time allows all these branches to develop equally. But undoubtedly, it is affected also by the opinions and concepts, the trends and demands, the character and idiosyncrasies of each age.[65]

The fetters of our own time and place bind us all.

Davies, at times, does appear to recognize the impossibility of escaping the constraints of both personal and cultural biases and presuppositions, but then also suggests that through the application of the principles of criticism the objectivity of one's work can be trusted. "The surface of the mirror is always distorted," he writes, "but we can conceptualize the image being reflected if we examine the surface of the mirror."[66] Actually, Davies is entirely correct; everyone, scholar or not, should practice a hermeneutic of suspicion. But this will include suspicion of secular as well as sacred biblical studies.

Here is a small matter, but one that indicates something of Davies' own quite subjective approach. After insisting on how methods used in the social sciences can be helpful to the study of ancient societies, Davies offers a rebuttal to scholars who criticize the use of these methods. He says, "Knowledge is a social possession, and can be used to bestow or withhold power. Any reflective person living in Great Britain is aware of the paranoia that its government displays over the kind of access to information that citizens of the United States enjoy."[67] Davies' misreading of US history and American political dynamics is absolutely appalling. If, as a scholar applying the methods of the social sciences, he can't correctly interpret a contemporary society that speaks his own language, how is he, or other academicians of a similar mind, to be trusted in analyzing the people and culture of the Hebrew Bible?

A Systems Check

One of the most stunning and egregious failures to maintain academic integrity, where it would have been so incredibly easy to do so, is represented by the whole sleazy business of "The Gospel of Jesus's Wife"—the ragged piece of papyrus radiocarbon dated to the Medieval period with the words, "Jesus said to them, my wife" written in Coptic. This piece of papyrus, which

---

65. Cassuto, *Documentary Hypothesis*, 12.
66. Davies, *In search of Ancient Israel*, 14.
67. Ibid.

is written in ink consistent with that used between 400 BCE and 700 CE, is roughly the size of a business card, and translates from Coptic into English as:

> line 1: . . . not [to] me. My mother gave me life . . .
>
> line 2: . . . The disciples said to Jesus, . . .
>
> line 3: . . . deny. Mary is (not?) worthy of it. . . .
>
> line 4: . . . Jesus said to them, "My wife . . .
>
> line 5: . . . she is able to be my disciple . . .
>
> line 6: . . . Let wicked people swell up . . .
>
> line 7: . . . As for me, I am with her in order to . . .
>
> line 8: . . . an image . . .

There are apparently eight incomplete lines of writing on one side and the other side is badly damaged so that only three faded words and a few letters of ink are visible even with computer-aided enhancement.[68]

Professor Karen L. King, Hollis Professor of Divinity at the Harvard Divinity School, was given, or purchased through Harvard University, the scrap of parchment by Walter Fritz, a well-educated German man living in Florida with a life-long history as a con artist, a producer of fake antiquities, and as a pornographer who featured his own wife. This is better stuff than Dan Brown could make up. But I wouldn't want to spoil it for you. Read Ariel Sabar's article in the *Atlantic*. The gullibility of Karen King, her colleagues, and Harvard is, to use a current internet cliché, jaw dropping.[69]

Professor King thought the papyrus contained a fourth-century Coptic translation of "a gospel" probably written in Greek in the second half of the second century. However, it wasn't long before other scholars recognized the similarity of this papyrus to another fragment from the same anonymous owner, which scholars knew to be a fake. César Guarde-Paz of the University of Barcelona contested it on the basis of paleography. Craig A. Evans at Acadia Divinity School thought the letters oddly written and an indication they were probably by a modern hand. The writing, which does not seem to be of the quality of a professional scribe, is a form of Coptic no longer in use during the period from which the papyrus is reported to have come. There

---

68. Trifunov, "Gospel of Jesus's Wife"; "Was Jesus married?"; Bartlett, "Lessons of Jesus' Wife"; "The Gospel of Jesus's Wife," Harvard Divinity School, http://gospelofjesusswife.hds.harvard.edu.

69. Sabar, "Unbelievable Tale Of Jesus's Wife"; Pattengale, "How the Jesus' Wife Hoax Fell Apart"; Wangsness, "Harvard Theological Review"; Baden and Moss, "Curious Case of Jesus's Wife."

are puzzling spelling and grammatical errors, and, as noted, it seems to have been largely copied out of order and reassembled from a known publication of the *Gnostic Gospel of Thomas*. Andrew Bernhard observed, for example, that there is a close resemblance between Mike Grondin's interlinear Coptic/English translation of the Gospel of Thomas and the text of the papyrus that the forger, now known to be Walter Fritz, appeared to have used to compose the supposed fragment. Karen King has now made available the interlinear translation provided to her by Fritz, and Bernhard has shown that every line shows evidence of copying from Grondin's interlinear.[70]

Christian Askeland's linguistic analysis of the text shows that it is in a dialect which fell out of use well before 741 CE. He concluded that the text must have been written on a fragment of medieval papyrus by a modern forger. In addition, Askeland showed that the fragment is "a match for a papyrus fragment that is clearly a forgery." This second fragment, containing part of the Gospel of John belongs to the same anonymous owner, and is now overwhelmingly considered by scholars to be a fake. Askeland argues that this papyrus piece was written by the same person, in the same ink, and with the same instrument as the "Gospel of Jesus's Wife." Professor King said, "This is substantive, it's worth taking seriously, and it may point in the direction of forgery." King's use of the word "may" should be noted. The *Atlantic* reported that "even though King herself has refused to declare the case closed, for all practical purposes, judgment has been passed on the Gospel of Jesus's Wife: it's a fake."[71]

What is to be emphasized just now, and what is more than a little pertinent to this discussion is that, as a scholar of impressive credentials at one of the most prestigious universities in the world, Karen King was profoundly wrong about this piece of 1.6 × 3.1 inch papyrus at a number of significant points: (1) It was not written sometime between 301 and 400 CE—that is, sometime in the fourth century; (2) It was not a copy of a gospel probably originally written in Greek between 150 and 200 CE; (3) It does not reflect the belief of early Christians that Jesus had a wife; and (4) It is not a "gospel." A gospel is a specific genre of literature and this obviously does not meet the criteria—a tiny piece of paper with a tantalizing phrase and the name "Jesus" on it does not a gospel make.

King was wrong, of course, in her conclusions or suggestions, or whatever they were, because the scrap is a modern forgery, but the critical point here is that King, and the colleagues she initially consulted, AnneMarie

---

70. Bernhard, "Gospel of Jesus' Wife"; Bernhard, "How the Gospel of Jesus' Wife Might Have Been Forged."

71. Baden and Moss, "Curious Case of Jesus's Wife."

Luijendijk at Princeton University and Roger Bagnall at the New York University Institute for the Study of the Ancient World, were unable to do what we "peasant readers" are constantly told scholars are experts at—objectively and scientifically deciphering and verifying the authenticity of whole documents and fragments purported to be of ancient origins.

However, for just a moment let's imagine what it would mean from the perspective proposed here in this book had that scrap of papyrus "proven" to be authentic and even somehow warranted the conclusion that early Christians did believe Jesus was indeed married? I suppose, and I am just supposing of course, that the Roman Catholic Church might want to revise its insistence on clergy celibacy. It certainly wouldn't be some sort of a mark against either Jesus or the Christian faith. Especially at Christmas and Easter one is likely to read, hear, or see in the media some report or story revealing the "real" Jesus, or the facts of what really happened. For instance, "Did you know Jesus's hands were probably tied and not nailed to the cross?" Or, "Did you know Jesus may have been married to Mary Magdalene and that they had 2.4 children, a Fox Terrier named Jake, and a Blue Persian cat called Purr?"

I am a fan of the television detective series starring Tom Selleck as the acerbic Jesse Stone, the name from which the series derives its title. The mayor, who is chronically displeased with Jesse Stone, frequently tries to threaten Jesse, saying, "You know we can fire you." And Jesse will tersely reply, "Yes. You can. You just can't tell me what to do." When asked, in regard to a case he is investigating, "Is that what you think or what you know?" Stone typically answers, "Know, but can't prove." Debunking is primarily, as Rabbi Edwin Friedman, a pioneer in systems therapy and leadership, noted, a manifestation of the debunker's own inner existential anxiety. I would assert that applied to the Christian faith it does so by diminishing Jesus so as to make him more humanly manageable.

I obviously have no real way of knowing for certain why Karen King or Harvard University made such a colossal and ludicrous blunder—hubris, status, greed, political correctness gone awry, spiritual anxiety, or sheer incompetence. But I do know, as Jesse Stone knows, when something is "off." Especially disconcerting and symptomatic is King and Harvard's reluctance to acknowledge their complicity, wittingly or unwittingly, in the hoax of the so-called Gospel of Jesus's Wife fragment. After concluding his exhaustive investigation of the provenance of the Fritz papyrus, Ariel Sabar called to arrange a meeting with Karen King. Even though he was one of the four reporters she had chosen to give an exclusive and personal interview prior to releasing her original report at the International Association for Coptic Studies Conference, she now refused his request and expressed no curiosity in what he had found. Only after Sabar's devastating article, "The Unbelievable Tale of Jesus's Wife," came out in the *Atlantic* did she make the rather anemic concession that the evidence now "presses in the direction of forgery." Harvard's own self-serving response, also obviously forced by Sabar's piece in the *Atlantic*, sounds like something written by a communications or public relations expert and is not worth quoting here. Adam Marcus in *Retraction Watch* referred to it as: "a cop-out of—bear with us—biblical proportions."[72]

But I am probably beginning to sound too much like the cranky old man my wife sometimes accuses me of being, and that is certainly no way to practice apologetics. What I hope you will be able to do as an evangelist and apologist is gently assure someone, whose faith has been shaken or whose spirit has been distracted by this sort of trivia, that what you have discovered is that debunking is really nothing to fear or with which to be overly concerned.

Ahistorical

The quest for both ancient Israel and the historical Jesus are equally problematic. The insurmountable difficulty for any historian is that the Bible is testimony and not history as such. The Gospels are confessions. One can argue with the honesty or accuracy of a confession, but not with the experience of the confessor. John L. McKenzie makes a helpful distinction between history as event and history as record.[73] Both Judaism and Christianity believe their faith to be grounded in actual events, but it is obvious that these events have either no or only fragmentary records, and that much of what has been recorded has been by people whose primary concern was with the signs of transcendence in those events. How does one record *sensus divinitatis*? How does one record an ineffable experience? Every attempt to do so is, as T. S. Elliot noted, "a raid on the inarticulate."[74] McKenzie therefore writes,

> Did Israel have a secular history? The mention of gods in the chronicles of Egypt and Mesopotamia makes it clear that no ancient nation thought of itself as having a "secular" history. Not until the Greeks did such an idea arise; and even the secular histories written by Greek agnostics were not free of moralizing.

---

72. Marcus, "Coptic Cop-Out?"
73. McKenzie, *Theology of the Old Testament*, 142–43.
74. Elliot, *Four Quartets*, 31.

> The Israelites could not have grasped the idea and could not have produced such a secular history.[75]

It has become increasingly clear that for any one historian the relative probability of the various facts about Jesus varies considerably, and that the historical estimates made by different historians vary even more.

The word "confession" comes from the Latin *confessio* which at one time referred to the tomb of a martyr—the burial place of a man or woman who had been willing to say what she or he had experienced in his or her own life of the mysterious reality of God and of Jesus Christ, even though doing so meant torture and death. It is this, and not the profession of the God, or the No-god, of the philosophers, theologians, and academics that constitutes something of the essence of being Christian. Davies is correct, one who reads the Bible sitting in this placeless place reads it entirely differently from one who does not see God as, in Wordsworth's words, "a presence that disturbs with the joy of elevated thoughts; a sense sublime, and rolls through all things."[76] Not to find God, to see God, to feel God in all of reality is essentially the definition of what it means to be secular.

But confessional biblical studies, particularly when they fall along the evangelical to fundamentalist side of the theological continuum, are no less problematic. Of the challenges confronting conservative Christians in North America, Calvin Miller writes of evangelical scholars: "But they have willingly adopted a scholarly narrowness that at times keeps their heads buried in the scholarship of the past, and they are not necessarily informed of the arts or mysteries of our own times. . . . What about hyperscholarship is hastening our decline? Not much you can put your finger on, but it seems that passion and study do vary immensely."[77] Adapting Miller's pertinent questioning one may very well ask, "What is there about scholarship that tends to lead into an intellectual and spiritual cul-de-sac?"

Of course, an obvious and critical error made by secular scholars such as Phil Davies, Richard Dawkins, and Bart Ehrman is the identification of religious right-wing fundamentalism as representative of the beliefs and attitudes of all confessing persons. What is important to most mainline Christians in the United States is not the dramatic details of biblical stories, whether, for example, if captured on video they would look like something out of a Cecil B. DeMille's movie—Charlton Heston parting the Pacific Ocean—but whether there were events regardless of how outwardly "normal" they may have appeared, contained signs of transcendence. Thomas

---

75. McKenzie, *Theology of the Old Testament*, 143–44.
76. Wordsworth, "Lines Composed," 69.
77. Miller, *Vanishing Evangelical*, 38.

Cahill, who tells the story of Abraham and Sarah in a way that feels entirely natural and that acknowledges the stories of the Bible to be problematic and even contradictory at points, is still able to write,

> But there is in these tales a kind of specificity—a concreteness of detail, a concern to get things right—that convinces us that the writer had no doubt that each of the main events he chronicles *happened*. More than this, *that* they happened—that God spoke to Avraham and told him to leave Sumer for the unknown, that God spoke to Moshe and told him to lead the Israelites out of Egypt—is the whole point. These are not, like *Gilgamesh*, archetypal tales with a moral at the end: they share nothing essential with other ancient myths from *Gilgamesh* to Aesop to Grimms' fairy tales. If the stories of Cupid and Psyche or Beauty and the Beast never happened in real time, no one is the poorer for that. But if Avraham and Moshe never existed, or if they did not receive their commission from God, their stories have no point at all—nor does the genetic collection known as "the Jewish people," nor do Christians or Muslims, who also count themselves heirs of Avraham.[78]

It is this sense of calling, this sense of "deep calling to deep," this *sensus divinitatis*, that is the distinguishing mark, the "singularity" of the confessional reading of Scripture.

To reiterate, it is not that of these two approaches to biblical studies one is more scientific or more historical than the other, but that both are highly subjective and based on circumstantial evidence. N. T. Wright's work is ponderously academic and confessional, but honesty compels one to admit it is subject to the same limitations as any nonconfessional study. Larry Hurtado consistently attempts to defend the integrity of scholarship in general by emphasizing its "vetting" process and the credentials of professional academicians. Yet, when one browses his blog it becomes apparent even Hurtado himself is concerned with "zombie" theories—propositions that cannot be laid to rest even though discredited, and which continue to be advanced even by scholars highly respected in the academy.

In his polemic against confessional study, Davies raises the question of whether a person of faith understands the Bible any better than the secular person. And here is what he thinks a trick question, "Does the Christian understand the Old Testament better than the Jew?"[79] What Davies does not see from his secular perspective is that for the spiritual person this is a

---

78. Cahill, *Gifts of the Jews*, 127.
79. Davies, *Whose Bible Is It Anyway?*, 12.

spiritual question as well as an intellectual one. Those on a spiritual quest understand one another and the sacred writings of each in a way secular scholars, no matter how well they understand the discursive content, cannot.

From the perspective of secular biblical scholars, the contrast of non-confessional with confessional studies might be conceptualized something like this:

Secular Biblical Studies	Sacred Biblical Studies
scholar	preacher
academic discourse	propaganda
erudite	benighted
intellectually objective	intellectually biased

This, however, is a false dichotomy. It erroneously assumes that intellectual integrity, including the ability to change one's mind, resides in ideology rather than the person.

Conclusion

Scholarship, profane or sacred, is not about formal membership in the academy. It is, rather, about three things: 1) extensive knowledge of a particular field; 2) skill in thinking reflectively;[80] and 3) the possession of certain attitudes, such as teachability, openness, and humility. Neither the confessing or nonconfessing scholar has cornered the market on these qualities.

The task of both the confessing and nonconfessing scholar is to work with as much intellectual integrity as possible while remaining open to the risk of being terribly mistaken, not only about the Bible, but also about the most fundamental questions and realities of life. However, for the person of the confessing scholar, for his or her essential self, there is also something additional always at work—reaching for the *suprarational* that transcends the positivism, rationalism, and scientism of our age. For this there need be no embarrassment, and there is nothing reprehensible about the scholar who sometimes preaches or evangelizes, provided the scholarship is saturated with humility and the preaching soaked through and through with the naiveté of the second kind.

---

80. King and Kitchener, *Developing Reflective Judgment.*

CHAPTER NINE

Before the Sermon

There are prophets, there are guides, and there are argumentative people with theories, and one must be careful to distinguish between them.

—Peter Brook in *The Laughter at the Heart of Things*[1]

I VIVIDLY REMEMBER THE day when I realized that, in spite of all my aspirations, I would never be a biblical scholar. It was in Dr. Thomas Gillespie's course on Saint Paul's Letter to the Galatians. Gillespie, who later became president of Princeton Seminary, was explaining how Otto Betz had made an important discovery regarding the structure of Galatians one night while reading a Greek rhetorical manual before bed. I asked myself, "What kind of a person sits around late at night reading ancient Greek rhetorical manuals?" And immediately the answer came to me: "Someone who is a true scholar, and that is why you will never be a real biblical scholar." The truth is, I am nothing more than a left-handed Okie boy from Bakersfield, California. However, while recognizing the futility of my scholarly ambitions and personal academic limitations, I have retained until this very day the desire to read the sacred page with as much intellectual integrity as possible.

---

1. Luke, *Laughter at the Heart of Things*, 7.

Scripture Reading as an Obstacle to Faith

I have often identified, while reading Scripture, with the awe and wonder of the Prophet Ezekiel, "I saw, and behold a stormy wind come from the north, a great cloud and flashing fire, and a Glow round about, and from its midst a vision of the Speaking Silence" (Ezek 1:1—2:2, Aryeh Kaplan's translation in *Meditation and the Bible*).[2] I am well aware, however, that contrary to my own experience, reading the Bible is, for some, a serious obstacle to faith. Bart Ehrman's experience, for example, was along the latter lines. Ehrman tells how as a student at Princeton he was asked to write an interpretive paper on a passage of his choosing. He chose to write his paper on Mark 2:25-26. In that pericope, Jesus asks the Pharisees, "Have you never read what David did when he was in need and hungry, he and those who were with him: how he entered the house of God, when Abiathar was high priest, and ate the bread of the Presence, which it is not lawful for any but the priests to eat, and also gave it to those who were with him?" Jesus was referring to the story in 1 Sam 21:1-10 where in fleeing from King Saul, David entered the tabernacle and ate consecrated bread. In 1 Samuel it is not Abiathar but his father Ahimelech who assists David. King Saul vengefully murders Ahimelech, and Abiathar only later succeeds his father as high priest. Ehrman found this technical discrepancy troubling. It was the moment in which he pivoted away from faith to agnosticism. Ehrman says that once he came to the conclusion that Mark had made a mistake, "the floodgates opened. If there could be one picayune mistake in Mark 2, maybe there could be mistakes in other places as well. Maybe, when Jesus says later in Mark 4 that the mustard seed is 'the smallest of all seeds on the earth,' maybe," says Ehrman, "I didn't need to come up with a fancy explanation for how the mustard seed is the smallest of all seeds when I know full well it isn't."[3]

I grew up in quite a conservative denomination. I know what it is to be afraid that one may lose his or her sanity, or soul, over some small matter. It is a prison from which some never escape—a mind-set stronger than steel bars.

One such imprisoning notion is the idea that Scripture is absolute, word-for-word truth or it is not sacred. Scripture is either inerrant (we used the word infallible) or it is not Scripture. The discovery of mistakes, discrepancies, or errors in any ancient biblical text renders the whole of Scripture entirely unreliable. This, it seems to me, defies ordinary reality—defies

---

2. Kaplan, *Meditation and the Bible*, 44.
3. Ehrman, *Misquoting Jesus*, 9–10.

common sense. As an old man, my brother Tom liked to tell how he began working as a shoe-shine boy in our town when he was only eight years old. I know that the age he gives is well off the mark—know it for a fact. I also know that his story of that time, as a whole, is reasonably accurate. Whether he was eight or twelve when he became a shoe-shine boy really doesn't matter. It doesn't matter whether Ahimelech or Abiathar was the high priest who gave David consecrated bread to eat, or whether Jesus called the mustard seed, contrary to the scientific evidence of standard weights and measures, the smallest of all seeds.

Reading Organically

Scripture cannot be read like a bank statement or a computer printout—as if it is nothing more than inert data that we can master, control, and manipulate. Writing against this mechanistic interpretation of Scripture, Berkeley Mickelson asked, "What is inspiration? It is," he said, "the energizing power of God in the lives, discourses, and writings of God's servants so that from these writings men and women can see life with God as supreme."[4] I am not implying that the techniques developed by the various schools of biblical criticism are not at all useful. I am simply proposing that the sacred page must be read organically, as something living, by those on a spiritual quest.

As an undergraduate student I purchased a copy of *How Does a Poem Mean?* by John Ciardi. I have kept it and reread it many times because of its usefulness in considering the sacred text. Ciardi said that analysis can never be a substitute for the poem itself. What analysis can do is to help one read the poem more perceptively. The reason for taking a poem apart is so that the reader, once the analysis is complete, can put the poem back together in a way that restores its simultaneity and so read it more richly.

> WHAT DOES THE POEM MEAN? is too often a self-destroying approach to poetry. A more useful way of asking the question is HOW DOES A POEM MEAN? Why does it build itself into a form out of images, ideas, rhythms? How do these elements become the meaning? How are they inseparable from the meaning? As Yeats wrote:
>
> *O body swayed to music, O quickening glance,*
> *How shall I tell the dancer from the dance?*
>
> What the poem is, is inseparable from its own performance of itself. The dance is in the dancer and the dancer is in the dance.

---

4. Mickelson, "The Bible's Own Approach to Authority," 84.

> Or put in another way: where is the "dance" when no one is dancing it? And what person is a "dancer" except when dancing? Above all else, poetry is a performance.[5]

I would add that it is a living performance.

An organismic approach to the interpretation of the biblical text, approaching it as a living performance, is liberating in that it frees one from the sorts of intellectual dilemmas inherent in either mechanistic or magical readings. Over time, I have become increasingly convinced that the more literal, dramatic, or spectacular shape a biblical story or saying takes in our own mind, the more we see it like something out of a movie. The more that event or saying becomes intellectually problematic for many of us who don't realize our struggle is not with the story but with our own imagination. Conversely, when I can look at a text organically, when I can see it as something quite "natural," when I can see "how it means," then I am more receptive to its cosmic, transcendent significance.

I used to think at times about the story of Samson. I am not sure why that story was something of a focal point for my doubts, but it was. I would think about how it says Samson killed a thousand Philistines with the jawbone of an ass. I would think, "Uh-uh! I don't think so." And the business about his losing his strength when sexy Delilah cut his long hair while he slept on the bed of their lovemaking sounded like something out of a fairy tale to me (absent the fairies). Then I quit reading the story as a fairy tale and saw something that didn't look strange or bizarre or fantastic at all. Could there have been a great warrior, powerful in personal combat, a champion of his people who was the death of many of their enemies (maybe not a thousand before eating breakfast but several), someone consecrated to God? What would happen to the prowess of such a person as a warrior if his or her life lost focus, was dissipated, if shorn of the very symbol of a vowed life? For me, that leaves the story intact, understandable, and something practically applicable to my own life and spirituality.

Alan Richardson's book *Religion in Contemporary Debate* is now over fifty years old and still worth reading. Richardson notes,

> In the New Testament, stories with profound symbolical significance are told in a matter-of-fact way which misleads the literalistic Western mind. St. Luke's story of the Ascension is a good example: we are simply told that the Risen Jesus was "taken up" into heaven and that a cloud received him out of the sight of the disciples (Acts 1:9). We have little idea what, in fact, were Luke's cosmological notions, but we may be sure that he is not

---

5. Ciardi, *How Does a Poem Mean?*, 667–68.

telling about the ascent of a physical body to a place above the sky. Heaven is not a place for the biblical writers, and there is no need to suppose that St. Luke is an exception to the rule.[6]

Luke used, says Richardson, traditional symbols such as clouds to represent divinity, as a way of explaining truth that is beyond the power of words to convey.

The Bible, as everyone is aware, was written over many hundreds of years and its many different authors who wrote it simply accepted the cosmology of their culture. But this constitutes no real problem for Christian belief. When I took my first college religion course, the professor delighted in making us aware of any information that might diminish our devotion to Scripture. That's where I learned of the quaint and, to us now, ridiculous notion of the three-storied universe. What took me a while to grasp was that the concept of the three-storied universe mattered only if one were a literalist and thought that if a biblical author entertained a scientifically incorrect cosmology one's whole faith was in danger of collapsing in a heap. But as Richardson noted, "It is impossible to construct a biblical cosmology, for many stages of cosmological development are represented in the various parts of the Bible; and, since what they were talking about was neither science in general nor cosmology in particular, the truth of what they said is not bound up with the validity of any particular scientific world view."[7] The biblical authors were writing of something, or rather someone, who transcends space and time, and drew on the poetic metaphors they had at hand in order to do so. Luke, for example, in writing of the ascension wasn't thinking about the arrangement of the physical universe, but drawing on a metaphor of an Oriental court where the Grand Vizier was elevated to sit at the right hand of the king. Ultimately, there is no conflict between scientific descriptions and the poetic language of spiritual mystery. But there may very well be a quite serious clash between measurable scientific observations and the literalist imagination.

A mechanistic, literal, one-dimensional, or fantastic reading of the sacred text comes from a rather limited, "earthbound," one-dimensional understanding of inspiration. If God inspired the text, it is reasoned, the original autographs would have been immaculate, inerrant, and perfectly preserved over the centuries. The fact that the biblical manuscripts contain errors must, therefore, mean that the Bible is an entirely human document and not the book God breathed; that, in fact, there may be no inspiring God. No dance, and no dancer to dance the dance.

6. Richardson, *Religion in Contemporary Debate*, 70.
7. Ibid., 71.

This was the conclusion to which Bart Ehrman came. When his fundamentalist belief in the inerrancy of the Bible collapsed his belief in God also collapsed into a kind of "fundamentalist agnosticism." Ehrman has now spent his professional career attempting to demonstrate that the Bible is a human book only. In *Misquoting Jesus* he attempts to persuade his readers that the Bible is so full of errors that it cannot possibly be trusted. Ehrman first points to the many simple accidental errors made by early copyists. He does acknowledge that such errors are no great matter, but by the time he makes that acknowledgment the well has been poisoned. He then points to changes that are "intentional" and include theological alterations.[8] Actually, Ehrman's book proves the opposite of what he intends—errors are, in fact, easily detected, as Ehrman's book itself demonstrates, and no error, given the entire context of Scripture, changes anything. But what Erhman really doesn't get is that the issue of copyists' errors or alterations is a problem only for those who hold to a particular theory of inspiration, which demands absolute certainty rather than embracing probability, and which confuses what God could have done with what one thinks God should have done. I can witness the dance and I can even enter into it—I don't get to choreograph it.

The historicity, the *happenedness*, of certain events does matter, but it does not matter for the person of faith in the same way it does for the secular historian or academic. When I read a text I want to know several things: (1) Is the historicity of what the text describes important, or can it be regarded as a literary work—like the book of Job; (2) Did anything like what is described take place? The historicity of the event does not depend on whether what happened transpired precisely as described in the text or as I have imagined it in my own mind; (3) Other than for exegetical and homiletical purposes I am not terribly concerned with the exact words spoken by the characters in the text. The work of the Jesus Seminar is largely irrelevant since what I want to know is not whether the Gospels record the precise words Jesus used but, "Did Jesus say anything at all like this?"

Sacra Pagina

As we have seen, Philip Davies, the minimalist academic formally at Sheffield, argues that biblical scholarship ought to be pursued in the same manner as "secular" science—physics, linguistics, or biology. Consequently, Davies, in complaining about the discrepancy between what Jewish and Christian leaders learn in university theology departments or denominational

---

8. Ehrman, *Misquoting Jesus*, 98–99.

seminaries and what they teach in synagogue and church, writes rather one-sidedly, inaccurately, and prejudicially:

> What they will learn in most modern textbooks written by biblical scholars is that the stories of Abraham and Moses are largely or entirely legend, not history; that the books of the prophets contain a great deal not written by those prophets; that David did not write all the Psalms (if any); that ancient Israelites probably once worshiped a goddess alongside their god; that Jesus was probably born in Nazareth, not Bethlehem; and that the stories of his birth and resurrection appearances display awkward contradictions and may well not be based on eyewitness accounts.... I cannot think of any other university subject whose graduates *disguise* from the public what they have learned.[9]

Every time I read this I find myself smiling. It is a confessing scholar at Fuller Theological Seminary, Christopher B. Hays, professor of ancient Near Eastern studies, who suggested I read Davies. My personal experience, at places like Iliff School of Theology, has taught me that secular biblical scholars are far more likely to disguise and to limit the scope of material that students pursuing honest inquiry are exposed to than are confessing scholars.

While they can and should, but often do not, involve rigorous intellectual discipline, historical, archaeological, and biblical scholarship are not, as we have already found, scientific fields in the same way as, say, chemistry. Even dating the Exodus, for example, is far from precise, and archeological artifacts are notoriously difficult to interpret by themselves or even in relation to the written record—as classical scholars seem to know. I remember a classicist asking if in five thousand years archaeologists were to excavate Chicago, finding volume G of an encyclopedia, a number of sites with "golden arches," and a copy of Mark Twain's *Huckleberry Finn*, what would they think? The encyclopedia would tell them about the arches of Gothic cathedrals, they would have "golden arches" as artifacts, but Mark Twain would say nothing about either Gothic cathedrals or McDonald's. Archaeology sheds enough light to sometimes make some good guesses, but hard conclusions based on guesswork are not part of the scientific method.

If the Gospel of Jesus's Wife had somehow proven to be authentic rather than a forgery, it would remain impossible to have come to the sort of conclusion to which Karen Kind and the news media quickly came. A few cryptic words with blank spaces and written in an illegible hand may, like the shorthand notes I scribble to my wife, mean almost anything.

---

9. Davies, "Do We Need Biblical Scholars?" See also, Davies, *Whose Bible Is It Anyway?* and Davies, *In Search of "Ancient Israel."*

Source criticism is fraught with difficulties. Scholars claiming to use the same "scientific procedures" come to wildly different and contradictory conclusions. The mind-boggling number of sources added to the documentary hypothesis, to JEDP, the sheer complexity of its explanations, and the contradictory and debatable nature of its results make it as difficult to believe that anyone can accomplish what scholars confidently assert they can accomplish in reconstructing a text as it is to believe a bunch of space aliens created the pyramids. I am not saying that the academics are entirely wrong, only, as I have already argued, that their work is not science and should not be received as such. Believing that anyone can delineate the various strata of a nonexistent document (Q), and even determine something about the community that produced that nonexistent document, in the words of Pete Hogwallop from the film *O Brother, Where Art Thou*, "Just don't make no sense." Furthermore, the exaggerations and false claims frequently made regarding the Gospel of Thomas are unworthy of anyone claiming to represent the world of scholarship.[10]

Davies laments the light regard in which biblical scholars, meaning secular biblical scholars, are held; yet, his essay, "Do We Need Biblical Scholars?" is more a caricature of people of faith, of history, and of the Bible itself than it is a serious intellectual reflection. That the stories of Abraham and Moses possess legendary qualities does not mean they are pure fabrications. That there are inconsistencies in the Gospel accounts of the resurrection does not mean there was no resurrection. That the Israelites were not exclusively monotheistic, as we understand the term, is hardly news to anyone who has ever read the Hebrew Scriptures. And Davies' denial of the eyewitness character of the Gospels is most assuredly disputed by scholars every bit as intelligent and competent as Davies. Davies is absolutely correct in arguing that the Bible does not belong to the fundamentalist, to the ignorant, to the superstitious, or to the institutional church. What he does not get is that neither does it belong to the scholars, or the intellectuals, or the academy. From a religious or spiritual perspective, the Bible does not "belong" to anyone, and the more we see it as a document to be mastered, controlled, and read entirely for information rather than transformation, the more irrelevant it becomes.

I am not at all suggesting that the Bible cannot be sensibly read from a secular point of view. It most certainly can. Doing so may even be helpful, like deconstructing a poem and putting it back together again "more richly." The fact that if a particular biblical event were caught on high definition

---

10. *O Brother, Where Art Thou*; Goodacre, *Case against Q*; Hill, *Who Chose the Gospels?*; Kostenberger and Kruger, *Heresy of Orthodoxy*; Cassuto, *Documentary Hypothesis*; Coogan, *Old Testament*; Bauckman, *Jesus and the Eyewitnesses*.

video from multiple angels it might appear quite mundane is not important. What could have looked more ordinary in the time of Abraham and Sarah than a caravan moving along the trade routes from Mesopotamia to Canaan? The significant question is how does it organically mean? Are there signals of transcendence in the story? Does the narrative have a theological purpose or a spiritually transformative function? Does it represent a movement, a step forward, in the continuing process of a larger purpose? For the religionist this may be manifested historically—best seen in looking backward. However, that there was an event does matter. The entire Judeo/Christian tradition begins with Abraham and Sarah on a journey of many adventures. Each adventure, each event, leads to an ever-growing sense of trust and intimacy with the God whose call they first heard in Ur of the Chaldees. Intimacy, and the trust required for its realization, occurs only in the context of real events. In Christianity, historicity matters. If certain events did not take place, whether their precise nature is understood or not, then the stories lose all significance.

The Nature of Scripture

The Princeton scholar B. B. Warfield argued in an 1881 article, "Inspiration," that contrary to the assertions of the "higher biblical criticism" being proposed in Germany, the Bible was inspired, and not only was it inspired, it was inspired in all its parts including its very words, and was therefore "errorless." Warfield used "errorless" or "without error" eleven times in his article. Charles Augustus Briggs, a Presbyterian pastor and seminary professor who had been trained in Germany, soon responded to Warfield and his colleague Charles Hodge with an article of his own in which he maintained that the whole of Scripture was not in fact "inerrant" as Warfield and Hodge had claimed—that its thoughts but not its words were inspired. Briggs argued that the theory that the Bible is inerrant was "the ghost of modern evangelicalism used to frighten children." Not long afterward, in 1893, Briggs was tried and convicted by the Presbyterian Church of heterodoxy. This means that the idea of verbal plenary inspiration and inerrancy is little more than a hundred years old as opposed to twenty-one centuries of Christian history without inerrancy as a part of its tradition. If in conversation with someone from a fundamentalist background, the apologist needs to be prepared to gently point out that for over two thousand years it has been possible to be an orthodox Christian without believing Scripture to be inerrant; or if on the other hand, someone from an agnostic or theologically far left background holds up Warfield's theory as Christian tradition in order to call the Christian faith itself into question, the apologist needs to be able to point to that genuine and ancient tradition which is more open, more realistic, and deeper.

Warfield was simply incorrect in both what Scripture claims for itself in regard to inspiration, and in the nature of inspiration itself. 2 Tim 3:16, along with 1 Pet 1:20–21, constitute the primary texts in considering the Bible's self-understanding of inspiration.

> All Scripture is inspired by God and is useful for teaching, for reproof, for correction, and for training in righteousness. (2 Tim 3:16 NRSV)

> First of all, you must understand this, that no prophecy of Scripture is a matter of one's own interpretation, because no prophecy ever came by human will, but men and women moved by the Holy Spirit spoke from God. (2 Pet 1:20–21 NRSV)

The first observation that needs to be made is that the verb "to be" is not in the original Greek text of Timothy—there is no "is." 2 Tim 3:16 does not say "all Scripture is inspired," but "all inspired Scripture is profitable." A second observation is that the Greek word translated into English as "Scripture" is *graphe*, which just means "writing." And "inspired" is literally "God-breathed." So, the text can easily be translated as: "All God-breathed writing is profitable." As Bishop Peter Elder Hickman of the Ecumenical Catholic Communion notes, this leads to a number of puzzling questions.

> The writer gives no indication of which writings are considered inspired in his mind and which are not. From this verse we come to know only one thing; that there are some writings that are God breathed and by implication there are some writings which are not. The question remains: What writings are indeed inspired and what are not? This is not the same as asking what writings are canonical and what writings are not. Then follows the next two questions: 1) Are there inspired writings not included in the Jewish and Christian canons? And 2) are all canonical writings inspired? Could a given biblical document have portions that are inspired and other portions that are not?[11]

The Second Epistle of Peter simply says the same thing in different words.

Again we learn that, by definition, all genuine prophecy is written by those who have been "moved" or "borne along as on the wind." In both ancient Hebrew and Greek, as you probably remember, the word for "spirit" is "wind" or "breath." In the end, there is something mysterious

---

11. Hickman, *Word Made Alive*, 82–83.

and unfathomable, something not amenable to human explanations, about God-breathed writing. Where 2 Pet 1:20–21 is concerned, the same questions raised in 2 Timothy remain: "Are all biblical and canonical writings and texts, indeed any and all written words, in the Bible prophetic?"[12] In writing the above, Hickman is recognizing that our wisdom and authoritative guide for the life and work of Christ's beloved community is not an imagined inerrant book, but Christ as known through Scripture, tradition, reason, and experience—and not just of the individual but of the historic and ecumenical Christian communion.

The prophets and apostles and holy men and women of the Old and New Testaments believed God was speaking to them in specific events and so they listened and confessed God. In this way the human response became fused with the Word, with the reality, of God. Writing this down, or inscripturating it, is part of the process of making revelation historical. And so I return to Berkley Mickelson's explanation of inspiration as one which is both orthodox and comprehensible to contemporary men and women. "What is inspiration? It is the energizing power of God in the lives, discourses, and writings of God's servants so that from these writings men and women can see life with God as supreme."

Furthermore, the authors of the Old and New Testament speak of this encounter with the Divine Mystery with a degree of reliability that gives us assurance of its essential truthfulness—the basic truthfulness of the event, the inner truth of its meaning, and its ultimate source as residing in the unfathomable energy and being of God so that when we read Scripture we experience it in the depths of our own being as nothing less than God's Word. The Bible is, then, both a genuinely human and Divine book. It is a guide for Christians in their life and in their spiritual work, it is for them authoritative and crucial to their sense of identity.

Postmodern men and women are quite capable of recognizing Scripture as Wind-borne, as Spirit-borne, as the product of those filled with the breath of Holy Wisdom as they wrote of their experience of Divine Mystery. Marcus Borg stated it like this:

> The Bible is thus both sacred Scripture and a human product. It is important to affirm both. To use stereotypical labels, both conservatives and liberals within the church have sometimes been reluctant to do so. Conservative Christians resist affirming that the Bible is a human product, fearing that doing so means it will lose its status as divine authority and divine revelation. Liberal Christians are sometimes wary of affirming that the Bible is

---

12. Ibid., 84–85.

sacred Scripture, fearing that to do so opens the door to notions of infallibility, literalism, and absolutizing. But a clear vision of the Bible and its role in the Christian life requires seeing it as both sacred Scripture and human product. It is human in origin and sacred in status and function.[13]

I mostly agree with Borg—it is important to see the Bible as both a sacred and human book.

Where both the mystic and the person rooted in the ancient orthodox faith will find Borg unsatisfying is in his perception that it is the "status" given the Bible and the way it has "functioned" in the Christian community and not its origin that make it Holy Scripture.

What Borg does not want to have to say, perhaps because he erroneously feels it must inevitably lead to literalism, notions of inerrancy, and absolutizing, is that Scripture is holy because its origins are to be found in the Holy One—in God. He cannot allow himself to say Scripture is sacred because it is inspired—or again as the writer of 2 Timothy put it—"God breathed" (2 Tim 3:16). It can, of course, be a tricky business to say that "Scripture is 'true' because it comes from God."[14] But if God is not merely passive but somehow active in any way in the divine human encounter, and if true truth ultimately comes from a source deeper than or from beyond the human condition, then the Bible is sacred, not because I give it a cherished status or find it foundational to my tribe, or because it is inerrant, but because it has been birthed by the Mysterious Beyond.

In the age of quantum mechanics with all its "spooky" manifestations, such as the fact that the observation of one object can instantaneously influence the behavior of another object at a very great distance, though no physical force connects the two, or that observing an object to be in one place causes it to be there while it can also be in two or even many distant places at once, and that what is found there seems to be there only upon (conscious?) observation, it is not terribly difficult to believe that the ultimate source of Scripture is a reality greater than any human or superhuman author. These are, to be sure, strange facts, but facts nevertheless. Niels Bohr said, "Anyone not shocked by quantum mechanics has not understood it." Rosenblum and Kuttner write in *Quantum Enigma*, "There are intriguing hints of the world we call physical with that which we call mental." In the end, quantum mechanics leaves us with the question of whether the only "real" reality is consciousness.[15] Is it strange then that the illumination we

---

13. Borg, *Heart of Christianity*, 48.
14. Borg, *Reading the Bible*, 7.
15. Rosenblum and Kuttner, *Quantum Enigma*, 12–13.

experience in Scripture might have its origins in the light of "that than which no greater can be conceived," and therefore is in a very real sense "inspired" of God whose being is its very source. You will, of course, recognize that I am speculating with the hope of convincing you that the sacredness of Scripture, the transcendent light and beauty the mystic finds within it, does indeed emanate from its source and is not entirely dependent on the status a human community gives it or on how it functions among them—although it certainly includes those two elements.

Signs of Integrity

The essential reliability of the New Testament is to be found, or experienced, at a number of points. It is to be experienced in the beauty of its teachings, but again if we have not experienced that beauty for ourselves, and the truth to which that beauty is linked, we cannot share it with anyone else. "What does not live in us cannot live around us."

What I am obviously positing as helpful to the academic enterprise, useful to the practice of evangelization, and beneficial to the spirit is a more contemplative or mystical way of understanding Scripture. Bernard McGinn writes of the Bible and mysticism:

> Christian Mysticism is rooted in the reading of the Bible. The mystic, however, does not seek an academic understanding of the scriptural text; nor is he or she content with viewing the Bible only as a repository of doctrinal and moral regulations. The mystic wants to penetrate to the living source of the biblical message, that is, to the Divine Word who speaks in and through human words and texts. This means that the Bible has been both the origin and norm of Christian mystics down through the ages.[16]

None of this is meant to disparage the role of reason in Christian spirituality. A true Christian spirituality will cultivate both our intuitive capacities and our rational powers. Mysticism values the knowledge of every intellectual discipline, of every field of study, and of every art, but it also seeks to transcend the sort of rationalism characteristic of modernity.

Among the pieces of evidence pointing to the integrity of the New Testament documents we find:

1) The sort of things one expects from eye-witness accounts—an experiential vividness, details about people's emotions, gestures, times,

---

16. McGinn, *Essential Writings*, 3.

places, and geographical locations. This isn't to say that everything written was written by someone actually present to everything that happened, but that what is related appears to have come from people who were there.[17]

2) Stories are often characterized by details that go against self-interests. The inclusion of women at the center of the resurrection story, for instance, could only have worked against the spread of the Christian message in that first-century world.

3) The presence of material that is irrelevant to the later developing church is striking, as is the absence of material that would have been highly relevant to the developing church. For example, if the Church created stories about what Jesus said and did in order to answer questions asked at a later time in its history, and then read or wrote them back into the gospels, then why are such issues as circumcision, charismatic gifts, the role of women in ministry, and what foods are kosher, all hot issues in the developing church, not addressed definitively.

4) Jesus and his disciples spoke Aramaic. Many of the sayings of Jesus in the Gospels appear to be Greek translations of Aramaic words; for example, the saying about straining out a gnat and swallowing a camel, in which "gnat" and "camel" sound almost identical in Aramaic, indicate that the Gospels are correct in crediting the sayings of Jesus to an Aramaic-speaking person rather than the creative imagination of a Greek-speaking church.

5) Archaeological evidence tends to confirm the New Testament record. The reference to the pool of Bethesda in the Gospel of John was once doubted, but has now been discovered and confirmed.

6) The Gospels represent a remarkably stable and unified framework—a stability we know from the books of Acts and the chronology of the Apostle Paul's work was easily achieved in probably no more than four years after the death of Jesus. This means that the story of what Jesus said and did, and what it all meant, did not evolve slowly and incrementally over a long span of time but occurred suddenly, and far too rapidly for the sort of creative process that has often been hypothesized.

7) If Jesus died in 33 CE then the Gospels, indeed the entire New Testament, was completed in roughly thirty-five to seventy years after his death—a very early date even if the outside mark is used. Again, far

---

17. Bauckham, *Jesus and the Eyewitnesses*.

too short a time for fabrications of the sort often proposed to develop. The distinguished and quite liberal New Testament scholar John A. T. Robinson thought the entire New Testament had to have been written before 70 CE. Otherwise, Robinson thought, there was no way to explain why no book of the New Testament points back clearly to the Fall of Jerusalem and the Destruction of the Temple in that year as the fulfillment of Jesus's prophecy.

The Question of Canon

The Christian canon of Scripture is a set of twenty-seven books considered authoritative within the Christian community. Originally, the word "canon" referred to a reed that was used as a measuring stick. The canon then is the rule or measuring stick which establishes the biblical books as legitimate and authoritative. The epistles or letters of the Apostle Paul were circulated as a collection by 100 CE. They circulated prior to that time individually but collectively around 100 CE. The Four Gospels, Matthew, Mark, Luke, and John, circulated as a collection by 160 CE, and by 200 CE a set of Christian writings very similar to the New Testament as we know it was in circulation. In his Easter Letter of 367, Athanasius, Bishop of Alexandria, Egypt, gave a list of books exactly like the New Testament as we have it today and referred to them as canonized. Synods and councils meeting in 393, 397, and 419 all regarded the canon as closed. So the process of canonization was a long, slow, time-tested process.

To be recognized as canonical a book had to meet four requirements: (1) It had to be apostolic in origin; that is, it had to be attributed to or based on the teaching of the first generation of the apostles or their close companions; (2) It had to have universal acceptance, meaning that it had to have been acknowledged by all the major Christian communities in the ancient world by the end of the fourth century; (3) It had to have been used liturgically—read publicly as the Christian communities gathered to celebrate the Lord's Supper during their weekly worship service; and (4) It had to have a consistent message; it had to be consistent with, similar to, or complementary to other accepted Christian writings.

A number of scholars have argued that the canon was actually a late creation of the church and was imposed on it by political forces. Michael J. Kruger in *The Question of Canon: Challenging the Status Quo in the New Testament Debate,* challenges this notion, arguing for an "intrinsic" model of the canon in which it emerged naturally out of the historical essence of

Christianity.[18] I would suggest you read Kruger's book along with C. E. Hill's book *Who Chose the Gospels? Probing the Great Gospel Conspiracy*.[19] This is a very useful book that deals with a question we have already touched on; namely, how were the Four Gospels chosen? Did fourth century councils and powerful bishops rewrite history to make it look like their version of Christian faith was the one true version? Kruger's work actually offers three helpful and complimentary definitions of "canon."

> All three of these definitions make important contributions to our understanding of canon and therefore all three should be used in an integrative and multidimensional manner. The exclusive definition rightly reminds us that the canon did not fall in place overnight; it took several centuries for the edges of the canon to solidify. The functional definition reminds us there was a core collection of books that functioned with supreme authority in early Christian communities. And the ontological definition reminds us that books do not just become authoritative because of the actions of the church—they bear authority by virtue of what they are, books given by God. When all three perspectives on the canon are considered in tandem, a more balanced and more complete vision of the canon is realized. Thus, we should not be forced to choose between them.[20]

When all the evidence has been sifted we will not have come to an indisputable conclusion, but we will, I think, discover a reasonable and satisfying confidence in the spiritual essence of Christian faith and hope.

Advent of Abraham & Sarah

As previously noted, Philip Davies maintains that Abraham and Sarah are "entirely legendary figures." Miller and Hayes believe, considering the limited evidence, that anything said about the time of the patriarchs in connection with the origins of Israel is largely "guess work," and, therefore, decline to reconstruct the earliest history of the Israelites.[21] There is, however, no particular reason to doubt the reality of Abraham and Sarah or the other Genesis characters. As the great Oriental scholar John Albright observed over fifty years ago, "The figures of Abraham, Isaac, Jacob, and Joseph appear before us as real personalities, each one of whom shows traits and qualities

18. Kruger, *Question of Canon*.
19. Hill, *Who Chose the Gospels?*
20. Kruger, *Question of Canon*, 42–43.
21. Miller and Hayes, *History of Ancient Israel and Judah*, 78–79.

which suit his character but would not harmonize with the characters of the others."[22] And it can still be credibly maintained, as Albright did then, that there is plenty of evidence indicating northern Mesopotamia as the original home of the Hebrews. The names of Abraham and Sarah's ancestors correspond to the names of towns in the vicinity of Harran, the fifteenth-century Nuzian documents show that the customs and laws as pictured in the Genesis stories of the patriarchs match Nuzian practices better than later Israelite practices. And the discoveries made at Mari provide numerous other parallels in proper names and language. While it is certainly true that the early analysis of the documents found at Nuzi was flawed, the basic conclusions remain intact.[23] Furthermore, it would appear that the stories of Eden, of the Deluge and Noah, and the tower of Babel are all still more ancient stories brought from Babylon. Even the God Abraham worships very likely is traceable back to Mesopotamia as the divinity embraced by Terah's family.

It requires no blind leap of faith to believe there was a man who thought he was called by the god his family worshipped to make the long journey from Ur of the Chaldees to the Land of Canaan. It would be difficult for me to believe that God appeared and spoke to Abraham in the way the cigar-smoking George Burns did to John Denver in the movie *Oh God!* But it is not at all difficult for me to see Abraham as a person hearing and seeing God in profound dreams and mystical visions (Gen 15:1). And it is easy for me to believe that his understanding of life, of reality, of himself, of God, and of his relationship to God was radically transformed by those dreams, visions, encounters, and experiences on his way to Canaan and beyond. Indeed, it is in the radical discovery made by Abraham and Moses and the Jewish people of a life based on the possibilities of the new rather than the ever-turning wheel, and of a life of faith as trust in the friendship of God, that I find what is most real and convincing about the story as a historical space/time event.

Thomas Cahill's, book, *The Gifts of the Jews*, pictures the story of Abraham and Sarah in a wonderfully organic and natural way, but also as about something cosmic, transcendent—revolutionary in the spiritual history of humanity.

> So, *wayyelekh Avram* ("Avram went")—two of the boldest words in all literature. They signal a complete departure from everything that has gone before in the long evolution of culture and sensibility. Out of Sumer, civilized repository of the predicable, comes a man who does not know where he is going but goes

---

22. Albright, *From the Stone Age to Christianity*, 236–49.

23. Kitchen, *On the Reliability of the Old Testament*. See also, Millard and Wiseman, *Essays on the Patriarchal Narratives*.

forth into the unknown wilderness under the prompting of his god. Out of Mesopotamia, home of uncanny, self-serving merchants who use their gods to ensure prosperity and favor, comes a wealthy caravan with no material goal. Out of ancient humanity, which from the dim beginning of its consciousness has read its eternal verities in the stars, comes a party travelling by no known compass. Out of the human race, which knows in its bones that all its striving must end in death, comes a leader who says he has been given an impossible promise. Out of mortal imagination comes a dream of something new, something better, something yet to happen, something—in the future.[24]

The Exodus

The story of Moses, Hebrew enslavement, and the Exodus is another place where the evidence is quite limited. There are, to be sure, some serious clues, but nothing as set and solid as we would like. But if the number of Israelite slaves in Egypt was relatively small, we would not necessarily expect to find them mentioned in Egyptian sources. However, the name Moses, as well as other Egyptian names, antiquarian details that would seem as inexplicable as inventions of a later time, the apparent discovery of the store cities of Pithom and Ramesses in the Nile Delta as named in Exod 1:11, the scene of Palestinian slaves found in the tomb of Rekhmire, the inclusion of the story in J. P. and E.,[25] and the literary difficulties that would be created in leaving the story out, all point to Hebrew slaves in Egypt and to Moses as more than figures of pure folklore.[26] Indeed, to be somewhat redundant, there is no more reason for doubting the actual existence of Moses as formative in the history of Israel than doubting the role of Buddha as the founder of Buddhism.

---

24. Cahill, *Gifts of the Jews*, 63.

25. Scholars using the criteria of source criticism divide the Pentateuch, the first five books of the Bible, into J. E. P. and D. J stands for the Yahwist. These were authors who primarily used Yahweh as the name of God. The Elohist (E) spoke of God as Elohim so that this is the distinctive characteristic of their writing. P stands for the Priestly, and reflects primarily the interests of the Hebrew priesthood. D stands for the Deuteronomist and is found only in the Book of Deuteronomy. In time, according to the theory of source criticism, various "editors" combined and intertwined these four different sources in what we now know as the books of Genesis, Exodus, Leviticus, and Deuteronomy. When scholars find the inclusion of a story in more than one of these "sources" it adds, for them, considerable weight to the story.

26. Provan, Long, and Longman, *Biblical History of Israel*, 119–236.

The Ipuwer Papyrus, officially Papyrus Leiden I 344, is a poetic description of Egypt in a time of chaos and multiple disasters. The date of the poem's composition is disputed. It was probably written between 1850 and 1600 BCE. The precise date for this present discussion is irrelevant. The Ipuwer Papyrus parallels the plagues preceding the biblical exodus at several points. Some of the more striking parallels have to do with the Nile turning to blood, and the frequent reference to servants abandoning their subordinate status (Ipuwer 2:10; 3:14—4:1; 6:7–8; 10:2–3). What I am suggesting is not that this is a description of the plagues afflicting Egypt at the Exodus, but how a time of crisis and chaos in Egypt could be, and was, pictured in language that no matter how metaphorical is similar to Old Testament language portraying the Exodus. It cannot, therefore, be unreasonable to conclude that the plagues of Exodus may well be a description of Egypt at a time of national distress—an opportune time for escaping slaves. To put it a little differently, it is not unreasonable to conclude that the plagues at the time of the Exodus refer to a real situation—just not the one pictured in wild imaginations.

One possible reconstruction of the Exodus, one that may seem more natural and less fantastic, goes like this: Under the leadership of Moses, Hebrew slaves (how many doesn't matter) escape from their forced labor. They make for one of the swamps or wetlands (the Reed Sea). At low tide the Children of Israel, on foot, are able to cross the swamp, but the Egyptians in their chariots become mired in the mud, and with the rising tide the danger of drowning becomes very real. For the Egyptians, with all the wealth and triumphs of their long history, this would not have been a terribly significant event, but for the Hebrews it would have been a glorious, miraculous victory.[27] Such a reconstruction need not be seen as disproving the Bible, or of diminishing its theological significance. There is a real event, but its significance is in its paradigmatic nature—in its relevance to the experience of God.[28]

Israel in Canaan

The difficulty most often mentioned in regard to the conquest narrative of Joshua is that it does not appear there was any major violent invasion of Canaan during the period most often assigned to the Exodus and Israel's

---

27. Coogan, *Old Testament*, 95.
28. McKenzie, *Theology of the Old Testament*, 133–51. See also, Cahill, *Gifts of the Jews*, 121.

entrance into Canaan as described in Joshua. A number of theories, or models, have been offered as explanations of Israel's emergence in Canaan.[29]

1. The conquest model, which takes seriously the traditional picture of a sudden military conquest, depends on a different dating for the destruction of certain sites named in Joshua, and on a more literal and somewhat simplistic reading of Joshua, than may be warranted; for example, the destruction may not have been nearly as massive as imagined.

2. The peaceful infiltration model maintains that Israel's entrance into Canaan was gradual rather than sudden and violent. This model has been faulted for not recognizing the ethnic character of Israel, and for not understanding how pastoralism actually worked in the ancient world—as a symbiotic relationship.

3. The revolt model holds that Israel did not enter from outside Canaan but through a sociocultural process from within. In this model, as Canaanite culture collapses, disaffected Canaanite people defy the establishment while fugitive slaves from Egypt, appearing with their egalitarian God, further polarize the opposing forces. This creates the motivational energy for the preexisting social units in Canaan to overthrow the authorities in the dominant complex of cities. There are a number of problems with the revolt model, but here I will only refer to what Provan, Long, and Longman indicate; namely, that there is nothing intrinsically implausible about the idea that Israel began as a family, which became the core into which other people were incorporated at the Exodus (Exod 12:38), maybe before, and certainly after. As R. Hess points out, "The possibility of foreign groups joining in with Israel on its journeys and after its entrance into the land might be remembered in the reference to the Midianites (Num 22–25), the Kenites (Judg 4:11; 1 Sam 15:6), the Gibeonites (Josh 9), and others."[30]

4. The ideological construct model is a theory argued by Philip Davies, which asserts that "biblical Israel" never existed other than as an ideological construct of the exilic or postexilic period.[31] This radical position of Davies can only be maintained by erroneously assuming that a theological cast to a text invalidates its ability to communicate historical information. Contrary to Davies, it can be said that the fact that a scribe finds a biblical "recital" to have a meaning applicable to

---

29. Provan, Long, and Longman, *Biblical History of Israel*, 138–47.
30. Ibid., 143.
31. Davies, *In Search of "Ancient Israel."*

his own day does not falsify the historicity, nor does it render either the old or new interpretation incorrect.[32]

Michael D. Coogan, in his historical and literary introduction to the Old Testament, probably offers the most balanced summary of Israel's emergence in Canaan. "Military activity was almost certainly part of the process by which Israel gained control of the land, and it is possible that some of the victories described in the book of Joshua may have occurred.... However, the emergence of Israel was slow and complicated, also involving the peaceful incorporation of some Canaanites into Israel."[33]

Again, what is important is that Israel did come to possess Canaan, not that there was a conquest resembling a Hollywood version of the book of Joshua.

Reading Scripture as Myth

Neither the people of ancient Israel nor the earliest Christians thought of themselves as writing "secular history." These people believed their faith rested on real events, not the records of those events. That the memories and written sources for such events might be fragmentary or use imaginative language was of no great consequence to them, they simply did not have the same positivistic interest in the records we have. John McKenzie, therefore, writes of the modern secular historian:

> The modern historian who attempts to produce a secular history faces some real problems, especially if he or she shares the Jewish or Christian faith. Both of these faiths have incorporated the Israelite belief in God's acts in Israel into their own creeds. If the historian is not a believer, he or she has the problem of interpreting sources which are entirely motivated in their narratives by their belief. It seems safe to say that the history of Israel, like the life of Jesus, does not yield to the quest of a historical Israel. The secular historian cannot overcome the embarrassment of the fact that no one else ever wrote this kind of history.[34]

McKenzie goes on to suggest that these events are best apprehended by the symbolic form of myth—that which lies outside experience.

Reading the sacred page organically means recognizing it as the existential expression of objective reality. John Knox, the twentieth century

---

32. McKenzie, *Theology of the Old Testament*, 142.
33. Coogan, *Old Testament*, 206.
34. McKenzie, *Theology of the Old Testament*, 143–44.

theologian who taught at Union Theological Seminary, in explaining the nature of biblical myth, said every biblical myth contains two essential elements—the *existential expressive* and the *objective explanatory*.[35] The existential expressive is the use of imaginative language to express the deepest reality of life as we experience it. The first three chapters of Genesis, Knox said, are not happenings to which we could give times and dates and locations in earthly or interstellar space if we only knew enough. They are imaginative stories that are truly expressive of the human existential condition. The creation stories of Genesis are not, however, merely parables, instructive fables, metaphors, or similes. They are truly explanatory in an objective sense. Biblical myth is comprised of more than an emblematic meaning. "To find it true means finding it carries at its heart an objective or factual truth which can be expressed in no other way." It contains the objective explanatory as well as the existential expressive; indeed, in a truly biblical myth the two cannot be separated. "There is undoubtedly a difference," Knox insisted, "between a story which came into being to express the inner meaning of a known fact in nature or history, and a story which alters, or even invents the fact itself. In the one case we have a fact creating a story, in the other a story creating a fact."[36]

It should perhaps be further noted that Knox did not see every miracle story as possessing the character of true myth. A true biblical myth, Knox asserted, must be a "cosmically significant act of God," that is, it must be an act of "decisive importance for the world." Consequently, "not every miracle story deserves to be called a 'myth.' Only the indispensable story is worthy of the name."[37]

I have never been able to fully embrace the argument that miracles are impossibilities only if you think of the universe as a machine that works in one entirely predictable way as a closed system. I have always been more inclined to Marcus Borg's notion of "the limits of the spectacular." Although it is important, says Borg, "not to draw the limits too narrowly"; that "more things are possible, and more things happen, than the modern world view allows." Borg thinks, for example, that Jesus did perform paranormal healings that cannot simply be explained away as psychosomatic. "But," he asks, "do virgin births, multiplying loaves and fish, and changing water into wine ever happen anywhere?"[38] The healing miracles, therefore, seem entirely possible to me precisely because, apart from money grubbing faith healers,

35. Knox, *Myth and Truth*, 30.
36. Ibid., 69.
37. Ibid., 36.
38. Borg, *Reading the Bible*, 46–47.

astonishing healing events can and do occur. Neither do I find it difficult to believe that even some of the "nature miracles" of Jesus may be based on strange, but not impossible, actual events.

I am rather skeptical when it comes to what appears to be a suspension or reversal of the laws of nature—although the quantum physicists do give me considerable pause here. For instance, John Polkinghorne, physicist and Anglican priest, maintains in his book, *Quantum Physics and Theology: An Unexpected Kinship*, that the universe is not quite the closed mechanistic system it was once thought to be; that, indeed, novel phenomenon are real and possible. He writes, "Thus, the problem of miracle is not strictly a scientific problem, since science speaks only about what is usually the case and possesses no *a priori* power to rule out the possibility of unprecedented events in unprecedented circumstance."[39] Polkinghorne goes on to say,

> The attitude to miracles being taken here corresponds to the way in which John's gospel speaks of them as "signs" (John 2:11) and so on, events that are windows opening up a more profound perspective into the divine reality than that which can be glimpsed in the course of everyday experience, just as superconductivity opened up a window into the behavior of electrons in metals more revealing than the discoveries of Professor Ohm had been able to provide. Claims for the occurrence of miraculous events will have to be evaluated on a case-by-case basis. There can be no general theory to cover the character of unique events, but the refusal to contemplate the possibility of revelatory disclosures of an unprecedented kind would be an unacceptable limitation, imposed arbitrarily on the horizons of religious thought.[40]

If this rather postmodern perspective is placed alongside Knox's understanding of myth and miracle we are perhaps left with the view that belief in every miracle recorded in the Bible, however one chooses to define the miraculous, is not essential to the faith. But the possibility of astonishing phenomenon of a revelatory nature remains open and viable. The real question with any event, even one that seems mundane and of little consequence, is whether its mysterious transcendence is perceived.[41]

---

39. Polkinghorne, *Quantum Physics and Theology*, 33–37.
40. Ibid., 36.
41. Lewis, "Myth Became Fact," 63–67.

The Fallacy of Misplaced Concreteness as Mystic Signpost

Nearly all theological, biblical, and religious investigation, when done entirely in the context of modern Western rationalism, materialism, and scientism, struggles in the sticky web of the fallacy of misplaced concreteness—an old concept that was restated freshly in Alfred North Whitehead's process philosophy; namely, the mistake of taking what is an abstraction and treating it as if it were a concrete reality.

Whitehead saw his work as "speculative," by which he meant not the pursuit of bizarre notions or weird hunches, but speculative in the sense of a rigorous exploration of how everything, absolutely everything, fits together or coheres. Whitehead's philosophical interest, unlike the analytical philosophers of the early twentieth century who focused narrowly on analysis, was in the synthesis of ideas and the experience of reality; that is, in how they cohere.

> Coherence, as here employed, means that the fundamental ideas, in terms of which the scheme is developed, presuppose each other so that in isolation they are meaningless. This requirement does not mean that they are definable in terms of each other; it means that what is indefinable in one such notion cannot be abstracted from its relevance to the other notions. It is the ideal of speculative philosophy that its fundamental notions shall not seem capable of abstraction from each other. In other words, it is proposed that no entity can be conceived in complete abstraction from the system of the universe and that it is the business of speculative philosophy to exhibit this truth. This character is its coherence.[42]

For Whitehead, this lack of synthesis, neglect of coherence, or misplaced concreteness was more than a little problematic.

The organization of knowledge, as Herman Daly and John Cobb note, requires a high degree of abstraction; consequently, the more successful and established an academic discipline in its development, and the more its practitioners are socialized to think in these abstractions, the more elaborate the abstractions themselves become. In time, conclusions are confidently applied to the real world without realizing the degree of abstraction involved. "First, a discipline abstracts a discrete subject matter from the totality, treating it as if its connections with the remainder of the world were

---

42. Whitehead, *Process and Reality*, 3.

not important. Second, it develops a method suitable to the study of the subject matter that abstracts from those features accessible to the method."[43]

As a mathematician, Whitehead was well acquainted with the importance of abstractions, but he was also aware that treating abstractions as if they were concrete and possessed functions they cannot have leads to both scientific and metaphysical confusion. Daly and Cobb observe,

> Those shaped by the disciplinary organization of knowledge usually speak and act as if the disciplines additively covered the whole range of what is to be known. This assumes that the real world is made up additively of the elements and aspects into which it has been divided by the disciplines. But since each has been abstracted from its relations to all the others, what are here added together are not the elements and aspects themselves but only those features that for some particular purpose were abstracted from those relationships. The addition of those abstractions provides a great deal of information. It does not provide understanding.[44]

In saying this, Daly and Cobb are thinking primarily of economics as an academic discipline, and even suggest that other sciences, particularly the social sciences such as historical studies, are less susceptible to this sort of reification.

However, I am proposing that the cul-de-sac in which contemporary biblical studies finds itself has a great deal to do with the fallacy of misplaced concreteness. God is an abstraction and as soon as we speak of God concretely it is no longer God of whom we are speaking. This is, of course, just as true for process philosophy and theology as it is for any other system of thought. For example, as soon as process theologians begin to discourse on whether God can know the future, or on the temporal, mutable, and passable qualities of divinity, they are already caught in the fallacy of misplaced concreteness. Both the "Christ of faith" and the "Jesus of history" are abstractions. The cosmic Christ is beyond all concepts, and while academicians may invent various methods for the study of the person of Jesus, the results are frequently contradictory and provide information with little spiritual understanding. I appreciate what Frederick Denison Maurice said somewhere, "People are hungry for God, but instead we give them a system." Biblical and theological studies provide systems based on, as Lao Tsu might have put it, ten thousand fallacies of misplaced concreteness. But yes, the mystics turn toward the "moon."

---

43. Daly and Cobb, *For the Common Good*, 25, 121.
44. Daly and Cobb, *For the Common Good*, 121.

Process theology advocates for what is sometimes thought of as a "dipolar theism," which suggests God must be conceived as embodying opposing characteristics:

> One—Many
> Transcendent—Immanent
> Eternal—Temporal
> Mutable—Immutable
> Merciful—Just
> Simple—Complex.

This tends, of course, to lead to the problem in modernity which both Paul Tillich and John A. T. Robinson saw so clearly—it tends to reduce God to a bundle of concepts and catch God in the snare of misplaced concreteness. Indeed, it can easily reintroduce the problem of God as a "being" to be apprehended by human thought, emotion, and imagination. However, on the plus side of this unsolvable equation, it affirms what the mystics have always said: "That which is most profoundly spiritual is paradoxical and quite beyond all our words, thoughts, imaginations, and concepts. "Here," we say. "I have it right here in my cupped hands. Do you want to see?" And we open our hands only to expose that they are empty.

As John Cobb, who is one of the two foremost proponents of process theology, points out, Whitehead believed there is truth that can not be expressed in ordinary English. More than two thousand years ago the Buddhists encountered a similar problem; that is, they realized the insights they had discovered could not be expressed by their own language, and, consequently, developed techniques of meditation meant to break through discursive thinking.[45] "There are," as process thought acknowledges, "many methods of understanding that no academic discipline affirms."[46]

It does not seem at all unreasonable to conclude that process philosophy as a whole, and the fallacy of misplaced concreteness in particular, is an unambiguous gesture toward a more mystical, spiritual understanding of reality. If, as Christian Scripture asserts, "it is in God we live, move, and have our being" (Acts 17:28), and if "God is above all, through all, and in all" (Eph 4:6), then what can this mean other than that ultimate reality is One, and that the Mystery we call God is both the source of this unity and the Oneness itself. Everything is connected and is truly known only in the totality of its relations. Further, to paraphrase Saint Paul, if spiritual things must be spiritually discerned (1 Cor 2:14), then genuine understanding and the sort of wisdom that works for the common good of humanity and expands

---

45. Cobb, *Whitehead Word Book*, 8.
46. Whitehead, *Process and Reality*, 128.

spiritual awareness, requires, without ignoring the results of well-conducted research or the reasonable demands of intellectual inquiry, a more contemplative and genuinely theological orientation.

Conclusion

One sometimes hears Scripture needs to be read with "radical skepticism." But radical skepticism is as much of a dead end as radical credulity. What I am suggesting is that insofar as is possible, we read the Bible intelligently, studiously, and organically—with a certain willingness that allows a text to tell us about itself rather than imposing our own argumentative theories. The question then becomes: "How do the images, ideas, rhythms, and events of a passage organically mean?"

CHAPTER TEN

Progressive Orthodoxy in Eight Sermons

Knowing

How can I describe this generation? They are like children sitting in the market place and calling to each other, "We piped for you and you would not dance. We lamented and you would not mourn." For John came neither eating nor drinking, and people say, "He is possessed"; the Son of Man came eating and drinking, and they say, "Look at him! A glutton and a drinker, a friend of tax collectors and sinners! Yet God's wisdom is proved right by its results.

—Matt 11:16–19 REB

Carl Jung was once asked in a BBC interview whether he believed in God. His rather cryptic reply was, "I don't need to believe, I know." It has been a long time since I studied German and it's another one of those areas in my education where I have now forgotten more than I learned. But I suspect that while Jung answered the question in English he may have been thinking in his native Swiss German, where the word for "belief" can convey greater uncertainty than it does in English—something more akin to an opinion. Jung thought that a God he could not experience and that had no real impact on his life either did not or might as well not exist. So what Jung was saying was that he didn't really have an intellectual opinion as such about the theoretical existence of God, but rather knew God, experienced God, as a living reality.

This pericope, this Gospel reading, concerns not only who Jesus is, but also what we expect Jesus to look like when he appears to us. Chapter 11 begins with John the Baptist, now nagged by doubts, worrying whether he has been mistaken about Jesus. Alone and vulnerable in the sinister shadows of Herod's dungeon, John manages to get word to his disciples to ask Jesus one critical question, "Are you the Expected One, or shall we look for someone else?" Jesus's answer as to who he is, which includes his assessment of John, might be paraphrased something like this: "It all depends on what you are looking for. Were you looking for a celebrity, for someone powerful, for someone sophisticated or magical or impressive in the eyes of the world? If so I'm not the one. If you are looking for a messiah who brings healing, who encourages those who have lost heart, who teaches mercy and forgiveness and self-sacrifice in a world riddled with greed, violence, competitiveness, and narcissism, then I am the one you are looking for—the one you are hoping for."

The people, "the multitudes" as Matthew calls them, have their doubts about both Jesus and John. They said, and I am, of course, again paraphrasing, "You know John was a strange guy—a little crazy. Like a lot of other religious hermits out there in the desert, he was a little 'different.' And this Jesus is supposed to be a holy person, the Son of Man, but he's just a freeloader. All he does is eat and drink—a lot."

"Well," says Jesus, "here is how I see you. You are like children who want to be in charge of how the game is played. You want everyone to dance and sing to your tune. You're angry because neither John nor I allow you to define us—who I am is not determined by your expectations." These people, like many we may know, have their obscurantist theories about what messiah ought to be, and consequently cannot see the Christ even when staring him in the face.

Jung's interviewer was asking something like this: "Dr. Jung, you are a brilliant person, we are all in awe of you. Could you tell us what you believe, what you have figured out about God?" Jung's reply was, in effect, "I haven't figured anything out about God. It is not possible to contain God in some theoretical box in our mind, but I have discovered in my own experience that mysterious reality we call God." It is highly unlikely that we are ever going to find some definitive mathematical proof for the existence of God, or of Jesus as the cosmic Christ, but it is possible for any one of us to discover and to know the reality. The great Jewish scholar and mystic Abraham Joshua Heschel once said, "God is not a being whose existence we can prove with our syllogisms, but a reality, in the face of which, when becoming alive to it, all concepts become clichés."

Discovery, both scientific and spiritual, is made possible when we assume the attitude of humility, the attitude of attentive listeners. Science itself, physical science, has made the most progress when men and women, thirsty for knowledge, have set aside their own presuppositions and biases as best they can, and instead have been open to what nature itself has presented to them. I think it was Einstein who said that what we must learn to do scientifically is allow the universe to simply tell us about itself. This is equally true of the quest for wisdom, for spirituality, for the essence of religion and theology.

You may be familiar with C. S. Lewis's wonderfully humorous story in *The Great Divorce* about the ghost who takes a bus trip from hell on an excursion to heaven. The ghost chooses to return to the joyless city, the grey town, rather than stay in heaven because he cannot or will not give up his intellectual affectations. Here is what he says:

> But you have never asked me what my paper is about! I'm taking the text about growing up to the measure of the stature of Christ and working out an idea I am sure you'll be interested in. I am going to point out how people always forget that Jesus was a comparatively young man when he died. He would have outgrown some of his earlier views you know, if he'd lived. . . . I'm going to ask my audience to consider what his mature views would have been. . . . What a different Christianity we might have had if only the Founder had reached his full stature!"

The humor of Lewis's point in this caricature is somewhat lost today in its uncanny resemblance to the actual state of contemporary "Jesus studies." Did you know that Jesus's grave has been found, that there are better sources for studying the life of Jesus than the Four Gospels, or that there is a conspiracy to conceal the truth about Jesus—what he taught, what he did, what he was like? Did you know that Jesus said less than twenty-five percent of the sayings attributed to him in the Gospels?

During my two years at Bakersfield Community College I was on the debate squad, captain of the debate team. One of the main things I learned from debate is that there is no proposition, regardless of the facts, that cannot be plausibly debated. Now that is less true, not impossible but less true, when we are dealing with hard science, but biblical scholarship is not science. The fields of biblical studies, archaeology, and historiography can and should, but often do not, involve rigorous academic discipline. But they are not hard science. Biblical scholars using the same techniques get wildly different results. Conjectures based on exaggeration and manipulation are often asserted and assumed as proven fact. Nevertheless, many people find them convincing. Secular biblical scholars working at various academic institutions advocate an attitude of "radical skepticism" as a kind of scientific principle. But an attitude of radical skepticism is no more helpful in the search for truth than radical credulity. Neither attitude will help you in your search for truth—if truth is what you want.

We will never come to the kind of "knowing" Carl Jung was talking about if we become entangled in an endless web of academic speculation. If you are on a "head trip," you will never arrive in the realm of the Spirit—not because this sort of knowing contradicts reason but because it transcends it.

The people Jesus addresses in this passage do not believe, for the simple reason that Jesus is not what they want in a messiah. Someone speaking on a college campus was once asked, "If God is real and Jesus is the Christ, why do most intellectuals not believe?" She answered, "Most intellectuals do not believe for the same reason most nonintellectuals don't believe. They do not want to surrender to what that would mean." If you are looking for a Jesus who will dance to your tune you will never find him—never know him.

The way to know Jesus, with this Jungian and biblical sort of knowing, is to open our mind, heart, soul, spirit, whatever you want to call it, to the immediate and self-authenticating presence of Christ's Spirit. Jesus said, "What I teach comes from the One who sent me. Anyone who follows my teachings will know whether I have made these things up myself, or whether they come from God."

There is a story that has grown in importance to me in proportion to the length I have traveled this path. In the year 155, when the Romans arrested and demanded that Polycarp, bishop of Smyrna, renounce Christ and acknowledge Caesar as Lord or burn at the stake, Polycarp responded, "For eighty and six years I have served Christ as Lord and he has never done me anything but good. How can I renounce him now?" And when they went to tie Polycarp's hands before setting him on fire, he said, "You do not need to tie my hands. Do you think that I cannot endure your fire for the love of Christ?" And unfettered in body, mind, or spirit he died there in the flames. Polycarp died well, and dying well, dying free, depends on living well, and living well depends on an attitude of openness to an experiential knowing that transcends restless belief and transforms the spirit. *Amen.*

The Ancestors of Our Faith

This is an account of the descendants of Abraham's son Isaac. Isaac's father was Abraham. When Isaac was forty years old he married Rebecca, daughter of Bethuel, the Aramaean from Paddanaram and sister of Laban the Aramaean. Isaac appealed to the Lord on behalf of his wife because she was childless; the Lord gave heed to his entreaty, and Rebecca conceived. The children pressed on each other in her womb, and she said, "If all is well, why am I like this?" She went to seek guidance of the Lord, who said to her, "Two nations are in your womb, two peoples going their way from birth. One will be stronger than the other; the elder will be servant to the younger." When her time had come, there were indeed twins in her womb. The first to come out was reddish and covered with hair like a cloak, and they named him Esau. Immediately afterwards, his brother was born with his hand grasping Esau's heel, and he was given the name Jacob. Isaac was sixty years old when they were born.

—Gen 25:19–26 REB

"These are the descendants," our reading from the ancient book of Genesis begins, this is the story of Abraham, Isaac and his wife Rivka, and the twin boys, Jacob and Esau, to whom she gave birth and who became two nations. But what is that to us, we may wonder; or, as a rather restive teenager once put it to me in a youth group, "Why should we care about a bunch of people that have been dead for a long time?" Regardless of where her question came from or the attitude with which it came, it was a good one, pertinent to our exploration of this text—to our swirling doubts and beliefs.

A therapist, in one way or another, says to everyone entering counseling, "Tell me your story." Spiritual directors invite people to share the story of their faith journey. "When, if ever," they may ask, "have you experienced a sense of Divine Mystery, a feeling for what is transcendent and infinitely sacred? Tell me the history of you and God." Our memories are an integral part of who we are. Henri J. M. Nouwen said, "When we cut down our memories to a pleasant, comfortable size, we become strangers to ourselves." Our memories are not, of course, just recollections of inert bits of data, they are profoundly emotional connections with other people who matter to us. Psychologists tell us that family issues are actually transmitted from one generation to another. Forbearers of whom we may have no direct knowledge have played a part in who we are today. My father died when I was an infant. My older brother, who is my only surviving sibling, still tells me stories of the father I never knew—stories that are, in some strange way, integral to who I am. It's not just the stories that predate my own personal memory, but the interwoven lives of these people, this family, from whom and from whence I came, that has shaped and formed me. So Scripture repeatedly says, "Here is the story that shapes and forms the people of God, experiences that if you are a Jew or a Christian form your own story. Here are your spiritual ancestors and the bearers of your spiritual genetics.

But can we have confidence in these stories, in these memories? There are biblical scholars who argue that the answer is "no," that the stories of Abraham and Sarah, of Isaac and Rebecca, of Jacob and Leah and Rachel and their twelve sons and one daughter are pure legend—that these people, this family, never existed except in imaginative folklore. And, it is true that outside of the Bible there is little information regarding the time of the patriarchs and matriarchs of our faith. Much of what we do know comes from archeological finds at places like Nuzi, located in modern Iraq, and Mari, which was once a thriving city in northern Syria. At one time it was asserted that the customs described in the patriarchal narratives were so strange that the stories themselves could not possibly be true. After years of debating the finds at these two sites, as well as others, it is pretty clear that the laws and customs we read about in the patriarchal stories of Genesis accurately reflect the laws and customs of the biblical patriarchal period, and not those of a later time in which it has been argued they were composed.

The names of people, places, and cities cited furnish strong links between the Hebrew patriarchs and their traditional home in northern Mesopotamia. The characters Abraham and Sarah, Isaac and Rebecca, Jacob and Leah and Rachel, and Joseph and his brothers, all have the feel of real and individual personalities—with whose struggles and quirks we can identify, admire, or criticize. All of this has led many scholars to abandon the idea that the patriarchal stories are the inventions of a much later period in Israel's history. It is now common to hear that these stories are indeed ancient traditions that have been edited centuries later so as to furnish guidance and help in times of national and ethnic crises. I am not sure why some automatically assume this should negatively affect our trust in the text. Isn't this what we do all the time in sermons?

Here is a very simple example of what I mean: A couple of years ago Community Resource Center, which coordinates revolving homeless shelters, asked if our church would host the two weeks before Christmas—not a convenient time. But I remember the vestry, with some humor and appropriating the nativity story in the Gospels, responding, "What are we going to say—that there is no room in the inn?" Now, if some scholars were reading about this two thousand years from now and plying their expert methods they might argue: "These people in Encinitas, California, were, around 2009 CE, concerned with the lack of homeless shelters and with the problem of providing shelter at an inconvenient time. Consequently, they edited the older story of Jesus's nativity in such a way as to find guidance for their own situation." The truth, of course, is that the answer to a contemporary problem was readily found in an ancient text. We look at a text and we see a meaning for our own situation, answers to our own questions in our own time. A text may, in fact, have several layers of meaning. There is a difference between applying a biblical story to the here and now and making up a story that is then applied.

This leads to the question of whether it matters if the stories of the patriarchs, whether any biblical story, is true. A Native American shaman is often quoted as having said, whenever he began to tell tribal stories, "I don't know that this happened, but it is a true story." In this sense, a story of something that never happened may be true in that it expresses a positive sentiment or offers wise advice on how to live. We can say, then, that the story of the three little pigs never happened, but it is a true story. But if Abraham and Sarah, and Isaac and Rebecca and their children and their children's children, never lived, if they never experienced anything remotely like what we are told, then "the great cloud of witnesses" of which Scripture speaks dissipates and disappears in the blue air. God has not acted, and regardless of our happy jingles, lovely slogans, or lofty sentiments, there is no purpose to anything other than what we invent. Like a solitary sailor lost on a raft at sea, we are alone, drifting in the dark cosmic void, making up cheerful songs to trick ourselves into feeling better. Quite frankly, I don't quite know why any of us would want to be in a place like this church gathering—read a self-help book, go for a jog or a cup of coffee with a friend, relax with a round of golf, or go sit on the beach. But if these were real people who encountered God in real experiences then that is another matter entirely.

In the second millennium BCE, most, perhaps all, of the world was bound in its thinking by the concept of the eternal return—an endlessly reoccurring cycle of birth, life, and death. No beginnings and no ends, just an endlessly turning wheel—everything important already decided, nothing new ever happening. The only advice to be given anyone is like that in the psychedelic song by the rock group Blood, Sweat, and Tears, "Spinning wheel got to go round. Ride a painted pony. Let the spinning wheel spin." But in Ur of the Chaldees a man and woman, who have strange dreams and experience mystical visions, come to believe that their God is calling them to end their old, predictable, comfortable life and to begin an arduous journey into a new land. Little by little in their ordinary lives, we begin to see signs of something transcendent. As they listen and as they journey, they begin to realize their journey is a journey into the future—into infinite new possibilities. And little by little, they learn to trust God for this great unknown future. And the more they trust God, the more they experience God as friend.

I close with these words from *The Gifts of the Jews* by Thomas Cahill:

> Since it cannot be proven that God exists, it can hardly be shown that God spoke to Avraham, Moshe, or Isaiah. Each person must decide if the Voice that spoke to the patriarchs and the prophets speaks to him, too. If it does, there is no question of needing proof, any more than we require proof of anyone we believe in. For in the last analysis, one does not believe *that* God exists, as one believes that Timbuktu or the constellation Andromeda exists. One believes *in* God, as one believes *in* a friend—or one believes nothing.

Amen.

Strength When the Power is Doubted

Nor was it out of deference to anyone else that you gave them amnesty for their misdeeds, for no one can say, "What have you done?" Who can challenge your verdict? Who can appear against you in court to plead the cause of the guilty? For there is no other god but you; all the world is your concern, and there is none to whom you must prove the justice of your sentence. There is no king or other ruler who can outface you on behalf of those whom you have punished. But you are just and you order all things justly, counting it alien to your power to condemn anyone to undeserved punishment. For your strength is the source of justice, and it is because you are Master of all that you are lenient to all. You show your strength when people doubt whether your power is absolute; it is when they know it and yet are insolent that you punish them. But you, with strength at your command, judge in mercy and rebuke us in great forbearance; for the power is yours to exercise whenever you choose.

—Wisdom of Solomon 11:17 REB

I WANT TO FOCUS on just one sentence from one verse of the Wisdom of Solomon: "For You, O Lord, show Your strength when people doubt the completeness of Your power." At times, it feels like the pain and sorrows of this world will overwhelm goodness and kindness. In Norman Mailer's novel *The Naked and the Dead*, General Cummings tells young Lieutenant Hearn, "In the future, the only morality will be the morality of power." He means, of course, that in the future it will be those who have learned to wield a dark and brutal power who will prevail. Sometimes when watching the news or reading the papers it is easy to feel like Cummings's fictional prophecy has come to pass—there is so much greed, so much violence, so much deceit, and so much hunger and disease and death caused by it all. Or, in the words of an old song, "Games People Play" by Joe South, so much evil done in the name of morality:

> *People coming up to you*
> *singing glory hallelujah*
> *And then they sock it to you*
> *in the name of the Lord.*

In our own personal lives there can be so much darkness that we lose hope that anything good will ever happen again. This verse from the Wisdom of Solomon is about people like the sadistic General Cummings, but it is also about people like those tormented by him. It is about a loss of confidence in the completeness of the Power that is greater than ourselves. "For You, O Lord, show Your strength when people doubt the completeness of Your power."

Although ultimately this text encompasses everyone, an Adolph Hitler, an Edi Amin, a secular, decadent, rich, and powerful twenty-first century America, and every man and every woman on this planet, it refers here specifically to Pharaoh and it refers to the people already there in Canaan with their cruel practices of child sacrifice and drunken sex orgies as worship, so arrogant and seemingly invincible with their walled cities and their heavily armored soldiers. "Oh," said Moses's spies, "the people there are like giants and we are like grasshoppers, insects, before them." "For You, O Lord, show Your strength when people doubt the completeness of Your power."

So Pharaoh doubted the Power. You know the story. The Hebrews, once welcomed guests in Egypt, have been enslaved. There is not much outside the Bible about Hebrew slavery in Egypt. But if the Hebrews were small in number we would not expect to find them much mentioned. There is a scene of slaves, including Palestinian slaves, which has been found in the tomb of an Egyptian official. The discovery of the store cities of Pithom and Ramesses in the Nile Delta, as named in Exod 1:11, also point to Hebrew slaves in Egypt and to Moses as more than figures of pure folklore. There is no more reason to doubt the actual existence of Moses as formative in the history of Israel than for doubting the role of Buddha as the founder of Buddhism. Moses courageously asks Pharaoh to release the captives, to let the people go so that they can worship God and so that they can follow along the way that God has called them to follow. Pharaoh arrogantly responds, "So who is this god that I should listen?" Pharaoh is brutally obstinate. There are plagues of grasshoppers and frogs, hail, blood flowing in the Nile, and the deaths of the firstborn. The Ipuwer Papyrus, probably written between

1850 and 1600 BCE, is a poetic description of Egypt in a time of crises and parallels the plagues of exodus at several points—crocodiles gorge themselves on bodies floating in a bloody Nile. Passover night comes and Moses leads the Hebrews in flight out of Egypt, but pursued by the Egyptian soldiers, they are quickly trapped with their backs against the Red Sea. Then something astounding happens to these vulnerable, frightened, desperate runaway slaves, Moses raises his arms and the waters part, and as they pass through the waters to the safety of the other side, Moses lowers his arms and the walls of water collapse on the threatening soldiers—"death," as the New Testament puts it, is indeed, "swallowed up in victory." "For You, O Lord, show Your strength when people doubt the completeness of Your power."

You may have heard the story of the little boy who went to Sunday school and on the way home his mother asked him what he had learned that day. "Well," he said, "we learned how Moses and the Jews escaped from Egypt. The Egyptian army trapped them at the edge of the Red Sea. So Moses had the corps of engineers throw up a pontoon bridge. Pharaoh's soldiers in their tanks and Humvees were chasing them across and just about to catch them. But when the last person got across, Moses had his commandos blow up the bridge with plastic explosives. The soldiers and their tanks all splashed down in the sea and drowned, but Moses and all the people were safe." His incredulous mother asked, "Is that really what your teacher said?" "No," the little boy answered, "but if I told it to you the way she told us you would never believe it."

I have come to think that the more dramatic, spectacular, or literal shape a biblical story takes in our own mind, if, for example, we picture this story like something out of a Cecil B. De Mille movie, Charlton Heston parting the Pacific Ocean, then the more problematic it becomes for those of us with something of a skeptical bent to our nature. We think that our intellectual struggle is with the event itself when in reality it is with our own imagination. If you have difficulty with the Exodus story, try to picture this: Imagine Egypt in a time of crisis, suffering from multiple disasters, plagues, and violence that can be described in the same poetic language as that used in the Ipuwer Papyrus. Under the leadership of Moses, Hebrew slaves, how many doesn't matter just don't picture an evacuation of Los Angeles, flee from their forced labor. They make not for the Red Sea itself, which is an inaccurate translation, but for the Sea of Reeds, one of the swamps or wetlands. At low tide, the Children of Israel, on foot, are able to make it across, but the Egyptians in their chariots become mired in the mud. It is a deadly blunder. As the tide rises, men and horses drown. For the powerful Egyptians, with their long glorious history, it is not a terribly significant event, but for the Hebrews, it is a miraculous, breathtaking deliverance. "For You,

O Lord, show Your strength when people doubt the completeness of Your power." It is not the theatrical aspects of a biblical event that matter most, but the signs of something transcendent in it.

The same is true of the settlement of Canaan to which this text alludes. If you read the book of Joshua like a fantasy conquest it may very well seem unreal—and difficult to square with the archaeological record. Archeology is not a hard science, but it is an academic discipline and can't simply be ignored. Military activity was certainly part of the process by which Israel gained control of the land; however, the emergence of Israel was slow and complicated, and involved, as the Bible itself seems to indicate, the peaceful incorporation of some of the Canaanites. For the people of Israel this too was miraculous—an act of God. To think that they, the people who had been slaves in Egypt, now possessed the land of Canaan was a sign of a Power greater than themselves. "For You, O Lord, show Your strength when people doubt the completeness of Your power."

Let me ask you this: When you look back over your own life are there any transcendent moments, times when you felt trapped, helpless, or afraid, and yet discovered within them the very presence and power of God. Let me share with you again what the young Jewish psychiatrist Viktor Frankl wrote after his liberation from the Nazi death camp at Auschwitz.

> One day, a few days after the liberation, I walked through the country past flowering meadows, for miles and miles. . . . Larks rose to the sky and I could hear their joyous song. There was no one to be seen for miles around, there was nothing but the wide earth and sky and the lark's jubilation and the freedom of space. I stopped, looked around, and up to the sky—and then I went down on my knees. At that moment there was little I knew of myself or of the world—I had but one sentence in my mind—always the same: "I called to the Lord from my narrow prison and he answered me from the freedom of space." How long I knelt there and repeated this sentence memory can no longer recall. But I know that on that day, in that hour, my new life started.

"For You, O Lord, show Your strength when people doubt the completeness of Your power." *Amen.*

The Bread We Eat

After leaving that region Jesus took the road by the Sea of Galilee, where he climbed a hill and sat down. Crowds flocked to him, bringing with them the lame, blind, dumb, and crippled, and many other sufferers; they put them down at his feet, and he healed them. Great was the amazement of the people when they saw the dumb speaking, the crippled made strong, the lame walking, and the blind with their sight restored, and they gave praise to the God of Israel. Jesus called his disciples and said to them, "My heart goes out to these people; they have been with me now for three days and have nothing to eat. I do not want to send them away hungry; they might faint on their way." The disciples replied, "Where in this remote place can we find bread enough to feed such a crowd?" "How many loaves have you?" Jesus asked. "Seven," they replied, "and a few small fish." So he ordered the people to sit down on the ground; then he took the seven loaves and the fish, and after giving thanks to God he broke them and gave hem to the disciples and the disciples gave them to the people. They all ate and were satisfied; and seven baskets were filled with what was left over. Those who were fed numbered four thousand men, not counting women and children. After dismissing the crowd, he got into a boat and went to the neighborhood of Magadan.

—Matt 15:29–39 REB

At its first reading, this story, in spite of its talk of the miraculous, feels rather straightforward and simple. On a solitary hill away from the villages and towns, Jesus, in response to the most basic of human needs, provides the most basic of human necessities—bread to eat. But a closer reading reveals multiple allusions—subtle, polyvalent, profound.

It alludes to Israel's wanderings in the desert and to God's feeding all the people with *manna*—"bread from heaven." It alludes to Elisha's miraculous feeding of the hundred. It contrasts the banquet of Jesus with the banquet of Herod. At Herod's banquet there is opulence, arrogance, scheming, and murder. At Jesus' banquet there is simplicity, healing, generosity. It is worded in such way that its allusions point both back in history and forward—forward to the Last Supper and the Christian Eucharist. We can't read it without being caught by the liturgical formula of the mass—took, blessed, broke, gave. But its forward movement continues on, transcends space and time in alluding to the divine kingdom pictured in both Jewish and Christian spirituality as the great heavenly banquet.

Every year when this story of the Feeding of Four Thousand appears in the lectionary, the Episcopal Diocese of Colorado celebrates Loaves and Fishes Sunday. In all the parishes people fill grocery bags, bring them to church, place them around the altar, bless them, and when the service is over they are distributed to food banks or in whatever way the parish desires. Among the first sermons we heard in an Episcopal Church was one preached on Loaves and Fishes Sunday. The priest explained that there was nothing supernatural about this story, that what happened is that in the willingness of the few to share what they had, everyone was inspired to share, and all were fed and their hunger satisfied. A lovely interpretation, and perhaps true. The well-known and respected New Testament scholar Daniel Harrington asks in his commentary on the Gospel according to Matthew, "Was there an event behind this highly symbolic narrative, and what was its nature?" His own answer to that question is, "This is probably a case in which we will never be absolutely certain about the event behind the text, and it is fruitless to spend too much time and effort in worrying about it." Harrington does note that this story meets the test of multiple attestations. It occurs in all four gospels, and the more places in which a story appears the more likely it is at least based on some objective reality. It's just that there is no way to know exactly what happened or how—only that something astounding transpired. Whether a miracle of generosity or the supernatural multiplication of one loaf of bread that became two and then a thousand doesn't really matter. What matters is where it points. You may be familiar with the Zen saying, "The one who watches the finger pointing to the moon misses seeing the moon." I love what the Jesuit William Johnston at Sophia University in Japan wrote.

> Christ is the moon because the people who wrote the Gospel are leading their readers to a vision not only of the historical Jesus but of the risen Christ, the cosmic Christ, the Christ who was

there at the beginning. . . . The risen Christ is so far beyond all concepts that we find Paul struggling with all kinds of words to express the inexpressible. . . . For Paul, Christ is a "secret" or a "mystery" or whatever you want to call it, and Paul keeps pointing one finger after another at the moon that no human eye can descry. The poor scholars get all tied up in Paul's fingers; the mystic turns toward the moon.

So what do we see when we look to where this reading is pointing? We see the face of God in the historical Jesus, the man Jesus, whose life is absolutely centered—centered in the Father, in the quiet awareness of God's presence, a presence stretching beyond the furthest horizon but closer and more intimate than our most inward thought.

Upon hearing of John's death, Jesus seeks out a desert place, a quiet place to be alone with the Alone. The highest form of prayer, of praise and of communion with God in the Old Testament is silence. "Commune with your hearts and be still," says the Psalm, and, "To Thee silence is praise." From Habakkuk, "The Lord is in His Holy Temple; let all the earth keep silence before Him." God is known and experienced in the Hebrew Scriptures in attentive silence, watchful stillness, and calm wakefulness. What do we see? We see Jesus communing with God, at one with God, in the great silence.

We see Holy Scripture pointing to the face of God in the historical Jesus, in the man Jesus—the compassion and healing of God revealed. "When Jesus went ashore He saw the multitude and had compassion for them." Compassion involves the qualities of love and sympathy and empathy. It is the desire to do something about the suffering of others. But it is not a feeling or a desire alone; it is what moves us to act to relieve suffering, doing something for the lonely, the frightened, the desperate who have little or no resources is compassion. All of the great religions of the world teach compassion. Some urge compassion on the basis that all humanity is one, or that we are all in this thing called life together, but the Judeo/Christian tradition urges compassion on the basis that the very nature of the one we call God is somehow mysteriously, warmly, personal, loving, and caring. That's what we see when we see Jesus.

We see, the Divine healing of compassion in Jesus. "But for you who revere my name," says the Prophet Malachi, "the sun of righteousness will rise with healing in its wings." Zacharias, the father of Saint John the Baptist, may be alluding to Malachi in his own prophecy when he says something very similar in the Gospel of Luke, referring to "the tender mercy of our God, with which the Sun from on high shall visit us." Biblically, "to visit" is not to make a social call, but to be a helping presence. There is pretty much a consensus among scholars that, at the very least, Jesus was known by those who encountered him in his own day as someone of profound and powerful presence—a healing presence.

The healings of Jesus could be interpreted psychosomatically. But if by that it is meant that both the disorder and the healing were entirely "in someone's head," then that is not a very satisfactory explanation. But if we mean that someone radiating hope, confidence, and caring might be able to cure even organic diseases then that is a much stronger interpretation. Scientifically, we are just at the edges of recognizing the curative properties of hope. Be that as it may, the people who witnessed these healing events, whether we agree or disagree with the accuracy of their account, were convinced that there was a spiritual force that flowed from God through Jesus to the sick, the hungry, the lonely, the discouraged, and the afraid. This story, this lesson, then points to the healing, compassionate One.

The most powerful vision, the most profound symbol, the strongest allusion in this reading is to the Eucharist. Implied by that allusion in this reading, but made explicit in John's extended narrative, is that Jesus is Himself the Bread of Heaven—the Bread of Life. "I am the living bread," says Jesus, "that came down out of heaven. Those who eat of this bread shall live forever." What a mind-boggling self-assertion to make unless the person making it is a hopeless narcissistic, a megalomaniac, or knows something that no one else knows, and knows it simply and sanely.

Of course, there is that haunting question from Jesus Christ Superstar:

> Jesus Christ, Jesus Christ
> Who are you? What have you sacrificed?
> Do you think you're what they say you are?

Who did Jesus think he was? What was His intention? Did he know what he was doing or did things just race crazily out of control? Did he really think He was the Messiah, the Son of God, and the very "Bread of life?" Those are complex questions, but the simple answer is this: If you mean did Jesus know He was divine in the same way that I know I was born the youngest of four children in Bakersfield, or that I'm bald, or had oatmeal for breakfast this morning, then the answer is no. However, Jesus clearly believed that he was called to do and to be for the oppressed people of Israel and the world what only God can do and be. Jesus believed passionately that it was His vocation to accomplish what Scripture declared only God alone can accomplish. This is a different sort of knowing than a supernatural, magical sort of awareness. It is something that can only be known by living into it. I know that Brenda loves me, but how do I know that? There is no scientific way to objectively prove it beyond all possibility of doubt. I know only by living into it day-by-day, month-by-month, year-by-year. Jesus's knowledge of divinity, of Himself as Messiah or Christ, Son of God, Son of Man, Lord of Life, and Bread of Heaven was grasped in faith, supported in prayer, tested in confrontation and suffering, and implemented in compassion. And that's the same way that you can know who Jesus is—the same way in which Jesus can become for you the Bread of Life—you have to live it to know it. We only know we are eating good bread when we eat it. *Amen.*

Calm in the Storm

As soon as they had finished, he made the disciples embark and cross to the other side ahead of him, while he dismissed the crowd; then he went up the hill by himself to pray. It had grown late and he was alone. The boat was already some distance from the shore, battling with a head wind and a rough sea. Between three and six in the morning he came towards them walking across the lake. When the disciples saw him walking on the lake they were so shaken they cried out in terror, "It is a ghost!" But at once Jesus spoke to them: "Take heart! It is I; do not be afraid." Peter called to him: "Lord, if it is you, tell me to come to you over the water." "Come," said Jesus. Peter got down out of the boat, and walked over the water towards Jesus. But when he saw the strength of the gale he was afraid; and beginning to sink, he cried, "Save me, Lord!" Jesus at once reached out and caught hold of him. "Why did you hesitate?" he said. "How little faith you have!" Then they climbed into the boat; and the wind dropped. And the men in the boat fell at his feet exclaiming, "You must be the Son of God."

—MATT 14:22–33 REB

I AM BY NATURE a skeptic—perhaps the result of being the youngest of two sisters and a brother who thought it their solemn duty to see to it that I was firmly grounded in reality, or maybe they just mischievously enjoyed spoiling fantasies. I never at any point in my life believed in Santa Claus or the Easter Bunny or in the stork that brings babies. I don't believe space aliens have visited us. I am not easily scammed, not even by people who claim they can grow hair on my head; although, I do sometimes permit myself to be scammed for the sake of the scammer. And I have serious doubt that anyone will ever discover intelligent life on Earth. To those who know this about me it probably seems incongruous with my rather orthodox Christian beliefs. I believe, as I declared in my ordination to the priesthood, that the Old and New Testaments contain all things necessary for my salvation—salvation not only in the evangelical sense, but also in the biblical sense of what is large, spacious, expansive, and free from anything that would narrow or constrict the life God has given me.

I have a friend, a Presbyterian chaplain, who says that whenever she recites the creed she crosses her fingers behind her back. I do not cross my fingers when I say the creed, but I open my heart so that it infuses me with an inexplicable strength. I believe Scripture is inspired, literally "God breathed," not in the fundamentalist sense of inerrancy but as, in the words of Berkeley Mickelson, "the energizing power of God in the lives, discourses, and writings of his servants so that from these writings we can see life with God as supreme, and that we ought to live, move, and have our being in relationship to God." I myself, of course, don't see anything at all incongruous in any of this. It is that skeptical part of myself that compels me to ask how the Bible can be read so that it makes sense to both the mind and the heart. How can it be read with integrity and faithfulness to the text? When my own doubts arise within me, I now recognize them as old friends who nag me into a deeper faith. Doubt is not the opposite of faith—"faithlessness is the opposite of faith." Doubt and faith dance together, performing many intricate and rhythmic moves until at last the moves are forgotten and nothing remains but the passion of the dance—divine intimacy. Many times in reading or listening to the sacred text, while dancing the dance, I have felt interfused with a powerful and loving presence that has lifted me up out of myself, and made God as real to me as anything I can see, touch, taste, or feel.

I am well aware, of course, that contrary to my own experience, reading the Bible or reading it in a particular way, is for some a serious obstacle to faith. The scholar Bart Ehrman, for example, tells how as a graduate student at Princeton he chose to write an interpretative paper on Mark 2:25–26 for one of his classes. In that pericope Jesus tells the story of how when David was in need and hungry, with King Saul in deadly pursuit, David went into the house of God, and with the help of Abiathar the High Priest, ate the sacred Bread of Presence. The problem is that as the story is told in the Old Testament it is Ahimelech, the father of Abiathar, and not Abiathar who is High Priest and who assists David. Only later when Saul murders Ahimelech in revenge does his son Abiathar become High Priest. Ehrman found this technical discrepancy troubling. In fact, it was the moment he rejected the Christian faith and embraced agnosticism. Ehrman says that once he came to the conclusion that Mark had made a mistake the floodgates opened. "If there could be one picayune mistake in Mark 2, maybe there could be others. Maybe when Jesus says later in Mark 4 that the mustard seed is 'the smallest of all seeds on the earth,'" says Ehrman, "I didn't need to come up with a fancy explanation for how the mustard seed is the smallest of all seeds when I know full well it isn't."

What Ehrman doesn't get is that it just doesn't matter whether Ahimelech or Abiathar was the High Priest who gave David consecrated bread to eat, or whether Jesus called the mustard seed the smallest of all seeds when we know that according to standard weights and measures it is not. Bart Ehrman is one of those scholars, and there are a number of them, who has renounced the Christian faith but continues to interpret Scripture from the fundamentalist perspective they learned in their youth. They try to read the Bible much like one might read a bank statement, thinking any one error renders the whole thing hopelessly wrong. They imagine that Scripture must be wholly inerrant or it is not Scripture. Whether coming from a fundamentalist belief perspective or a fundamentalist agnostic perspective, conclusions about the nature of Scripture rooted in such perceptions are largely irrelevant.

I once wrote an article for a journal on a bit of denominational history that required original research. I did personal interviews, read stacks of papers stored in old barns in Oregon, explored crumbling documents in locked library archives, and here is what I found that is pertinent to our discussion: Different people described the same events from different perspectives—sometimes varying from one another in details. But that didn't mean the event did not happen. Secondly, there were things I could have left out, comments and stories, and it would have made no difference to the overall veracity of what I had written. All truth is true, but not every truth is of equal significance. Most of you will show more understanding in what you hear than Bart Ehrman, for all his erudition—that is, you will be able to distinguish between what is meant to be heard as hard fact and what is meant to be heard in a more literary sense. Someone who owns a racehorse might say, "My horse is really fast." That is the basic fact. They might also say, "My horse is really fast—can run the quarter of a mile in twenty-one seconds," or, "My horse is really fast—as fast as polished steel." Both statements are factual; they just express the fact in a different way.

So we have this challenging story of Jesus walking on water, calming stormy wind and waves. The text obviously raises numerous questions: Was Jesus walking on the water like you might walk across the hardwood floor? Or, as some New Testament scholars argue, was Jesus out in the rough surf, in the strong current? Did Jesus, as the text indicates, invite Peter to join him? And did Peter, losing confidence, almost drown? Did Peter have to be saved by Jesus? Is this one story or two that have been joined? With Jesus's stilling words, with his prayer of peace, did the sea become a dead calm or did the storm simply lessen in its fierce intensity? Certainly the disciples were no longer so tossed about by fear. Was there a surreal quality to whatever actually happened? And was this a pivotal moment for the disciples—a moment of danger and opportunity, a very real crisis and a very real saving that was then told more poetically, more metaphorically, in the New Testament Gospels? Was this a real event and a true sign pointing to something, or someone, transcendent?

Many years ago a man who was going through difficult times, he had made and lost a lot of money, requested to take Brenda and me to lunch one Sunday after church. His wife was a member but I had never seen him much before this crisis in his life. When we were settled in at our table in the restaurant he said, "You know I have been coming to church lately, and I have been thinking quite a bit about baptism. What I want to know is how much I have to believe before I can be baptized?" At first that sounds like a funny question, but it is a good one. What he had recognized was that there seem to be some values, convictions, beliefs, and commitments that are essential to the Christian life, but others that are not so central or necessary. The stories of Jesus walking on the water and stilling the storm are not absolutely crucial for our faith. You could take them out of the Bible and it would essentially change nothing; nevertheless, they point to something very real and significant, and they tell us something magnificent about Jesus and the character of God.

Just what any event tells us spiritually tends to depend, of course, on our preconceptions. We will ordinarily see nothing miraculous, no "God signs" as Saint John calls them, in any experience or in any event if we have already adopted a philosophy which excludes the "supernatural."

In the cult film *Pulp Fiction*, not to be viewed as a family film, Jules and Vincent, two professionally violent mobsters, are sent by their powerful gangster boss, Marsellus Wallace, to retrieve a mysterious attaché case from rather foolish, middle-class looking young men in a hotel room. Jules and Vincent first casually and cruelly play with, intimidate, and frighten the young men and then ruthlessly shoot them to death. One of the boys however has been hiding in the bathroom the whole time with a handgun—a .44 magnum. Suddenly, he springs from the bathroom screaming obscenities and fires all five rounds at Jules and Vincent from almost point-blank range. Incredibly, he misses with every shot. Jules and Vincent are themselves astonished, but respond with their own barrage of bullets that do not miss.

Later in a coffee shop Jules and Vincent have a theological discussion about their strange experience—their unbelievable escape from death. Jules calls it a miracle, but Vincent says what he witnessed was merely a "freak occurrence." Vincent explains, "A miracle is when God makes the impossible possible. But this morning," he says, "I don't think it qualifies."

"Vincent," insists Jules, "don't you see? That don't matter. You're judging this the wrong way. I mean it could be that God stopped the bullets, or He changed Coke to Pepsi, or He found my car keys. You don't judge stuff like this based on merit. Now whether or not what we experienced was an 'according to Hoyle' miracle is insignificant. What is significant is that I felt the touch of God. God got involved." Quantum physics has shown that the universe may not be as closed or as predictable as once thought so that the surprising and new may indeed occur—top down and bottom up causality may be at work together. But Jules is right: "That stuff don't matter." What matters is, whether logically explicable or inexplicable, God is in it, God is involved—if we experience "the touch of God."

It is night on the sea; the friends of Jesus are caught in a sudden storm. They are blown about by the wind and the waves wash over the sides of the boat. They are helpless and frightened in the storm until Jesus comes to them and calms the wind and the waves. "Take courage," says Jesus reassuringly, "It is I"—an expression used in the Old Testament to speak of God's helping, rescuing, sustaining presence. Jesus is the loving strength of God that is always and everywhere available to us—the hand of God reaching out, as it does here to Peter, to pull us to safety when the waves are splashing over our head and we are drowning. "Take heart, it is I. Have no fear." Jesus is the calm in the storm.

The Hebrew word for "sea" suggests primordial darkness and chaos, with some monstrous evil lurking in its depths. And when the Hebrews wanted to express their belief that only the power of God could save them in a time of darkness, crisis, confusion, and desperation they sang of the Divine mastery, power, and authority over this sea. The boat itself reminds us of the ark of Noah—no surprise that in Christianity a boat is a symbol of safety. The disciples' cry for help, the whole story, is a reverberation of Ps 107 where the poet writes:

> Some went down to the sea in ships,
>   doing business on the great waters;
> they saw the deeds of the Lord,
>   his wondrous works in the deep.
> For he commanded, and raised the stormy wind,
>   which lifted up the waves of the sea.

> They mounted up to heaven, they went down to the depths;
> > their courage melted away in their evil plight;
> > they reeled and staggered like drunken men,
> > and were at their wits' end.
> > Then they cried to the Lord in their trouble,
> > and he delivered them from their distress;
> > he made the storm be still,
> > and the waves of the sea were hushed.

So stories of Jesus's calming, appearing to master, wind and sea point to Jesus as the Lord of the church who saves his people when they turn to him for help. They symbolize Jesus as the Master of the Sea who saves his followers when they have been overwhelmed, capsized and are sinking down into the depths of chaos and terror. What was said of God's power and willingness to help in the Old Testament is now said of Jesus in the sea stories of the Gospels.

This story in the Gospels is, again, obviously an echo of Ps 107, but to speak of Jesus in this way is to say something astonishing about the direct impact he must have had on his friends and followers, and what they made of his words and actions, and, my friends and fellow travelers, what we may ourselves experience, discover, and possess in our darkest and most desperate hours—what we ourselves may come to know of Jesus.

But notice also how Jesus holds a mirror up so that along with Peter and the others we can see ourselves—see what is in our own hearts. "Oh," says Jesus, "your faith is so small. Why did you doubt?" Peter thinks it is the strong wind and the surging waves that have made him afraid, but Jesus names Peter's lack of inner confidence, trust, faith, and belief as the problem. It is not the storms of life that make us afraid, but what we think about them. Doubt is fuel for fear, belief in Jesus, both as mental assent and trust, is the calm in the storm. Anne Lamott is correct when she says, "Here are the two best prayers I know: 'Help me, help me, help me,' and, 'Thank you, thank you, thank you.'"

In Jules's and Vincent's fictional coffee shop conversation at the end of *Pulp Fiction,* Jules says, while sitting there eating his muffin and drinking his coffee and thinking about the miracle, that what for Vincent was nothing more than "a freak occurrence," was for him an epiphany, a decisive, "kairotic" moment—what Jules notes "alcoholics call a moment of clarity." He will return the mysterious attaché case to Marsellus and tell Marsellus he is "quitting the business." Like Caine in the television series *Kung Fu,* perhaps a kind of Christological metaphor here, Jules will "walk the earth," "talk to people," and "have adventures." He will wait patiently, wait "even if it takes forever," for God "to put him where God wants him." In more explicitly religious or spiritual language, it could be said that Jules has had a conversion experience, renounced his old life, the life of violence and greed and power and exploitation and evil, and he will wait in utter simplicity to know the will of God. Jules longs to become a "shepherd." He will, we might say, become a friar, an itinerant monk, like Caine, like Jesus and the disciples, preaching justice and compassion. Vincent says all that really means is that Jules has "decided to become a bum." I remember reading somewhere long ago a line that goes something like this: "There will come a time when people will go mad, and they will seize anyone who is not mad saying, 'You are not like us! What is wrong with you? You must be mad!'" Saint Paul says that we are made poor and fools for Christ's sake. Be wary of miracles, they can do that to you if you're not careful—make you a bum, a poor, mad fool. *Amen.*

The Koan

Jesus then left that place and withdrew to the region of Tyre and Sidon. And a Canaanite woman from those parts came crying out, "Sir! Have pity on me, Son of David; my daughter is tormented by a devil." But he said not a word in reply. His disciples came to Him and urged: "Send her away, see how she comes shouting out after us." Jesus replied, "I was sent to the lost sheep of the house of Israel." But the woman came and fell at his feet and cried, "Help me, sir." To this Jesus replied, "It is not right to take the children's bread and throw it to the dogs." "True, sir," she answered, "and yet the dogs eat the scraps that fall from their master's table." Hearing this Jesus replied, "Woman, what faith you have! Be it as you wish!" And from that moment her daughter was restored to health.

—Matt 15:21–28 NEB

The story of the Canaanite Woman is a riddle that contains a riddle— a kind of lived parable. There are many difficult passages in Scripture— some difficult to believe, some difficult to understand, and some difficult to live even if we do understand them. The narrative of the "Syrophonecian lady," as Mark calls her in his parallel text, and her encounter with the teacher, holy man, prophet, and healer from Israel is a difficult lesson. The problem is in verse 26 of Matt 15: "Jesus said to her, 'Let the children be satisfied first; it is not fair to take the children's bread and throw it to the dogs.'" This reading grates on our modern sensitivities. It sounds chauvinistic and therefore offensive. We promise in our baptismal vows "to respect the dignity of every human being," and so it's hard for some to reconcile this verse with the Jesus of unconditional, extravagant grace and love.

Countless preachers of every denomination will attempt to integrate this perceived insult with the kinder, gentler Jesus with whom we are more familiar. There are basically four proposals one hears in such attempts:

- Jesus learned something new here—learned something new about acceptance and inclusivity.
- This is the day Jesus was bested in an argument.
- Jesus's remark is not as bad as it sounds. It was simply good-natured banter with a person of wit.
- Jesus was tired and wanted to get away. Pressured while on retreat he became irritated and responded in a way that was out of character. The woman's clever reply brought him back to himself.

Each of the attempts to explain this verse assumes that Jesus's remark was an ethnic or racial slur. In the late sixties and early seventies I became acquainted with the work of the evangelical writer Francis Schaffer, and although I disagreed with much of what he said and found his interpretation of a number of philosophers, thinkers, and theologians simplistic, I found his writing helpful in thinking about what the church is called to be in the modern world, how the thinking of contemporary artists of all sorts filters down to the person on the street, and especially I learned the importance of at least attempting to identify my own presuppositions—the assumptions that lie behind and influence my thinking.

Notice that each of the four explanations above, except for the third one, diminishes, at least humanly speaking, the spiritual, emotional, and intellectual maturity and stature of Jesus as we meet and come to know him in Scripture. Personally, I don't find any of these explanations satisfying even from a purely literary perspective. The Jesus they describe is so out of character as to be jarring and unbelievable in its incongruence. But more than that, I wholeheartedly concur with the early church father Origen, who said, "Scripture must be interpreted in a way worthy of God."

So, if our presupposition is that Jesus was simply a great teacher (which he was), something of a social activist (which he was), or an advocate of the ethic of love and acceptance and nonviolence (which he was), but not someone essentially different, even on the human level, from the rest of us, then we will probably find one of these four interpretations satisfying.

If we are not Christian and don't believe Jesus is the Christ, then we may even find no problem in thinking Jesus a bigot.

If our perception of Scripture is that it is rather like a self-help book, perhaps containing useful insights and helpful hints and suggestions, but nothing definitive for life, or that its meaning is only on the surface, like whip cream on mocha, then we will most likely quickly exhaust any relevance this reading has for our existence.

If in Scripture we do not assume we are hearing the ring of authoritative and authentic truth, that we human beings can somehow sit in judgment of Scripture, critiquing it with our own opinions and personal or cultural sensibilities, rather than allowing it to challenge us in the very depths of our soul, then it is unlikely that anything truly and personally transformative will be discovered in this story.

If we approach Scripture with any of these presuppositions, which make it possible for us to domesticate and therefore control Christ, we will probably remain good, decent, and worthwhile people, but we are also likely to miss something we may not want to miss.

The other night Brenda and I watched the 1994 movie *Immortal Beloved*. It is a very fictionalized film about Ludwig von Beethoven and his music. My favorite scene is toward the end of the film where Beethoven, as a young boy, runs in the night from his abusive father. The dark sky is filled with billions of dazzling stars. Young Ludwig comes to a pool of water in a clearing in the forest, takes off his shirt, wades out into the pool, and floats on his back. The stars are, on this clear night, reflected in the pool so that from above it looks like Ludwig is floating in the starry heavens while the sound of Beethoven's magnificent "Ode to Joy" rises up. I do not know what you want, a lot of the time I don't even know what I want, but in this moment I hope to float in the starry sky to the joy of celestial music.

So as I begin to read this text, I come to it with the presupposition that it has something deep, and true, and beautiful, and infinitely desirable to tell me, and that it ought to be interpreted in a way worthy of the Spirit of Jesus Christ.

Notice how the story begins. "And Jesus went away from there and withdrew into the district of Tyre and Sidon." Matthew's description makes it clear, and Mark's even more so, that Jesus's leaving for the region of Tyre and Sidon is purposeful. Even going to this place where Jews were fiercely hated suggests some significant intention in Jesus's mind. It is rather ludicrous to think that Jesus decided it would be a good idea to take a relaxing vacation, as some have suggested, among hostile people whom he could insult if they annoyed him with desperate cries for help. It just doesn't fit the character of Jesus.

A woman from that place, a Canaanite woman, began following Jesus and his friends around, kept following them persistently, kept calling out, "Have mercy on me! Help my daughter!" Strangely, "Jesus does not answer her at all." It's driving the disciples crazy, they beg Jesus to do something to get rid of her. But Jesus remains quiet. This is a common teaching technique employed by the sages of every wisdom tradition. They have an uncanny sense of how to wait and how to leave the seeker waiting until the right moment, the teachable moment, arises.

And so this woman in longing, hope, and distress is left waiting. She will not give up her quest. She is not only quick-witted, as seen by her reply, but unusually perceptive. Above all, she demonstrates that self-emptying sort of humility that is the essence of all spiritual progress—she is willing to receive as a child. Jesus recognizes these qualities of receptivity, and although he seems to be doing nothing at all, mysteriously works with them to bring about the emergence of a deeper spiritual awareness within her, waits like a midwife for the moment of natural birth—the birth of enlightenment.

The woman asks help for her daughter, and Jesus starts talking about bread. Bread, or *artos* in the original Greek, is an archetypal symbol. It symbolizes here the Eucharist, *manna*, in the wilderness, and the miraculous feeding of the five thousand, but especially the way in which the Gospels see Jesus as not only the bread-giver, but as the bread itself—the bread of heaven. What Jesus wants to give this woman is not only bread to eat, not only physical healing for her daughter, but the gift of himself—the gift of the divine life.

And here it comes: "It's not fair," answers Jesus somewhat playfully, "to take the children's food and throw it to the dogs." I say playfully because Jesus uses the word for household puppies, and not snarling street scavengers. Jesus's playfulness is part of an invitation to this woman to seek wisdom with him—to seek the wisdom in her distress.

Jesus's response, "It is not fair to take the children's food and throw it to the dogs," is, I believe, the first half of a proverb. In ancient Israel people might gather at the village gate to evaluate the events of the day in reference to traditional folk wisdom. Now and then someone would come up with a new proverb to cover a new situation, and all the villagers were free to contribute to and refine it until it came to embody the collective wisdom of the village. What parent is here who does not feel this woman's desperation? But she has neither heard nor faced the question of real faith, the faith that is Ultimate Concern, the faith that can sustain her in every time of desperation, until Jesus confronts her with this proverb, or, rather, with the first half of a proverb that she extends so that it sounds like this:

> *It is not right to throw the bread of the children to the pups under the table.*
> *Yet, even the puppies eat the crumbs that fall from the table.*

What we see here, then, is a collaborative *mashal* or proverb that breaks her out of conventional thinking, ends the cycle of alienation and hostility at all levels, and brings her to a new experience of faith and hope and love. A Zen master might say, "Ahhh. She solved the *koan*." The point of a koan is to make it impossible for someone to continue to think discursively, to think using ordinary logic, so that thinking becomes more intuitive, more of an experience of reality. I have a friend who did a lot of *koan* work. One day when it was raining his teacher asked something like, "Where is the master when it rains?" His reply was to begin drumming with his fingers on the hardwood floor where they sat. And that was an acceptable answer. It was an acceptable answer because it showed he was not thinking about what the right answer might be, or how to please the teacher, but simply had entered into an experience of the rain.

This woman's answer: "Yes, but even the puppies eat the crumbs that fall from the table," demonstrates that, for her, faith and grace and hope and love are not merely theological concepts but inexplicable transcendent experiences. For her, this is not the day she met a rude healer from Nazareth, but the day she discovered the sage and Lord who showed how she could float beautifully in the spiritual cosmos, to the joyful sound of "silent music." *Amen.*

Sensus Divinitatis

> "And you," he asked, "who do you say I am?" Simon Peter answered: "You are the Messiah, the Son of the Living God."
>
> —Matt 16:15–16 REB

I WONDER WHETHER AFTER the question there was a breathless pause—a moment when hearts seemed to stop beating and the normal spinning of thoughts was suspended. Perhaps not. It is after all for good reason that we are afraid to gaze at the sun—even when eclipsed by the moon. And I sometimes wonder where the answer came from. How did Peter know? How did he reach such a conclusion? Our daughter, Carolyn, did her senior thesis on homological algebra. It was seventy-five pages of mathematical symbols held for a long time to our refrigerator door by a couple of strong magnets. I couldn't follow it, of course, although I thought the symbols aesthetically pleasing, but I knew it followed some rigorously logical process approved by her professor, Dr. Goro Kato, who was, I always thought, a kind of mathematical samurai. But how did this fisherman, Peter, know what he knew?

Some professional philosophers, the logical positivists, argue that if what we say cannot be put into precise mathematical form it is meaningless. If you say a painting is beautiful or a piece of music sublime, you are speaking nonsense. For such statements to mean anything they would have to be a mathematical description of the electrochemical processes in your brain. I have never met anyone, I have never heard of anyone, who can actually live as if that is true.

There have been others, many others, who have thought quite differently. The brilliant medieval thinker Thomas Aquinas, tediously logical and rational in his writing, believed that we are born with an inner spiritual awareness, born with what has often been called the *sensus divinitatis*—the "sense of the divine." It is what Saint Augustine, writing late in the fourth century, meant when he said, "O Lord, you have made us and drawn us to yourself, and our heart is unquiet until it rests in you." Augustine was probably not only poetically and spiritually correct, but scientifically as well. There is a good deal of research that suggests we are "hardwired" for God—that there is some sort of a genetic disposition to the experience of God. In his book *The Awakened Heart*, the psychiatrist and spiritual director Gerald May writes about the innate human longing for Love. A good deal of the time May capitalizes the word "Love." He wants us to understand that he is not talking about love as narrowly defined, but Love as the Ultimate and Divine Mystery. He writes this:

> There is a desire within each of us, in the deep center of ourselves that we call our heart. We were born with it, it is never completely satisfied, and it never dies. We are often unaware of it, but it is always awake. It is the human desire for love. Each person on this earth yearns to love, to be loved, to know love. Our true identity, our reason for being is to be found in this desire.

The *sensus divinitatis* is understood as a faculty, like perception, memory, or reason by which we come to knowledge of the truth. Like reason or memory or perception our *sensus divinitatis* can be wrong, and so has to be tested in as many ways as we can. But here is a more specific modern example taken from another book by Gerald May, *Will and Spirit*. It is an anecdote about a corporate lawyer and the experience that brought him to the acknowledgment of life's profoundly mysterious and spiritual quality. In this attorney's words here is what happened:

> I was on vacation in the mountains. Two friends and I had hiked most of the morning and we were very tired. I lay down by a tree stump and slept. When I awoke it was late afternoon and everything had become quiet. The crickets and cicadas had silenced their chirping, and even the breeze stopped. All I can say is the moment was an eternity, and it was the moment of my birth. I was forty-five years old, but in those few minutes I was born. I had no thought at the time—everything was just there. I had no reaction except for a deep quiet and peace. This is hard for me to say, but at some point I remember thinking, "There is a God, there is a God." And my life hasn't been the same since then. I still practice law, and keep the same friends. I still worry about money and politics. I still snap at my wife when I've had a hard day, but I'm different. Somewhere deep down something

has changed. Now I look for God—I seek the wonder of life, and while I appreciate being here on the face of this earth more than ever before, I also fear death less. I sit alone sometimes, and now and then I enter that moment again.

"Who do I say you are?" We might imagine Peter questioning, thinking, something like this in his own heart: "I can only say what I have experienced in your presence, what I feel when you speak, what happens to me when I see your compassion, your healing, your caring, your courage. It is something I have found nowhere else. I don't know where else I could go and find the life that flows in you, and through you, and around you, and catches me up in its power. I can only use the best language I have available to me. I can only stammer out, 'You are the Christ, the Son of the Living God.'"

Peter's response is not argument, it is confession. The Latin word *confessio* originally referred to the tomb of a martyr—the burial place of a man or woman willing to speak of the truth, of the reality, they had experienced in Christ even if doing so meant torture and death. The word "gospel" simply means "the good message." The Gospels, then, are not philosophical discourses, or proofs, or arguments, they are testimonies of faith, hope, and love lived in Christ. They are expressions of the *sensus divinitatis*. I suppose that one thing I have been attempting to do in this little series of sermons is to offer reassurance that there is nothing unreasonable about our faith, our Christian faith; and, that the *sensus divinitatis* is, itself, a legitimate way of knowing. Nothing has been found, when tested or reasonably interpreted, in biblical studies, science, philosophy, or theology that renders belief in Jesus as Lord and Christ irrational.

The Gospels obviously do contain some apparent discrepancies, which at this point in history are difficult to analyze. But there are no discrepancies or errors that make any real difference in what we believe about Jesus. There is more reason, regardless of any doubts about details, to trust the historical core of the New Testament than there is for many of the historical events we accept without question—for example, the Battle of Marathon. The Gospels were written very early, and Saint Paul's Letters even earlier. Unlike the apocryphal gospels you may have read, or read about, which were written much later, such as the gospel of Judas or James or Mary Magdalene or Thomas, the canonical Gospels of Matthew, Mark, Luke, and John contain strong internal evidence that eyewitness reports lie behind their writing. What matters is not whether Jesus spoke the exact words, uttered the precise sentences we have in the Gospels, but whether he said anything like what they report.

When I was a kid I thought my mother's red-letter edition of the Gospels special. I thought the actual words of Jesus were right there in the beautiful cadence and poetry of King James English—spelled out in red letters to be given particular reverence. As an adult I know that it's not possible to create a red letter edition of the New Testament, but I also know that isn't necessary in order to encounter Jesus as the Christ—or when we read or hear these words to sense Christ as the Holy One, Sacred, Transcendent, Life-abundant and everlasting.

If Ann Lamott happened to be at the flea market in Sausalito across the Bay from San Francisco between eleven and one on Sundays, she could hear gospel music coming from a ramshackle building across the street—Saint Andrew Presbyterian. She began stopping in about once a month to listen to the music, but always left before the sermon. To her, Jesus made about as much sense as Scientology or dowsing.

In April of 1984, Pammy, Ann Lamott's best friend, took Ann in for an abortion. Ann was sadder than she had been anytime since her father died. When she got home that night she went upstairs to her loft with a pint of Bushmills and some codeine the nurse had given her for pain. She drank until nearly dawn.

She didn't go to the flea market the week of her abortion. She stayed home and smoked dope and got drunk, and tried to write a little, and went for slow walks along the salt marsh. A week later, very drunk and just about to take a sleeping pill, she discovered she was bleeding heavily. She thought of calling a doctor or Pammy for help but was depressed and disgusted that she had gotten so drunk one week after her abortion. Too sad and too afraid to take another drink or pill she got into bed, smoked a cigarette, and turned off the light. As she lay there she became aware of someone with her, hunkered down in the corner. At first she assumed she was feeling the presence of her father—a presence she had often felt when frightened and alone. The feeling was so persistent and so strong that she turned on the light to make sure no one was actually there. But after a while, lying there in the dark, she knew without any doubt that it was Jesus—as real to her as anything physical. She was appalled. What would her smart, sophisticated, hilarious friends think of her if she became a Christian? That was the one thing that must not happen. She turned to the wall and said out loud, "I would rather die." She felt him just sitting there on his haunches in the corner, watching with patience and love. She squinched her eyes shut, but that didn't help because that's not what she was seeing him with.

Finally she fell asleep, and in the morning he was gone. But she was badly spooked. She thought maybe it was an experience born of alcohol, drugs, emotional stress, and the loss of blood. But then she found that everywhere she went she had the feeling that a little cat was following her—wanting her to reach down, pick it up, open the door, and let it in. She knew, of course, where that would lead. Let a cat in, feed it a little milk, even just one time, and it stays forever.

When she went back to church, she was so hung over that she couldn't even stand up for the songs. Nevertheless, this time she stayed for the sermon, which she thought so ridiculous, like someone trying to convince her of the existence of extraterrestrials, but there was something about the last song, so deep and raw and pure, that she could not escape.

She started to cry and left before the benediction. As she raced home she felt the little cat running along at her heels. She says, "I walked down the dock past dozens of plotted flowers, under a sky as blue as one of God's own dreams, and opened the door to my houseboat, and I stood there a minute, then I hung my head and said, '[Bleep] it. I quit.' I took a long deep breath and said out loud, 'All right. You can come in.' So this was the moment of my beautiful conversion."

> *Sensus divinitatis*
> Who do you say I am?
> *Sensus divinitatis*
> You are the Christ, the Son of the Living God.
> *Sensus divinitatis*.
> Sensus divinitatis.
> Amen.

Hope of "Wretched Humankind"

From that time Jesus Christ began to make it clear to his disciples that he had to go to Jerusalem and endure great suffering at the hands of the elders, chief priests, and scribes; to be put to death, and to be raised again on the third day.

—Matt 16:21 REB

I DON'T READ A lot of fiction anymore. It's not that I don't enjoy it; it's just that I don't seem to have the time. When I do read fiction I find myself often reading, or rereading, *The Cadfael Chronicles,* a series of short novels set in a twelfth century Benedictine monastery in Shrewsbury, England. The main character, Brother Cadfael, a monk in the monastery who fought in the crusades and as a mercenary on the Mediterranean Sea, but who now follows the cross rather than the sword, tends the monastery's herbal garden, practices herbal medicine, prays the Hours, and solves murder mysteries. Bernard Ramm, my professor for Christology liked to say that the best psychologists are the novelists. And that's true of *The Cadfael Chronicles—* they are full of psychological insight and spiritual wisdom. Here is just a very short paragraph that is pertinent to this Gospel reading—to the theme of resurrection.

> So that is how it had ended, after all Mark's efforts and prayers, after all his own ineffective reasonings and seekings and faith. Cadfael got up in grieving haste. "I'll come," he said. "Now we have the whole battle on our hands, and little time left. . . . "Brother Mark fell in at their heels and followed to the gatehouse, altogether cast down and out of comfort, unable to find a hopeful word to say. He felt in his heart that this was sin, the sin of despair, not of despair for himself, but despair of truth and justice and right and the future of wretched humankind.

Why does Mark feel his despair is sin? The question is rhetorical. And the simplest and most obvious answer is, of course, that for Mark it is "sin" because despair so easily becomes the denial of faith as trust. Mark is a Christian, a young Benedictine monk, a believer who has committed his life, has given his heart, to the way of extraordinary trust and hope. As it is to be for all Christians, Mark is someone whose very existence is shaped by the love of the cross and the hope of Christ's resurrection.

There are at least three basic ways of seeing the resurrection of Christ from a Christian perspective:

The first view is that there was a literal physical event, a bodily resurrection, in which there was both an empty tomb and the flesh and blood body of Jesus brought to life. The strength of this view is its ability to make sense out of much of the historical data. For example, the theory that the tomb was empty because the disciples stole the body, or that the authorities transferred Jesus's body to a more secure location, or that the women went to the wrong tomb that morning, all fail to account for why the authorities did not produce the body when it would have been to their every advantage to have done so.

As a young graduate student, Frank Morison, an unbeliever but admirer of Jesus, conceived the idea of writing a short book on the most critical and last phase of Jesus's life. Morison wanted to show the pulsating drama of Jesus's life against the sharp background of antiquity, strip it of its primitive idea and beliefs, and show this great person, Jesus, as he really was. Ten years later, Morison had his opportunity to do just that. As he investigated the origins of biblical literature, sifted through evidence, and used his skills as an attorney to form his own judgments about the facts, it effected a revolution in his thinking. Instead of writing a book disproving the resurrection, he published *Who Moved the Stone?*. It was a very different sort of book than the one he originally intended—one that found the case for the resurrection of Jesus so compelling that Morison himself became a Christian.

The second view is that there was indeed an empty tomb and a number of appearances of the risen Christ, but what was seen was not the former body, but a new or spiritual body of which we can know very little. The emphasis is on the transformation of the physical body of Jesus. Just a casual reading of the resurrection narrative makes it obvious that if we regard Jesus as having an actual post-resurrection body it was certainly nothing like any ordinary body we know about.

The third view is that the resurrection was a real event, and consisted of a number of dramatic encounters in which the disciples were intensely aware of the presence of Christ. In some of these encounters, Jesus seemed to have a body, but from this perspective that is unimportant, as is the empty tomb. If Jesus's bones should be found in some Palestinian tomb, that discovery would not contradict the genuineness of the experience.

The popular scholar and writer Marcus Borg suggests that the appearances of Jesus may have been akin to visions—visions that are disclosures of reality. To anyone who says, "So the appearances were just visions," Borg replies, "No one who has ever had one would ever say, 'It was just a vision.'" Furthermore, he says, visions can involve the dimensions of seeing, and hearing, and touch. Consequently, a story in which the disciples see Jesus eat or touch him does not necessarily point away from a vision.

Now it is possible to adopt any of these perspectives and be Christian. We are never going to be able to say precisely what happened at the resurrection, nor are we ever going to be able to say exactly how it happened. What does seem clear is that something unique really happened to Jesus who had been dead for three days so that the disciples experienced Jesus as just as alive and just as present as they were to one another.

There are certain strands of evidence that support and give warrant to belief in Christ's resurrection. For one thing, the documents of the New Testament were written early in the history of Christianity. Because of the numerous manuscripts, fragments of manuscripts, and all the biblical quotations in the writings of the Early Church Fathers, textual scholars are able, with a great deal of facility, to detect errors and glosses by copyists so as to produce a highly accurate version of the original Greek New Testament. We can have a great deal of confidence in the reliability of the New Testament as the transmission of what the earliest Christians thought, believed, and confessed about Christ. More importantly, the written New Testament has a "ring of truth" about it.

John Bertram Phillips served the Church of the Good Shepherd during the London Blitz. With the bombs raining down nightly, he began asking himself what more he could do to care for the people in his parish. It came to him that maybe one of the most helpful things he could do would be to translate the New Testament with its message of faith and hope into modern English. He had taken a degree in classics from Emmanuel College, Cambridge, so he was well-suited for such work—much of which was done during the nights he spent in a bomb shelter. Later, he spoke of his own personal experience in translating the New Testament. He said he found the biblical text "extraordinarily alive"—unlike any experience he'd had with non-scriptural ancient texts. He referred to Scripture as having the "ring of truth," of authenticity, about it, and speaking to his own condition in an "uncanny way."

We can add to this how the canonical Gospels show every sign of having been based on eyewitness accounts—on the stories of people who were there and encountered Jesus. The work of scholars like Larry Hurtado, director of the Center for the Study of Christian Origins at the University of Edinburgh, offers persuasive evidence that the stories and the worship of Jesus did not evolve slowly over time, as often claimed, but rather exploded into the world. The question has to be asked, "What ignited that terrific explosion?"

Then there is the astonishing transformation of the disciples that has to be accounted for. They were not expecting Jesus to show himself alive after his crucifixion. They knew like everyone else that when someone dies they stay dead. Yet, with uncommon courage, wisdom, and love they insist they have seen, heard, touched the crucified one as now alive—filling them with hope and life, and their lives back up what they say.

The survival, the continuing existence and triumph of the church, the community of faith, against all odds, demands an event capable of having an impact of that magnitude. And what are we to say of all those through the centuries who have experienced Christ as living, divine, present? *Sensus divinitatis, sensus divinitatis.* What are we to make of Saint Francis of Assisi or Mother Teresa of Calcutta? *Sensus divinitatis.*

How do we know that God is caring and loving? How do we know life is stronger than death, or that goodness overcomes evil? How do we know that Yahweh is not like Zeus, or Aphrodite, or Dionysus—without pity or mercy? How do we know "wretched humankind" has a future? If we are Christian we know it, not as a theory we have spun out of longing imagination, but by the reality of the resurrection. Indeed, those who believe the good message, the Gospel of the Resurrection of Jesus Christ, find it the reality, which, when opening their heart to it, makes the supreme difference in their lives. In the words of the modern Christian monk and mystic Thomas Merton,

> So we are called
> not only to believe
> that Christ once rose
> from the dead,
> thereby proving that
> he was God;
> we are called to experience the Resurrection
> in our own lives
> by entering
> into this dynamic movement,
> by following Christ

who lives in us.
Come,
People of God.
Christ our Passover is sacrificed,
and in sharing his banquet
we pass with him
from death to life!
He has risen. . .
he is going before us into his Kingdom!
Alleluia!

Bibliography

Abbey, Edward. *Desert Solitaire: A Season in the Wilderness*. New York: Simon and Schuster, 1968.

Albers, Robert Herbert. "The Theological and Psychological Dynamics of Transformation in the Recovery from the Disease of Alcoholism." PhD diss., School of Theology at Claremont, 1982.

Albright, William Foxwell. *From the Stone Age to Christianity: Monotheism and the Historical Process*. Anchor Books. Garden City, NY: Doubleday, 1957.

Baden, Joel, and Candida Moss. "The Curious Case of Jesus' Wife." *The Atlantic*, December 2014. http://www.theatlantic.com/magazine/archive/2014/12/the-curious-case-of-jesuss-wife/382227/.

Bader, Christopher, et al. "American Piety in the 21st Century: Selected Findings from the Baylor Religion Survey." Waco, TX: Baylor University, 2006.

Bagnall, Roger S. *Everyday Writing in the Graeco-Roman East*. Berkeley: University of California Press, 2011.

Barclay, William. *The Gospel of Matthew*. The Daily Study Bible Series 1. Philadelphia: Westminster, 1975.

Barna Group. "3 Trends Redefining the Information Age." October 21, 2013. https://www.barna.com/research/3-trends-redefining-the-information-age/.

Barry, William A. *Paying Attention to God: Discernment in Prayer*. Notre Dame: Ave Maria, 1990.

Barth, Karl. "The Growth of the Community." In *Theological Foundations for Ministry: Selected Readings for a Theology of the Church in Ministry*, edited by Ray S. Anderson, 258–302. London: T & T Clark, 1979.

Bartlett, Tom. "The Lessons of Jesus' Wife." *The Chronicle of Higher Education*, October 1, 2012. http://www.chronicle.com/blogs/percolator/the-lessons-of-jesus-wife/31234.

Bauckham, Richard. "Bauckham on the Talpiyot Tomb Inscription." Larry Hurtado's Blog: Comments on the New Testament and Early Christianity (and related matters), April 6, 2012. https://larryhurtado.wordpress.com/2012/04/06/bauckham-on-the-talpiyot-tomb-inscription/.

———. *Jesus and the Eyewitnesses: The Gospels as Eyewitness Testimony*. Grand Rapids: Eerdmans, 2006.

Bauer, Walter. *Orthodoxy and Heresy in Earliest Christianity*. Translated by a team from the Philadelphia Seminar on Christian Origins. Edited by Robert A. Kraft and Gerhard Krodel. Philadelphia: Fortress, 1971.

Becker, Ernest. *The Denial of Death*. New York: Free Press, 1973.
Benedict XVI, Pope. *Apostolic Letter in the Form of Motu Proprio: Ubicumque et Semper*. Castle Gandolfo: Pontifical Council for Promoting the New Evangelization, 2010.
Bernhard, Andrew. "The Gospel of Jesus' Wife: 'Patchwork' Forgery in Coptic . . . and English." NT Blog, August 28, 2015. http://ntweblog.blogspot.com/2015/08/the-gospel-of-jesus-wife-patchwork.html.
———. "How the Gospel of Jesus' Wife Might Have Been Forged: A Tentative Proposal." October 11, 2012. http://www.academia.edu/25790869/How_The_Gospel_of_Jesus_s_Wife_Might_Have_Been_Forged_A_Tentative_Proposal_October_11_2012.
Black, James. *The Mystery of Preaching*. Grand Rapids: Zondervan, 1977.
Block, Ned. "On a Confusion about a Function of Consciousness." In *The Nature of Consciousness*, edited by Ned Block, Owen Flanagan, and Güven Güzeldere, 375–413. Cambridge: MIT Press, 1998.
Borg, Marcus J. *The Heart of Christianity: Rediscovering a Life of Faith*. San Francisco: HarperSanFrancisco, 2004.
———. *Jesus: Uncovering the Life, Teachings, and Relevance of a Religious Revolutionary*. San Francisco: HarperSanFrancisco, 2006.
———. *Reading the Bible Again for the First Time: Taking the Bible Seriously but Not Literally*. San Francisco: HarperSanFrancisco, 2001.
Brodie, Fawn. *No Man Knows My History: The Life of Joseph Smith, the Mormon Prophet*. New York: Knopf, 1945.
Broslavick, S. Chris. "St. Dominic's Nine Ways of Prayer." Racine Dominicans: A Community of Catholic Sisters and Lay Associates, n.d. http://www.racinedominicans.org/about-us/prayer.cfm.
Brown, Sally, and David R. Brown. *A Biography of Mrs. Marty Mann: The First Lady of Alcoholics Anonymous*. Center City, MN: Hazelden, 2005.
Brueggemann, Walter. "Where Is the Scribe?" *Anglican Theological Review* 93 (2011) 385–403. http://www.anglicantheologicalreview.org/static/pdf/articles/brueggemann.pdf.
Buber, Martin. *I and Thou*. Translated by Walter Kaufmann. New York: Scribner, 1970.
Bultmann, Rudolf. *Theology of the New Testament*. Translated by Kendrick Grobel. Vol. 2. New York: Scribner, 1955.
Buttrick, David. *A Captive Voice: The Liberation of Preaching*. Louisville: Westminster John Knox, 1994.
———. *Homiletic: Moves and Structures*. Philadelphia: Fortress, 1989.
———. "On Doing Homiletics Today." In *Intersections: Post-Critical Studies in Preaching*, edited by Richard L. Eslinger, 88–104. Grand Rapids: Eerdmans, 1994.
Cahill, Thomas. *The Gifts of the Jews: How a Tribe of Desert Nomads Changed the Way Everyone Thinks and Feels*. New York: Anchor, 1998.
Can We Trust the Text of the New Testament? A Debate between Daniel B. Wallace and Bart D. Ehrman. DVD. Center for the Study of New Testament Manuscripts, 2011. http://www.csntm.org/resources/dvd.
Cassuto, Umberto. *The Documentary Hypothesis and the Composition of the Pentateuch: Eight Lectures*. Translated by Israel Abrahams. Jerusalem: Magnes, 1972.
Charlesworth, James H. "Why Evaluate Twenty-Five Years of Jesus Research?" In *Jesus Research: An International Perspective*, edited by James H. Charlesworth and

Petr Pokorný, 1–15. Princeton-Prague Symposia Series on the Historical Jesus 1. Grand Rapids: Eerdmans, 2009.

Chaves, Mark. *American Religion: Contemporary Trends*. Princeton: Princeton University Press, 2011.

Chestnut, Glenn F. *God and Spirituality: Philosophical Essays*. New York: iUniverse, 2010.

Ciardi, John. *How Does a Poem Mean?* Boston: Houghton Mifflin, 1959.

Cobb, John B., Jr. *Theological Reminiscences*. Claremont, CA: Process Century, 2014.

———. *Whitehead Word Book: A Glossary with Alphabetical Index to Technical Terms in Process Reality*. Claremont, CA: Process Century, 2008.

Coogan, Michael D. *The Old Testament: A Historical and Literary Introduction to the Hebrew Scriptures*. Oxford: Oxford University Press, 2006.

Crick, Francis. *The Astonishing Hypothesis: The Scientific Search for the Soul*. New York: Simon and Schuster, 1995.

Daly, Herman E., and John B. Cobb Jr. *For the Common Good: Redirecting the Economy Toward Community, the Environment, and a Sustainable Future*. 2nd ed. Boston: Beacon, 1994.

Davies, Philip. "Beyond Labels: What Comes Next?" The Bible and Interpretation, April 2010. http://www.bibleinterp.com/articles/moore1357926.shtml.

———. "Do We Need Biblical Scholars?" The Bible and Interpretation, June 2005. http://www.bibleinterp.com/articles/Davies_Biblical_Scholars.shtml.

———. *In Search of "Ancient Israel": A Study in Biblical Origins*. London: T & T Clark, 1992.

———. *Whose Bible Is It Anyway?* London: T & T Clark, 2004.

Dostoyevsky, Fyodor. *The Brothers Karamazov*. Translated by Constance Garrett. New York: Barnes and Noble Classics, 1995.

Downing, David C. *Into the Region of Awe: Mysticism in C. S. Lewis*. Downers Grove, IL: InterVarsity, 2005.

D'Souza, Dinesh. *Life After Death: The Evidence*. Washington, DC: Regnery, 2009.

Ehrman, Bart D. *Misquoting Jesus: The Story Behind Who Changed the Bible and Why*. San Francisco: HarperCollins, 2005.

Elliot, T. S. *Four Quartets*. New York: Harcourt Brace, 1971.

Evans, Craig A. *Fabricating Jesus: How Modern Scholars Distort the Gospels*. Downers Grove, IL: InterVarsity, 2006.

Foster, Richard. *Celebration of Discipline: The Path to Spiritual Growth*. San Francisco: Harper and Row, 1978.

Frankl, Viktor. *Man's Search for Meaning: An Introduction to Logotherapy*. Newly rev. and enl. ed. of *From Death-Camp to Existentialism*. Translated by Ilse Lasch. Boston: Beacon, 1959.

Friedman, Edwin H. *Generation to Generation: Family Process in Church and Synagogue*. London: Guilford, 1985.

Gibbs, Eddie. *ChurchNext: Quantam Changes in How We Do Ministry*. Downers Grove, IL: InterVarsity, 2000.

Gibbs, Eddie, and Ryan K. Bolger. *Emerging Churches: Creating Christian Community in Postmodern Cultures*. Grand Rapids: Baker Academic, 2005.

Goodacre, Mark. *The Case against Q: Studies in Markan Priority and the Synoptic Problem*. Harrisburg, PA: Trinity Press, 2002.

———. "How Reliable Is the Story of the Nag Hammadi Discovery?" *Journal for the Study of the New Testament* 35 (2013) 303–22.

———. *The Synoptic Problem: A Way through the Maze*. London: T & T Clark, 2001.

———. *Thomas and the Gospels: The Case for Thomas's Familiarity with the Synoptics*. Grand Rapids: Eerdmans, 2012.

Goodacre, Mark, and Nicholas Perrin, eds. *Questioning Q: A Multidimensional Critique*. Downers Grove, IL: InterVarsity, 2004.

Gortner, David. *Transforming Evangelism*. New York: Church Publishing, 2008.

"The Gospel of Jesus's Wife: A New Coptic Gospel Papyrus." The Gospel of Jesus's Wife, retrieved September 19, 2012. http://gospelofjesuswife.hds.harvard.edu/.

Grinde, Bjørn. *Darwinian Happiness: Evolution as a Guide for Living and Understanding Human Behavior*. 2nd ed. Princeton, NJ: Darwin Press, 2012.

Hadaway, C. Kirk. "A Report on Episcopal Churches in the United States." New York: Office of Congregational Development, Domestic and Foreign Missionary Society, 2004.

Hamer, Dean. *The God Gene: How Faith Is Hardwired into Our Genes*. New York: Doubleday, 2004.

Hart, David Bentley. *The Experience of God: Being, Consciousness, Bliss*. New Haven: Yale University Press, 2013.

Hart, Larry D. "A Model for Relational Counseling through Expository Preaching at the Santa Cruz Church of Christ." DMin. diss., Fuller Theological Seminary, 1984.

———. *Numinous: Reflections on the Mystery of Preaching*. San Francisco: Blurb Books, 2010.

Hayward, John, ed. *The Oxford Book of Nineteenth-Century English Verse*. Oxford: Clarendon, 1964.

Herzog, William R. *Jesus, Justice, and the Reign of God: A Ministry of Liberation*. Louisville: Westminster John Knox, 2000.

Heschel, Abraham Joshua. *Quest for God: Studies in Prayer and Symbolism*. New York: Crossroad, 1993.

Hickman, Peter E. *The Word Made Alive: The Pastoral Writings of Bishop Peter Hickman*. Orange, CA: ABM, 2014.

Hill, C. E. *Who Chose the Gospels? Probing the Great Gospel Conspiracy*. Oxford: Oxford University Press, 2010.

Horsley, Richard A. "Jesus Movements and the Renewal of Israel." In vol. 1 of *Christian Origins*, edited by Richard A. Horsley, 11–39. A People's History of Christianity. Minneapolis: Fortress, 2010.

Hultgren, Arland J., and Steven A. Haggmark, eds. *The Earliest Christian Heretics: Readings from Their Opponents*. Minneapolis: Fortress, 2008.

Hurtado, Larry. *How on Earth Did Jesus Become a God? Historical Questions about Earliest Devotion to Jesus*. Grand Rapids: Eerdmans, 2005.

———. *Lord Jesus Christ: Devotion to Jesus in Earliest Christianity*. Grand Rapids: Eerdmans, 2003.

———. "You've Got to 'Accentuate the Positive': Thinking about Differences Biblically." *Scottish Bulletin of Evangelical Theology* 30 (2012) 21–29.

Jampolsky, Gerald G. *Love Is Letting Go of Fear*. Berkeley: Celestial Arts, 1979.

John of the Cross, Saint. *Saint John of the Cross: From Anabaptist Spirituality*. Translated by Hugo Zorrilla. Fresno, CA: H. Zorrilla C., 1993.

John Paul II, Pope. *Redemptoris Missio*. Washington, DC: United States Catholic Conference, 1990.

Johnson, Robert A. *Inner Work: Using Dreams and Active Imagination for Personal Growth*. San Francisco: Harper and Row, 1986.

Johnson, Vernon E. *I'll Quit Tomorrow: A Practical Guide to Alcoholism Treatment*. New York: Harper and Row, 1973.

Johnson, William A. "Constructing Elite Reading Communities in the High Empire." In *Ancient Literacies: The Culture of Reading in Greece and Rome*, edited by William A. Johnson and Holt N. Parker, 320–30. Oxford: Oxford University Press, 2009.

Johnston, William. *Lord Teach Us to Pray: Christian Zen and the Inner Eye of Love*. London: HarperCollins, 1990.

———. *Silent Music: The Science of Meditation*. San Francisco: Harper and Row, 1976.

Jones, Robert P. *The End of White Christian America*. New York: Simon and Schuster, 2016.

Jones, Tony. *The Church is Flat: The Relational Ecclesiology of the Emerging Church Movement*. Minneapolis: JoPa Group, 2011.

Kaplan, Aryeh. *Meditation and the Bible*. York Beach, ME: Samuel Weiser, 1978.

Keener, Craig S. *The Gospel of John: A Commentary*. Vol. 1. Peabody, MA: Hendrickson, 2002.

King, Patricia M., and Karen S. Kitchener. *Developing Reflective Judgement: Understanding and Promoting Intellectual Growth and Critical Thinking in Adolescents and Adults*. San Francisco: Jossey-Bass, 1994.

Kitchen, Kenneth A. *On the Reliability of the Old Testament*. Grand Rapids: Eerdmans, 2003.

Kittel, Gerhard, ed. *Theological Dictionary of the New Testament*. Translated by Geoffrey W. Bromiley. 10 vols. Grand Rapids: Eerdmans, 1964–1976.

Knox, John. *Myth and Truth: An Essay on the Language of Faith*. Charlottesville: University of Virginia Press, 1964.

Kostenberger, Andreas J., and Michael J. Kruger. *The Heresy of Orthodoxy: How Contemporary Culture's Fascination with Diversity Has Reshaped Our Understanding of Early Christianity*. Wheaton, IL: Crossway, 2010.

Kreider, Alan. *The Change of Conversion and the Origin of Christendom*. 1999. Reprint, Eugene, OR: Wipf & Stock, 2006.

Kruger, Michael J. *The Question of Canon: Challenging the Status Quo in the New Testament Debate*. Downers Grove, IL: InterVarsity, 2013.

Küng, Hans. *On Being a Christian*. Translated by Edward Quinn. Garden City, NY: Doubleday, 1976.

Langford, Michael J. *Unblind Faith: A New Approach for the Twenty-First Century*. Tunbridge Wells, UK: Parapress, 2010.

Lewis, C. S. *The Great Divorce*. New York: Macmillan, 1946.

———. *Mere Christianity*. New York: Macmillan, 1960.

———. "Myth Became Fact." In *God in the Dock: Essays on Theology and Ethics*, edited by Walter Hooper, 63–67. Grand Rapids: Eerdmans, 1970.

———. *Surprised by Joy: The Shape of My Early Life*. London: Harcourt, 1955.

Lewis, Nicola Denzey, and Justine Ariel Blount. "Rethinking the Origins of the Nag Hammadi Codices." *Journal of Biblical Literature* 133 (2014) 399–419.

Luke, Helen M. *The Laughter at the Heart of Things: Selected Essays*. New York: Parabola, 2001.

Luz, Ulrich. *Matthew: A Commentary.* Vol. 1, *Matthew 1–7.* Translated by James E. Crouch. Edited by Helmut Koester. Hermeneia—A Critical and Historical Commentary on the Bible. Minneapolis: Fortress, 2007.

Lycan, William G. *Consciousness and Experience.* Cambridge: MIT Press, 1996.

Marcus, Adam. "Coptic Cop-Out? Religion Journal Won't Pull Paper Based on Bogus 'Gospel.'" Retraction Watch, June 21, 2016. http://retractionwatch.com/2016/06/21/coptic-cop-out-religion-journal-wont-pull-paper-based-on-bogus-gospel/.

Marshall, I. Howard. *I Believe in the Historical Jesus.* Grand Rapids: Eerdmans, 1977.

Maurice, Frederick Denison. *Theological Essays.* 1853. Reprint, Memphis: General Books, 2010.

May, Gerald G. *The Awakened Heart: Living beyond Addiction.* San Francisco: HarperCollins, 1991.

McGinn, Bernard, ed. *The Essential Writings of Christian Mysticism.* Modern Library Classics. New York: Modern Library, 2006.

McKenzie, John L. *A Theology of the Old Testament.* Garden City, NY: Doubleday, 1974.

McKnight, Edgar V. "Contours and Methods in Literary Criticism." In *Orientation by Disorientation: Studies in Literary Criticism and Biblical Literary Criticism, Presented in Honor of William A. Beardslee,* edited by Richard A. Spencer, 53–70. Pittsburgh, PA: Pickwick, 1980.

Mead, Loren B. *The Once and Future Church: Reinventing the Congregation for a New Mission Frontier.* Washington, DC: Alban Institute, 1991.

Mickelson, Berkeley. "The Bible's Own Approach to Authority." In *Biblical Authority,* edited by Jack Rogers, 75–105. Waco, TX: Word Books, 1977.

Millard, A. R. "Methods of Studying the Patriarchal Narratives as Ancient Texts." In *Essays on the Patriarchal Narratives,* edited by A. R. Millard and D. J. Wiseman, 35–52. Winona Lake, IN: Eisenbraun, 1983.

Millard, A. R., and D. J. Wiseman, eds. *Essays on the Patriarchal Narratives.* Winona Lake, IN: Eisenbrauns, 1983.

Miller, Calvin. *The Vanishing Evangelical: Saving the Church from Its Own Success by Restoring What Really Matters.* Grand Rapids: Baker, 2013.

Miller, James Maxwell, and John H. Hayes. *A History of Ancient Israel and Judah.* Philadelphia: Westminster, 1986.

Moltmann, Jürgen. *The Church in the Power of the Spirit: A Contribution to Messianic Ecclesiology.* Minneapolis: Fortress, 1993.

Muggeridge, Malcolm. *The End of Christendom.* Grand Rapids: Eerdmans, 1980.

Nee, Watchman. *What Shall This Man Do?* Fort Washington, PA: CLC Ministries, 1973.

Nietzsche, Friedrich. *Thus Spoke Zarathustra: A Book for Everyone and No One.* Translated by R. J. Hollingdale. New York: Penguin, 1961.

O Brother, Where Art Thou? DVD. Directed by Joel Cohen and Ethan Cohen. New York: Mike Zoss Productions, 2000.

Pattengale, Jerry. "How the 'Jesus' Wife' Hoax Fell Apart." *Wall Street Journal,* May 1, 2014. http://www.wsj.com/articles/SB10001424052702304178104579535540828090438.

Patterson, Cecil Holden. *Relationship Counseling and Psychotherapy.* New York: Harper and Row, 1974.

Paul VI, Pope. *On Evangelization in the Modern World: Apostolic Exhortation Evangelii Nuntiandi.* Washington DC: United States Catholic Conference, 1976.

Peace, Richard. *Holy Conversations: Talking About God in Everyday Life.* Downers Grove, IL: InterVarsity, 2006.

———. *Witness: A Manual for Use by Small Groups of Christians Who Are Serious in Their Desire to Learn How to Share Their Faith.* Grand Rapids: Zondervan, 1976.

Peterson, Dwight N. *The Origins of Mark: The Markan Community in Current Debate.* Boston: Brill, 2000.

Peterson, Eugene H. *A Long Obedience in the Same Direction: Discipline in an Instant Society.* Downers Grove, IL: InterVarsity, 1980.

Pew Research Center. "Religious Landscape Survey." 2013. http://www.pewforum.org/religious-landscape-study/.

Plantinga, Alvin. *Warranted Christian Belief.* New York: Oxford University Press, 2000.

Polkinghorne, John. *Quantum Physics and Theology: An Unexpected Kinship.* New Haven: Yale University Press, 2007.

———. *Quarks, Chaos, and Christianity: Questions to Science and Religion.* New York: Crossroad, 1994.

Provan, Iain, V. Philips Long, and Tremper Longman III. *A Biblical History of Israel.* Louisville: Westminster John Knox, 2003.

Rahner, Karl. *Foundations of Christian Faith: An Introduction to the Idea of Christianity.* Translated by William V. Dych. New York: Crossroad, 1982.

Raines, Robert Arnold. *To Kiss the Joy.* Waco, TX: Word, 1973.

Ralph, Margaret Nutting. *Why the Catholic Church Must Change: A Necessary Conversation.* Lanham, MD: Rowman and Littlefield, 2013.

Rambo, Lewis R. *Understanding Religious Conversion.* New Haven: Yale University Press, 1993.

Richardson, Alan. *Religion in Contemporary Debate.* Philadelphia: Westminster, 1966.

Ricoeur, Paul. *The Symbolism of Evil.* Translated by Emerson Buchanan. Boston: Beacon, 1967.

Robinson, John A. T. *But That I Can't Believe!* London: Collins, Fontana, 1967.

———. *Honest to God: With Essays by Douglas John Hall and Rowan Williams.* 40th anniv. ed. Louisville: Westminster John Knox, 2002.

Robinson, Thomas A. *The Bauer Thesis Examined: The Geography of Heresy in the Early Christian Church.* Studies in the Bible and Early Christianity 11. Lewiston, NY: E. Mellen, 1988.

Roof, Wade Clark, and William McKinney. *American Mainline Religion: Its Changing Shape and Future.* New Brunswick: Rutgers University Press, 1989.

Rosenblum, Bruce, and Fred Kuttner. *Quantum Enigma: Physics Encounters Consciousness.* Oxford: Oxford University Press, 2006.

Saber, Ariel. "The Unbelievable Tale of Jesus's Wife." *The Atlantic*, July/August 2016. http://www.theatlantic.com/magazine/archive/2016/07/the-unbelievable-tale-of-jesus-wife/485573/.

Sacks, Oliver. *The Man Who Mistook His Wife for a Hat, and Other Clinical Tales.* New York: Simon and Schuster, 1985.

Sample, Tex. *The Spectacle of Worship in a Wired World: Electronic Culture and the Gathered People of God.* Nashville: Abingdon, 1998.

Schweitzer, Albert. *The Quest of the Historical Jesus: A Critical Study of Its Progress from Reimarus to Wrede.* Translated by W. Montgomery. 3rd ed. London: A & C Black, 1954.

Shore, John. *Penguins, Pain and the Whole Shebang: Why I Do the Things I Do*. New York: Seabury, 2005.
Steindl-Rast, David. *Gratefulness, the Heart of Prayer: An Approach to Life in Fullness*. New York: Paulist, 1984.
Stott, John R. *The Contemporary Christian: Applying God's Word to Today's World*. Downers Grove, IL: InterVarsity, 1992.
Taylor, Barbara Brown. "Physics and Faith: The Luminous Web." *The Christian Century*, June 2, 1999. https://www.christiancentury.org/article/2011-11/physics-and-faith.
Thompson, Thomas L. *The Mythic Past: Biblical Archaeology and the Myth of Israel*. New York: Basic Books, 1999.
Thoreau, Henry David. *Walden, Or Life in the Woods; On the Duty of Civil Disobedience*. New York: Rinehart, 1948.
Thornton, Martin. *Christian Proficiency*. London: SPCK, 1961.
Tickle, Phyllis. *The Great Emergence: How Christianity Is Changing and Why*. Grand Rapids: Baker, 2008.
Tiebout, Harry M. *Conversion as a Psychological Phenomenon*. New York: National Council on Alcoholism, 1944.
Tielhard de Chardin, Pierre. *The Phenomenon of Man*. Translated by Bernard Wall. New York: Harper and Row, 1959.
Tillich, Paul. *Dynamics of Faith*. New York: Harper, 1957.
———. *The Shaking of the Foundations*. New York: Scribner, 1948.
———. *Systematic Theology*. Vol. 1, *Reason and Revelation, Being and God*. Chicago: University of Chicago Press, 1951.
Trifunov, David. "'Gospel of Jesus's Wife' Revealed in Rome by Harvard Scholar." *Global Post*, September 18, 2012. https://www.pri.org/stories/2012-09-18/gospel-jesuss-wife-revealed-rome-harvard-scholar-video.
Twelftree, Graham H. *Jesus the Miracle Worker: A Historical and Theological Study*. Downers Grove, IL: InterVarsity, 1999.
W., Bill. *Alcoholics Anonymous: The Story of How Many Thousands of Men and Women Have Recovered from Alcoholism*. 3rd ed. New York: Alcoholics Anonymous World Services, 1976.
Wainwright, Arthur William. *The Trinity in the New Testament*. 1962. Reprint, Eugene, OR: Wipf & Stock, 2001.
Wangsness, Lisa. "Harvard Theological Review Won't Retract 'Jesus's Wife' Paper." *Boston Globe*, June 21, 2016. https://www.bostonglobe.com/metro/2016/06/20/harvard-theological-review-says-won-retract-gospel-jesus-wife-paper/6sSUniCZbOxBbnAgt2vOoO/story.html.
Ward, Keith. *God and the Philosophers*. Minneapolis: Fortress, 2009.
———. *Why There Almost Certainly Is a God: Doubting Dawkins*. Oxford: Lion, 2008.
"Was Jesus Married? New Papyrus Fragment Fuels Debate." *Sydney Morning Herald*, September 19, 2012. http://www.smh.com.au/world/was-jesus-married-new-papyrus-fragment-fuels-debate-20120918-265av.html.
White, James Emery. *The Rise of the Nones: Understanding and Reaching the Religiously Unaffiliated*. Grand Rapids: Baker, 2014.
Whitehead, Alfred North. *Process and Reality: An Essay in Cosmology*. Edited by David Ray Griffin and Donald W. Sherburne. Corrected ed. New York: Free Press, 1978.
Willard, Dallas. *The Spirit of the Disciplines: Understanding How God Changes Lives*. San Francisco: Harper and Row, 1988.

Williams, Michael Allen. *Rethinking "Gnosticism": An Argument for Dismantling a Dubious Category*. Princeton: Princeton University Press, 1999.

Williams, Oscar, ed. *The New Pocket Anthology of American Verse, from Colonial Days to the Present*. New York: Washington Square, 1961.

Wire, Antoinette Clark. *The Case for Mark Composed in Performance*. Eugene, OR: Cascade, 2000.

Wolinsky, Stephen. *Trances People Live*. Falls Village, CT: Bramble Books, 1991.

Woods, Richard. "Recovering Our Dominican Contemplative Tradition." *Dominican Life*, n.d. http://www.domlife.org/BeingDominican/Spirituality/contemplationwoods.html.

Wordsworth, William. "Lines Composed a Few Miles above Tintern Abbey." In *Oxford Book of Nineteenth-Century English Verse*, edited by John Hayward, 69. Oxford: Oxford University Press, 1964.

Wright, N. T. "Jesus and the Identity of God." *Ex Auditu* 14 (1998) 42–56.

———. *Jesus and the Victory of God*. Christian Origins and the Questions of God 2. Minneapolis: Fortress, 1996.

Yeakley, Flavil R. *Why Churches Grow*. St. Louis: Anderson's, 1977.